Accounting Ethics Education

Accounting Ethics Education: Teaching Virtues and Values gathers a diversity of contributions from invited, well-known experts. It promotes a comprehensive reflection around how ethics can and should be taught to accounting students, discussing and highlighting the most updated research on accounting ethics education, and it is an essential reference in the field.

The subject of accounting ethics education is critical to foster ethical awareness that may prevent the way in which one acts or behaves, especially towards others. The point is that accounting education cannot exist without ethical education and accountants must be technically proficient and ethically sensible since ethical behavior is vital to the status and credibility of the accountancy profession. And this sensibility must be developed while the future professional is still cultivating his or her moral and intellectual structure within the school learning environment: character and practical reasoning are crucial because they include not only knowledge of rules and principles, and their correct application but also values and virtues.

Examining multiple perspectives, *Accounting Ethics Education: Teaching Virtues and Values* advances the scholarly debate by providing cutting-edge and insightful research vital for all those interested and immersed in these matters. It begins with a historical perspective of accounting ethics education and continues by exploring challenges, opportunities and developments in the area. It will be of great value to academics, students, researchers and professionals in the fields of accounting, accounting education and ethics.

Margarida M. Pinheiro, PhD, is a Professor at the University of Aveiro (Institute of Accounting and Administration, ISCA-UA) and a Full Researcher at the Research Centre Didactics and Technology in Education of Trainers (CIDTFF), on the Policies, Evaluation and Quality research group. She is currently a member of the School Council and was a member of the Scientific Council and President of the Pedagogical Council of ISCA-UA. She has been publishing in the areas of learning and teaching methodologies, quality of education, knowledge construction and internationalization of universities. She serves on the editorial board of the *Journal of Higher Education Pedagogies*. She is a passionate researcher engaged in teaching at the level of higher education.

Alberto J. Costa, PhD, is a Professor at the University of Aveiro (Institute of Accounting and Administration, ISCA-UA), where he has been teaching ethics and deontology for several years now. He also teaches accounting and management control and is the Head of the Masters Degree in Accounting and Management Control. He is a Full Researcher of GOVCOPP (Research Unit on Governance, Competitiveness and Public Policies, of the University of Aveiro), on the Systems for Decision Support research group. He has been a certified accountant in Portugal since 1997 and member of GRUDIS—Portuguese Network of Accounting Research—since 2006. He researches in the fields of financial accounting and management accounting, particularly in the area of ethics and deontology. He has published papers in national and international journals.

Routledge Studies in Accounting

31. **Managerial Accountant's Compass**
    Research Genesis and Development
    Gary R. Oliver

32. **Institutions and Accounting Practices after the Financial Crisis**
    International Perspective
    Edited by Victoria Krivogorsky

33. **Corporate Environmental Reporting**
    The Western Approach to Nature
    Leanne J. Morrison

34. **Cost Management for Nonprofit and Voluntary Organisations**
    Zahirul Hoque and Tarek Rana

35. **Multinational Enterprises and Transparent Tax Reporting**
    Alexandra Middleton and Jenni Muttonen

36. **Accounting for M&A**
    Uses and Abuses of Accounting in Monitoring and Promoting Merger
    Edited by Amir Amel-Zadeh and Geoff Meeks

37. **Interventionist Research in Accounting**
    A Methodological Approach
    Edited by Vicki Baard and Johannes Dumay

38. **Accounting Ethics Education**
    Teaching Virtues and Values
    Edited by Margarida M. Pinheiro and Alberto J. Costa

For more information about this series, please visit www.routledge.com/Routledge-Studies-in-Accounting/book-series/SE0715

Accounting Ethics Education
Teaching Virtues and Values

Edited by Margarida M. Pinheiro
and Alberto J. Costa

NEW YORK AND LONDON

First published 2021
by Routledge
52 Vanderbilt Avenue, New York, NY 10017

and by Routledge
2 Park Square, Milton Park, Abingdon, Oxon, OX14 4RN

Routledge is an imprint of the Taylor & Francis Group, an informa business

© 2021 Taylor & Francis

The right of Margarida M. Pinheiro and Alberto J. Costa to be identified as the authors of the editorial material, and of the authors for their individual chapters, has been asserted in accordance with sections 77 and 78 of the Copyright, Designs and Patents Act 1988.

All rights reserved. No part of this book may be reprinted or reproduced or utilised in any form or by any electronic, mechanical, or other means, now known or hereafter invented, including photocopying and recording, or in any information storage or retrieval system, without permission in writing from the publishers.

Trademark notice: Product or corporate names may be trademarks or registered trademarks, and are used only for identification and explanation without intent to infringe.

Library of Congress Cataloging-in-Publication Data
Names: Pinheiro, Margarida M., 1961– editor. | Costa, Alberto J., editor.
Title: Accounting ethics education : teaching virtues and values / edited by Margarida M. Pinheiro and Alberto J. Costa.
Description: New York : Routledge, 2021. | Series: Routledge studies in accounting | Includes bibliographical references and index.
Identifiers: LCCN 2020024627 | ISBN 9780367337421 (hardback) | ISBN 9780429321597 (ebook)
Subjects: LCSH: Accounting—Study and teaching. | Accounting—Moral and ethical aspects. | Accountants—Professional ethics.
Classification: LCC HF5630 .A433 2021 | DDC 174/.9657071—dc23
LC record available at https://lccn.loc.gov/2020024627

ISBN: 978-0-367-33742-1 (hbk)
ISBN: 978-0-429-32159-7 (ebk)

Typeset in Sabon
by Apex CoVantage, LLC

Printed in the United Kingdom
by Henry Ling Limited

To my daughter Rita and her husband Sérgio, who, as doctors, are at the forefront of the battle against Covid-19.

Margarida M. Pinheiro

To my parents, who taught me ethics by their example.

Alberto J. Costa

Contents

List of Contributors	xi
Acknowledgments	xiv
Foreword	xvi
Preface	xix

PART 1
Accounting Ethics Education's Odyssey   1

1   Accounting Education and Ethics in the 15th Century   3
ALAN SANGSTER

2   The Long Strange Trip: A Reflection on the Historical Relativity of Accounting Ethics   31
TIMOTHY J. FOGARTY

3   Accounting Ethics Education Research: A Historical Review of the Literature   44
LAN ANH NGUYEN AND STEVEN DELLAPORTAS

PART 2
Challenges, Opportunities and Developments   81

4   Industry 4.0: Reimagining Higher Education and Value Transformation   83
PHILOMENA LEUNG

5   Educating the Next Generation of Accountants: How to Promote Ethical Consciousness Through Critical Thinking   100
ARIELA CAGLIO AND MARA CAMERAN

6 Ethical Virtues, Norms and Values in Accounting Education 120
   DOMÈNEC MELÉ

7 Building Moral Courage Through a Wisdom-Focused
   Accounting Ethics Course 137
   MICHAEL K. SHAUB

8 Moral Competence: What It Means and How Accountant
   Education Could Foster It 155
   GEORG LIND

   Index 175

Contributors

Ariela Caglio is Associate Professor of Management Accounting and Performance Measurement at Bocconi University and at the SDA Bocconi School of Management, Italy. Her research interests primarily rest in sustainability and integrated reporting, compensation design, performance measurement in interorganizational settings and the evolution of the accounting profession. She has published for prestigious academic outlets, such as *Accounting, Organizations and Society*, *European Accounting Review* and *Management Accounting Research*. She currently sits on the Management Committee of the European Accounting Association (EAA).

Mara Cameran, PhD, is a Tenured researcher of accounting at Bocconi University, Italy, an Italian CPA (*dottore commercialista*) and chartered auditor (*revisore contabile*), as well as a member of the European Auditing Research Network (EARNET) scientific committee and of the Standing Scientific Committee of the European Accounting Association (EAA). She serves on the editorial board of *Auditing: A Journal of Practice and Theory, Accounting and Business Research* and *Accounting Forum*. Her research interests currently focus on the regulation of the audit market and the development of the auditing process, as well as on the public perception of the accounting profession.

Alberto J. Costa, PhD, is a Professor at the University of Aveiro (Institute of Accounting and Administration, ISCA-UA), where he has taught ethics and deontology for several years now. He also teaches accounting and management control and is the Head of the Masters Degree in Accounting and Management Control. He is a full researcher of GOVCOPP (Research Unit on Governance, Competitiveness and Public Policies, of the University of Aveiro) in the Systems for Decision Support research group. He has been a certified accountant in Portugal since 1997 and a member of GRUDIS—the Portuguese Network of Accounting Research—since 2006. He researches in the fields of financial accounting and management accounting, particularly in the area of ethics and deontology. He has published papers in national and international journals.

Steven Dellaportas is a Professor of accounting at the Nottingham University Business School China, University of Nottingham Ningbo, China. Steven's primary area of research is professional ethics in accounting and education. Steven serves on several editorial boards, including as coeditor of the accounting and business ethics section of the *Journal of Business Ethics* and as associate editor of *Accounting Education*. Dellaportas is the lead author of two textbooks and has published several articles in international peer-reviewed journals on accounting ethics and related topics.

Timothy J. Fogarty is a Professor in the accountancy department at Case Western Reserve University, USA. He has published over three hundred articles in both academic and practitioner journals. His research interests include accounting education, the sociology of business organizations and the regulation of professionals. He serves on many editorial boards and in many capacities for the American Accounting Association and the American Institute of Certified Public Accountants. He is an attorney and a CPA.

Philomena Leung is Associate Dean, International Engagement and Professor of Accounting and Governance in the Macquarie Business School at Macquarie University, Australia. Leung has extensive achievements as a professional and academic leader in Hong Kong and Australia. She has published extensively in top quality journals, in the areas of ethics, auditing and accounting education. She was the joint editor for the SSCI publication *Managerial Auditing Journal* for over ten years and is the lead author for the book *Auditing and Assurance*, published by John Wiley, one of the two leading auditing texts. She also led the Ethics Education project commissioned by the International Federation of Accountants (IFAC) as the blueprint for accounting ethics education for over 160 countries. More recently Leung was awarded the highest honor—the Bob McDonald award by the Institute of Internal Auditors, Australia—for her contribution to the profession.

Georg Lind is Emeritus Professor of Psychology at the University of Konstanz, Germany, and is now a freelance author and teacher trainer. He has developed the behavioral *Moral Competence Test* (MCT), used worldwide for research and evaluation, and the *Konstanz Method of Dilemma Discussion* (KMDD), an affordable but very effective method for fostering moral competence. He offers workshops and on-the-job training. Lind is the author of *How to Teach Moral Competence* (2019).

Domènec Melé is Emeritus Professor of Business Ethics at IESE Business School, University of Navarra, Spain. He earned a doctorate in industrial engineering and another in theology. Over the past thirty years, he has taught and published extensively in business ethics, Catholic social teaching in economic and business, humanistic management and philosophy of management. He has authored or edited about fifteen books and fifty scientific papers. His latest book is *Business Ethics in Action: Managing Human Excellence in Organizations*, 2nd ed. (London: Red Goble Press, 2019). He has served as section editor of the *Journal of Business Ethics* for ten years and currently serves as a member of several editorial boards of journals related to his fields of expertise.

Lan Anh Nguyen, PhD, CPA, ACCA, is a Lecturer at RMIT University, Australia. She is a former professional accountant with extensive experience in financial accounting, management accounting and auditing in Europe and Asia. Lan Anh is a passionate researcher, engaged in both qualitative and quantitative research methodologies with an interest in business ethics, audit markets, accounting education and work culture.

Margarida M. Pinheiro, PhD, is a Professor at the University of Aveiro (Institute of Accounting and Administration, ISCA-UA) and a full researcher at the Research Centre Didactics and Technology in Education of Trainers (CIDTFF), on the Policies, Evaluation and Quality research group. She is currently a member of the School Council and was a member of the Scientific Council and President of the Pedagogical Council of ISCA-UA. She has been publishing in the areas of learning and teaching methodologies, quality of education, knowledge construction and internationalization of universities. She serves on the editorial board of the *Journal of Higher Education Pedagogies*. She is a passionate researcher engaged in teaching at the level of higher education.

Alan Sangster is a Professor of Accounting History at the University of Aberdeen, UK, and Editor-in-Chief of *Accounting Education*. An archival historian, he specializes in accounting, business practice and business education in late-Medieval and early modern Europe (c. 1200–c. 1800) and Luca Pacioli (1446/7–1517). His books include *De Raphaeli: Venetian Double Entry Bookkeeping in 1475* (Lomax Press 2018); *Libr. XV: Cotrugli and De Raphaeli on Business and Bookkeeping in the Renaissance* (Lomax Press 2014), and articles include "Pacioli's Lens: God, Humanism, Euclid, and the Rhetoric of Double Entry" (2018) and "The Genesis of Double Entry Bookkeeping" (2016), both in *Accounting Review*.

Michael K. Shaub is Clinical Professor of Accounting and Director of the Professional Program in Accounting at Texas A&M University, USA. Dr. Shaub's research focuses on ethical decision-making by accountants and auditors, professional skepticism, wisdom and moral reasoning, and accounting ethics education issues.

Acknowledgments

It took a lot of work by a lot of people to make a project like this come together. We'll begin with Routledge, an outstanding publisher with a superb team that believed, supported, encouraged and cherished this project from the beginning. Few books have been published on accounting ethics education; therefore, we applaud Routledge's foresight in publishing such a book.

We also offer our heartfelt appreciation to all the authors who were generous enough to share their knowledge and valuable time in adding very relevant contributions to the field of accounting ethics education and research. We feel extremely honored for having them on board and sincerely grateful for believing in this project.

Margarida M. Pinheiro and Alberto J. Costa

I personally want to thank Alberto for his commitment and ability to help make this book a reality.

Margarida

I am very appreciative of Margarida's enduring and unfailing support, for her friendship and for working with me to produce this book.

My most important thank-you goes to my wife, Rosa, the light of my life, for inspiring, supporting, encouraging and loving me every day and for being one of the most ethical human beings I know. She and our children, Anita, Duarte and Alice, remind me constantly that as long as we have each other, we have everything.

Alberto

Acknowledgments xv

"This work is financially supported by National Funds through FCT – Fundação para a Ciência e a Tecnologia, I.P., under the projects UIDB/CED/00194/2020 (CIDTFF – Research Centre on Didactics and Technology in the Education of Trainers) and UIDB/04058/2020 (GOVCOPP – Research Unit on Governance, Competitiveness and Public Policy).

Fundação para a Ciência e a Tecnologia

universidade de aveiro
theoria poiesis praxis

cidtff
centro de investigação
Didática e Tecnologia na Formação de Formadores

govcopp
universidade de aveiro
unidade de investigação em governança, competitividade e políticas públicas

Foreword

Can ethics be taught? What is the best way to teach ethics? How can we know if students are learning the lessons of ethics education? These are the salient questions accounting educators have thought about for many years. *Accounting Ethics Education: Teaching Virtues and Values* addresses these questions and more. I am delighted to write the foreword for this very important contribution to accounting ethics education and research.

During my forty-year career in academia, I have observed that the tools of accounting ethics education have changed from a rules-based approach that largely uses professional codes of conduct, to an approach that employs real and imagined case studies in the practice of accounting. Most recently, critical thinking assignments, such as short vignettes that ask "What would you do?" have become popular.

The chapters in this book describe the evolution of accounting ethics education, what might lie ahead, critical perspectives on the philosophical and developmental underpinnings of ethical behavior, the framework for ethics, values and attitudes of the accounting professional, how virtue connects to accounting ethics and the importance of moral courage and moral competence. The diversity of material in this book provides evidence that we can, indeed, teach ethics. Whether students learn the lessons are another matter. We can measure it, as some of the authors in this book suggest, but we may rely too much on what students believe is the right course of action rather than what they will do when faced with an ethical dilemma.

The increased coverage of ethics in the accounting curriculum can be traced back to a variety of financial frauds over the years. In recent times, failures at Enron and WorldCom (US), Satyam (India), Parmalat (Italy) and, most recently, BHS and Carillion (UK) have raised the question: where were the auditors? Perhaps a better question is why accountants and auditors didn't do the right thing.

Accounting traces its roots back to 1494 when Luca Pacioli, the father of modern accounting, first described the system of double entry bookkeeping used by Venetian merchants. Alan Sangster discusses the norms established by the guilds to protect against fraud in weights and measures, the sale of soiled produce, price fixing and other improper business practices. Here, we see the beginnings of an ethic of honesty, integrity, trustworthiness, prudence and due care in the performance of professional responsibilities, and the importance of protecting the public interest.

The notion of self-interest is counter to protecting the public interest. Timothy J. Fogarty looks at the processes of modernity and criticizes professional ethics codes as nothing more than the furtherance of self-interest. He examines the study of ethics from a critical perspective, concluding that much of it misses its mark because of its focus on simulation of attitudes such as ethical orientation and ethical sensitivity. If, as Fogarty suggests, "we have not fully incorporated context into ethical study", then observing what accountants do rather than attitudinal studies may have greater value.

Steven Dellaportas and Lan Anh Nguyen trace the evolution of accounting ethics education research from 1972 to 2018. They examine questions such as "What are the objectives of ethics education?" and "Which techniques are best to teach ethics to accounting students?" From the beginning, educators have debated whether to integrate ethics throughout the curriculum or teach it in a stand-alone course. There are good arguments for both. Using ethical decision-making models to teach ethics is well established in the literature. However, as the authors point out, "Ethics coverage has yet to reach the point of supporting students effectively in developing their moral attitudes".

The rapid pace of technological change has created new challenges for ethics education. Philomena Leung addresses the Fourth Industrial Revolution (4IR) that is changing the way individuals relate to society and the moral role of technologies. She proposes using a more "human-centered approach" that focuses on values and ethics. Accounting education should change as well due to the effects of new technologies on transaction flows, financial reports and auditing. Indeed, auditors need some level of proficiency in data analytics to analyze the data and interpret the information software provides.

Should we, as accounting educators, consider students' views of ethics in developing accounting ethics courses? Ariela Caglio and Mara Cameran asked their students: "Do you think accountants behave ethically?" Their study identifies several values that underlie the competent performance of professional services. A values-based approach to accounting ethics education fits well with Leung's suggestion and is consistent with the growing trend of addressing values, ethics and behavioral attitudes as the framework for professional judgment and professional skepticism.

Much like Fogarty, Domènec Melé points out that relying on professional codes of conduct to teach students about these characteristic traits of behavior do not go beyond answering the question: "What is legal"?

Ethics education should focus on "What is the right thing to do?" But, the traditional normative ethical theories (i.e., Kantianism and Utilitarianism) that address what is right according to a set of duties or consequences do not motivate students to act well. He suggests that values, moral duties and virtues arising from principles about right and wrong need to be anchored by the virtue of "practical wisdom". As he points asks: "What does it matter if students know how to reason well in ethics in accordance with a certain theory if they are not motivated to act ethically?"

Ethical intent and ethical action flow from the ability to deliberate well about ethical issues and reason through to a course of action. Michael Shaub uses Rest's Model of Moral Development to discuss moral courage, an important virtue for accounting professionals who are expected to approach an audit with a questioning mind. He believes that students may have the moral courage to do the right thing but they need to understand how difficult it may be to do what they generally believe they should do. Like Melé, Shaub believes that an accounting ethics course should transition students from moral reasoning to wisdom and moral courage by having students answer the question: "What will happen to me if I do that?"

How can we tell if our students have gained "moral competence"? Georg Lind characterizes it as "the ability to solve problems and conflicts on the grounds of moral principles through thinking and discussion, instead of using force and deceit, or submitting to an authority". He describes a Moral Competence Test (MCT) that produces a C-score: what proportion of the person's judgments is influenced by the moral quality of the arguments. Consistent with Melé and Shaub's discussions about wisdom and moral courage, moral competence helps to apply rules in everyday decision-making and solve the problems and conflicts that these rules may cause. Moral competence helps to make difficult decisions more swiftly such as when to blow the whistle on financial wrongdoing. As such, it is a critical component of ethical behavior for accounting professionals.

Accounting educators have a critical role to play in developing the ethical capacities of our students. We need to do everything in our power to develop the tools for students to act with moral courage when pressures exist in the workplace to deviate from ethical norms. Our students need to have the strength of character to act in accordance with the values of the accounting profession and protect the public interest. As researchers, we have an obligation to test existing paradigms and look for new ways to teach ethics. It is my hope and expectation that this book will provide a useful resource for accounting educators to thrive as ethics educators and researchers.

Steven M. Mintz, D.B.A.
Professor Emeritus California State University, San Luis Obispo

Preface

The story of this book began more than two years ago. It all started with the search for a double correspondence: create a cohesive editorship team and address a common and passionate topic in education, relevant enough to fill an existing gap and to interest teachers, researchers, students and professionals. We feel privileged to have met them both.

The combination of education, ethics and accounting came to us in a very spontaneous way. In fact, and as teachers at an accounting higher education institution, we feel the importance of providing students with ethics education. So, it was settled: accounting ethics education was the way. The next step led us to Routledge and to a proposal that was strong enough to attract several recognized authors and top experts in their fields. In fact, we had to split our original proposal in two in order to accommodate them all: this book is the first part of this endeavor and we are already working on the second book.

This book comprehends a careful reflection on what brought us here and what lies ahead and, we believe, meets all the conditions to be an essential and useful reference in the field. It will not make teachers, researchers, students or professionals more ethical, nor will it tell them how to judge others' behavior. Rather, its goal is to help them understand how ethics can be taught to accounting students and how they should be motivated to act ethically. If students achieve this, the accounting profession will be enriched and dignified, and they will excel at being responsible professionals with high technical standards and superior ethical sensibility.

Margarida M. Pinheiro and Alberto J. Costa

Part 1
Accounting Ethics Education's Odyssey

1 Accounting Education and Ethics in the 15th Century

Alan Sangster

1. Introduction

The 15th century marked the last century of medieval Europe. With its ending came the beginnings of the modern era, a shift in the balance of power, both in trade and in finance, and the beginnings of the spread of double entry bookkeeping across Europe made possible by the method being available in print. But, if bookkeeping was to become increasingly important, were the bookkeepers to be trusted? Did they know what they were doing? Did the journals and ledgers they maintained represent a true and fair view of the transactions they purported to reflect? To understand the answers to these questions, we need to look to the society in which they lived, the culture surrounding their work, who they were, how they were educated and to the work ethic of their craft. We begin by looking at the late medieval world of commerce.

2. Background

In the 13th century, Italian wholesale firms switched from a focus on international trade led by itinerant merchants to a business model based on sedentary merchants. They engaged in international trade through a network of permanent branches and a web of temporary agents spread across much of the continent and beyond, to London, Constantinople, Africa and the East. Banking was part of their activities and this change in business model resulted in a parallel international European banking network operated by Italian firms.

Economically, Italy was far ahead of the rest of Europe and the merchants had political control of Italy's towns and cities. With their sophisticated double entry bookkeeping supporting their control of credit and debt, Italians acted as virtually the only providers of banking services in Europe until the mid-15th century (Barnard, 1972), controlling the banking services at the international fairs of Flanders, Champagne and in the major centers of trade, including London, Paris and Bruges; and Italian merchants dominated both European trade with the East and trade within Europe (Spufford, 2006).

Double entry bookkeeping had first emerged in Italian banks no later than the early 13th century (Sangster, 2016). As a shortage of cash and bullion (Cipolla, 1956) created a need for a sound and reliable method of recording debt, its use spread to Italian merchants (Martinelli, 1974), primarily the larger international wholesale merchants, with their businesses heavily dependent on credit and relatively high volume of activity and transaction values. Because many of the international merchants also acted as agents for other merchants, this stimulated the need for "the comprehensiveness and orderliness which double entry did in a sense compel" (Lane, 1977, p. 191).

By the mid-15th century, the double entry system had standardized in each of the principal commercial regions of Italy: Lombardy, Genoa, Tuscany (including Florence) and Venice. However, whereas the basic concepts of double entry were clear and defined the method—in the ledger, make one debit entry and one equal credit entry for each transaction, include in each entry an indicator showing the location of the contra entry and record every entry in the same money of account—the construction of each entry, the accounts used, the manner in which each account was organized, how accounts were balanced and the ways in which books of account were organized was not standardized. Each firm did it differently. At a regional level, the double entry account books in use, the layout of the ledger accounts and the language used in entries varied between Lombardy, Genoa, Tuscany and Venice.[1] Small Italian businesses based on low-volume-low-transaction-value trade had little need for anything beyond a simple record of debt to survive. Many contented themselves with their own forms of single entry bookkeeping, such as can be seen in the surviving records of merchants in the Tuscan town of Prato in the 14th century (Marshall, 1999).

Whereas Italian merchants and bankers used double entry, they did not spread knowledge of the method to non-Italians. As a result, until the late 15th century, double entry was only used by Italians; their foreign agents; a few southern Germans who had been trained in Italy; and Catalans—the only region other than Italy that had established its own banks; and it had also copied the business methods of the Italians (de Roover, 1963; Edler, 1934).

2.1 Education

The Italians were considerably more advanced than the rest of Europe, not only in their development and use of double entry, but also in their Florentine-driven system of formal mercantile education: the *abaco* schools that began to emerge in the mid-13th century. This was the second stage in school education. It lasted approximately two years, depending on the student and was attended by boys, typically when they were 11–14 years of age (Cherubini, 1996; Goldthwaite, 1972; Grendler, 1989, 1990, 2002; Black, 2007).

Many, if not the majority of those who attended *abaco* school were sons of merchants or craftsmen who used the practical mathematics taught in these schools in their trade. As a result, they were taught the math they needed for business in school and either applied it in their fathers' work, or could be coached in its use by them. Male literacy levels in 14th- and 15th-century Florence, which was where the majority of these schools were located, were extremely high—at least 69 percent (Black, 2007)—making it by far the most highly educated region in Europe. Not surprisingly, Florence controlled the international financial markets of Europe from the mid-14th century (Mueller, 1997; Spufford, 2006). Venice, which controlled much of Mediterranean trade with the East was the dominant center of trade, importing spices and silk that was shipped across Europe in exchange for cloths, timber and a wide variety of staples and luxury goods (Postan, 1973; Braudel, 2002; Marino, 2002).

2.2 Bookkeepers and Bookkeeping

This was the environment in which bookkeepers worked between the 13th and late 15th century. During that period, most merchants were their own bookkeepers, even those operating internationally, many of whom acted as agents for other merchants in addition to buying and selling on their own behalf. However, there were some specialist bookkeepers in the larger firms. The earliest known double entry bookkeeper was Amatino Manucci, bookkeeper for the Florentine Farolfi company branch in Sabon, France in 1299–1300 (Lee, 1977; Smith, 2008). Another was Simone Bellandi, the bookkeeper of the international merchant, Francesco di Marco Datini in Pisa (1392–1394). He then moved to Datini's Barcelona branch as a partner and, although now a merchant, he continued to perform the bookkeeping in Barcelona (1394–1399) (Kuter, Gurskaya, Andreenkova & Bagdasaryan, 2018).

Italy's merchants and bankers who used double entry, not only did not disseminate double entry to non-Italians with whom they traded and banked, they did not teach other Italian merchants how to use it. This placed those who knew how to use double entry in a powerful position. Their double entry account books were considered legal documents and, because they were much better organized than single entry records, they created a potential problem for other merchants whenever debts were disputed.[2]

Any other merchants wishing to learn how to use double entry could not restart their careers by serving an apprenticeship. They had to find a different route to acquire the ability to use double entry.

3. Medieval Accounting Education

For many years, it was believed that accounting or, more appropriately at this stage of its development, bookkeeping, that is, double entry bookkeeping,[3] was first taught in the north-Italian medieval *abaco* schools of practical business mathematics. These schools were first founded in the mid-13th century to train future merchants in the mathematics they needed for their trade. A cursory glance at the literature confirms that this remains the dominant view among accounting historians and economic historians.

Evidence, if any, to support this conclusion is counterfactual: bookkeepers could do double entry in the late 13th century—all other things remaining equal, if they had not been taught double entry, they would not have been able to use it. It is also present-minded: double entry is taught in classrooms today—without classrooms where double entry was taught, merchants could not have learnt how to do it. And, it ignores the fact that until at least the mid-20th century, in the UK and many other parts of the world, bookkeepers in small businesses were typically self-taught, or 'learned with Nelly' by sitting beside an expert and watching how to do it. Others disagree. They point to the absence of instruction in bookkeeping from all of the c. 200 surviving *abaco* classroom manuals dating from before 1500 (Van Egmond, 1981): there is no evidence that any bookkeeping, double entry or single entry, was taught in an *abaco* classroom (Goldthwaite, 2009).

One aspect of some of those *abaco* manuals does, however, tell us that students in the *abaco* schools knew something about bookkeeping: several of the manuals contain examples of mathematical calculations that use accounting terms. Some even contain examples of bookkeeping entries that are used to present the data to which some mathematical calculation is to be applied, typically relating to annuities, loans, discounts and investments (Goldthwaite, 2015). It is as if bookkeeping has already been learned before stepping into the classroom at the age of 11–14. Perhaps that is not as fanciful as it appears.

According to the 15th-century international merchant, Benedetto Cotrugli, the only route to mastery of a trade or craft was through an apprenticeship (Carraro & Favero, 2017). In Venice, merchant apprenticeships started at age 12, but family members could begin their apprenticeship earlier (Molmenti, 1880). And, before beginning an apprenticeship, many would serve as *garzoni*, shop boys, watching and learning as they worked. Thus, many of those attending *abaco* school would already have heard the terms of bookkeeping and would have known what they meant. Some may have been shown the account books, either in the workshop or at home—several 14th- and 15th-century Florentine families kept household accounts, some in double entry. A student knowing any more than a few features of bookkeeping when entering *abaco* school for the first time would have been unexceptional.

But, double entry? In the 13th century, this is inconceivable. It was still developing and, based on the absence of surviving examples compared to examples of other simpler forms of bookkeeping, it was relatively rarely used. Anyone able to use it would have been able to command a much better income by doing so rather than teaching it, and surviving records indicate that those that did use it were primarily merchants who did their own bookkeeping, not specialist bookkeepers. However, in the 14th century, particularly in Florence, the most educationally advanced city of its day with male literacy levels of at least 69 percent, it is quite possible that a student entering *abaco* school might know at least how to record uncomplicated double entries in the books of account.

4. If Double Entry Bookkeeping Was Not Taught in *Abaco* School, Where Was It Taught?

It might be more appropriate to ask, 'how was it learned?' We do not know. It is not mentioned in any known documentation, merchant manuals or merchant guild statutes that have survived from before 1450. In the absence of any sign of formal classroom instruction, we can surmise that it was learned by sitting beside an expert in the workplace. This is consistent with the variety of approach within single firms over time reported by Martinelli (1974) in his study of double entry bookkeeping up to 1340; and it is evident elsewhere, for example, in the bookkeeping of the Pisan branch of the 14th/early-15th-century international merchant, Francesco di Marco Datini (Kuter et al., 2018).[4] It is also consistent with the description of the career of Francesco di Stoldo degli Strozzi in the first half of the 14th century, from shop boy to bookkeeper of the cash, to bookkeeper of the firm, then manager (Goldthwaite, 2009).

In Datini's case, examination of the ledgers reveals a method of recording double entry and a double entry system that changed relatively frequently over time as the bookkeeping increased in complexity and clarity. This was most noticeable when the bookkeeper in Pisa left in 1394 and his successor continued with virtually the same double entry method and double entry system, but then started to simplify it in ways quite clearly contrary to what his predecessor had done. The method had been learned from an expert but the new bookkeeper, with no need for sophistication and no longer an expert to guide him, settled on an approach presumably more suited to his own level of ability. Compared to his predecessor whose errors in the ledger entries were few and far between, the new bookkeeper struggled and his ledgers were increasingly error-ridden, something that Datini's correspondence reveals was not well-received by his employer. It is also, perhaps, indicative of why, as we shall see, double entry made its way into the classroom before the end of the 15th century.

This description of how the method of double entry was passed from expert to novice is also consistent with the relatively few examples of double entry that have survived from the 13th to 15th centuries compared to examples of other method of bookkeeping: you needed to know how to do double entry before you could train someone else. Double entry is predominantly to be found in the ledgers of international wholesale merchants, rather than in the ledgers of local retail merchants. These larger merchants could afford to employ bookkeepers, which meant that they had someone who could train a new bookkeeper. But, even a merchant with a large business of the scale of each of Datini's partnerships had little need for more than one bookkeeper in each location. Business was not large enough to merit it. However, the merchant also needed to know and understand the bookkeeping method in use. Not in case he suddenly lost his bookkeeper, but to be able to use it for the purpose it was maintained: to monitor and control credit.

4.1 Banks

Banks were different. Bankers needed to maintain scrupulously accurate bookkeeping records, but learning how to maintain a bank ledger was much easier than learning how to maintain the account books of an international merchant: all it contained was accounts for debtors and creditors and, perhaps, a cash account (Flori, 1636; Goldthwaite, 1985). When an international merchant also acted as a banker, the likelihood that the bookkeeper would be competent significantly increased, even if only in ensuring consistently that two equal and opposite entries were made for each transaction, which Datini's second bookkeeper in Pisa could not or did not do.

Datini only briefly operated a bank, for three years at the end of the 14th century and on a local level rather than in the international arena (Goldthwaite, 1985). Others, such as the Florentine Medici of the 15th century, set a new standard, both for banking with branches in the major trade centers of Europe and double entry (Fazzini, Fici, Montrone & Terzani, 2016). They were masters of the method of double entry as performed in Florence, refining the method and reaching new levels of competence and utility, with regular ledger closing, profit and loss accounts and balance sheets (Fazzini et al., 2016). Merchants did not share their trade secrets, including their system of double entry. Only if a bookkeeper left one merchant to enter the employment of another would this have occurred. Thus, for example, when a branch of the Medici family developed its double entry system in the early 15th century, it did so without knowledge of what Datini had done just a few years earlier (Edler, 1934).

Double entry's status as a trade secret resulted in a constant shortage of people—both merchants and bookkeepers—trained in the method. This was another reason why, as will be described in the next part of this chapter, it ultimately made its way into the classroom before the last quarter of the 15th century and then into print in 1494.

The 16th century author of two manuals on double entry, Alvise Casanova (1558), declared that a lot of people who professed to be bookkeepers were charlatans: they could do the basics but had neither the ability nor, perhaps, a desire to do the job well. This was a serious problem at a time when having an accurate ledger was paramount to the settling of any disputes over debt and one that needed to be addressed from a very early period, long before 1558. But, if *abaco* teachers did not teach bookkeeping outside the workshop, who did or who could? Only merchants or their bookkeepers. From the start, there was no alternative: once the method of double entry emerged, any teaching took place in the workplace (Sangster, 2018a).

5. Teaching Bookkeeping in the 15th Century Workplace

The first and only indication we have of how bookkeeping was taught in the workplace is contained in a five-page chapter on double entry bookkeeping in Benedetto Cotrugli's *Book of the Art of Trade*, a manuscript book written in 1458. The chapter is an overview of the double entry method, the bookkeeping system and the record-keeping system a merchant should maintain (Sangster & Rossi, 2018). It is not written for a small merchant, but for someone entering the business of an international merchant, which is what Cotrugli had been earlier in his life. The way it is presented resonates with what a merchant might have said to a new apprentice about the record keeping system he would soon be learning to use.

Cotrugli begins by emphasizing the importance of recording everything and leaving nothing to memory, describes what to record as debit and what to record as credit and gives an example involving cloth of the entries to be made in the journal and from there to the ledger. He describes how to maintain double entry accounts in two moneys of account, local and foreign, when using bills of exchange, use of which was fundamental to international trade, and he describes the other records that a merchant must maintain—contracts, letters and other important documents.

At the end of this five-page overview of the record-keeping system of the business, the apprentice would have been ready for instruction in double entry, at which point the bookkeeper, or the merchant himself, would have begun his training. For what happened next, as the example of Datini's bookkeeper from the 1390s illustrates, bookkeepers had to be (1) taught how to do double entry properly and then (2) monitored to see if they were 'fit for purpose'. It was a two-stage process: education followed by practical application in which ability and expertise was fine-tuned and acquired: an apprenticeship. It is likely to have involved the apprentice watching and learning by copying and attempting numerous examples until the bookkeeper was satisfied that the apprentice was ready. This process took between two and five years, depending on the complexity of the business (Sangster, 2018a). This example-based form of instruction was what was used when tutors began to teach bookkeeping outside the workplace.

6. The Tutors of Bookkeeping

We do not know when bookkeeping began to be taught outside the workplace but, we do know it was being taught by a private tutor named Marino De Raphaeli in Venice in 1475 (Sangster, 2015, 2018b). De

Raphaeli's manual on double entry has been preserved in the National Library of Malta (Sangster, 2014). It contains a brief overview of how to record double entries involving cloth, followed by 267 journal entries relating to various activities of a Venetian international wholesale merchant, showing how many different transactions are recorded. The examples are realistic in terms of price, measures, quantities, goods, moneys of account, taxes and the emphasis on accounting for voyages that was at the core of the Venetian economy.

We know nothing about the background or life of the student Zuan de Domenego. He became much better at arithmetic as he proceeded through the course of instruction (Sangster, 2018b), which suggests he may not by then have completed *abaco* school. If so, he was at most in his early teens. Of the tutor, little is known other than that he came from Ragusa (Dubrovnik), which was part of the Venetian republic at that time; and that before he started to teach his student, he travelled to Naples to prepare a copy of a manual on business, the *Book of the Art of Trade* by Benedetto Cotrugli, mentioned earlier.

Cotrugli's book was very apposite and complementary to De Raphaeli's double entry bookkeeping manual, not just because it contained a brief overview of the record-keeping system of a business and of double entry bookkeeping. It also included, in considerable detail, advice on how a merchant should conduct his business, his household, his family and himself, spiritually and ethically. De Raphaeli presented the copy of Cotrugli's book to Zuan de Domenego and the two texts were bound together defining, for the first time, what we today might recognize as a complete introductory text to business (Sangster, 2014).

No other bookkeeping tutors have been identified until 1510 and only three have been identified between then and 1540. The time for double entry bookkeeping to be taught by a significant number of tutors outside the workplace did not arrive until towards the end of the 16th century. Before then, the method, still a trade secret, needed to be released to a wider audience if more merchants were to be able to use it. This was accomplished in print.

7. The Printed Manuals

Pacioli (1494) identified a lack of expertise in double entry among local merchants and printed his manual on the subject in a book that consolidated all what was then known about applied mathematics for business: *abaco*. His book, *Summa Arithmetica*, was intended for that market (Sangster, Stoner & McCarthy, 2008) because, as indicated by Pacioli (1494), not many of them were very competent mathematicians. They also did not know how to do double entry (Sangster, 2018a).

Pacioli's (1494) manual served the needs of these small local merchants, not those of the international merchants for whom Cotrugli and

De Raphaeli had written. It was a manual for beginners and provided them with the tools to record what they needed, so that their account books would help them maintain control over their businesses *and* be sound evidence for a court should disputes arise with their customers, suppliers, debtors or creditors. It was the catalyst for all 882 editions of manuals on double entry that were printed before 1800 (Jeannin, 1991), and for the bookkeeping tutors who first emerged in significant numbers in Amsterdam in the late 16th century (Davids, 2004). Italian bankers were the first to develop double entry and Italian merchants were the first to use it in business, but it was print, not the Italian merchants or the Italian bankers that took it beyond Italian firms and into the businesses and classrooms of the rest of the world.

Within his manual, Pacioli (1494) delivered an ethical message for those merchants and bookkeepers. Cotrugli did so as well, but in a different way. Before considering what they both wrote, the ethics of medieval business needs to be considered for, as previously mentioned, most medieval bookkeepers were the businessmen themselves.

8. The Ethics of Medieval Business

Apart from their superior bookkeeping, the larger merchants also used highly developed postal systems to ensure they were always well informed of market prices and of changes in the business environment. They knew of bad news before everyone else and could adjust their prices and demand and supply to take advantage of changing prices long before the others. Consequently, they were often trading at an advantage compared to their competitors, their customers and their suppliers. (Braudel, 1972)

In addition, the vastly greater experience of the international merchants in dealing in credit, their knowledge of exchange rates and of the factors that caused them to change, gave them the skill to achieve high levels of profit from the less knowledgeable who required use of their services, through borrowing from them, lending to them either by granting credit in trade or by depositing funds in their banks or using their banking networks to transfer funds to other places using bills of exchange (Mueller, 1997).

For all these reasons, the scope these international merchants enjoyed for acting against the interests of the communities in which they traded was considerable. Offsetting that to some extent, with credit dominating trade not settled by barter, securing settlement of debt was a significant problem. Bad debts were a common feature both locally and internationally— in 1458, Cotrugli declared that debt loses 50 percent of its value in one year—devastatingly so for the three largest Italian international merchant banking firms of the 14th century, all of which failed because they failed to recover their debts (de Roover, 1954; Goldthwaite, 2009).

Consumers were protected to some extent through the rigors of the Catholic Church concerning adherence to a 'just price' and maximum prices set by guild statutes or State laws (Rosen, 2008); and interest rates were restricted, at least in theory, by the church's stance against usury and by state laws against it in major Italian centers of trade (Munro, 2003; Mueller, 1997).

The merchants controlled themselves through their guilds and their 'colonies' located in the major centers where they operated abroad. All the guilds, both merchant and craft, established norms within their community to protect their members and punish those that transgressed by fraud, use of false weights or measures, the sale of spoiled produce, price fixing, other sharp business practices, air pollution or noise pollution at night (Byrne, 2004). They also supported their "members and their families, through monetary charity, prayers, and burial" (Byrne, 2004, p. 478). Thus, for example, when four carpenters travelled from Parma to assist with the siege of Padua in 1388, members of their guild paid a levy so that the salaries of the four men could be paid to their families (Antinori, 1959).

These 'morally right' principles of the guilds benefited and protected both society in general and their members. However, there was another, darker side to the guilds. In contrast to the guilds' social morality, fairness, equality and desire to preserve the common good, an immoral selectivity for admission to membership was the norm, with entry restricted based on a range of requirements, including gender, ethnicity, social class, reputation and religion. Their mission was also predominantly self-serving and protectionist, intended only for the benefit of their carefully selected members. This was made possible by their enjoying monopolistic privileges, purchased from the state for whom the money received was a substitute for collecting and monitoring the collection of taxes. These privileges gave the guilds control over local trade and restricted access to local markets other than through their members—outsiders were unable to trade their goods to anyone other than with and through the guild (Ogilvie & Dessi, 2003).

Thus, whereas their existence was of significant benefit to their members and weeded-out those who failed to observe the norms of behavior laid-down in their statutes, their monopolistic power had an economically harmful impact on society by restricting consumer choice and causing consumers to pay more for their goods and services, less trade to take place because prices were high, less production because demand was suppressed and less employment.[5] It is, perhaps, not insignificant that when England and the Netherlands ceased to support the guilds in the 16th century, their economies flourished whereas the economies of other major European nations—France, Germany, Austria, Spain and Italy—none of which ceased supporting the guilds until the 18th and 19th century (Ogilvie & Dessi, 2003; Dessi & Piccolo, 2016), declined or stagnated (Braudel, 2002).

Other than their guilds, the principal guidance merchants followed came from merchant manuals. These were compendia of advice and instructions, important commercial facts—such as the timing of fairs and currencies, weights, measures, taxes, trading customs, products available from various trading centers and the ways to travel between them—and instruction in how to use financial instruments, such as bills of exchange. Of these, the best-known and most comprehensive manual of the medieval period was written by a factor of the Florentine banking house of the Bardi, Francesco Balducci Pegolotti. His manual, *La pratica della mercatura*,[6] was written c. 1340 and circulated in manuscript form before being published in print in 1766. However, it contained nothing relating to mercantile ethics. The first known manual for merchants that did was Cotrugli's *The Art of Trade*.

9. Cotrugli's *The Art of Trade* and Ethics

When he wrote his manual in 1458, Benedetto Cotrugli had spent many years as an international merchant, a statesman and was currently an ambassador to the King of Naples, which is where he lived. He had fled from the city to escape the plague, which, he wrote at the end of the book, had given him the time to write it. It was not printed until 1573, in an edition heavily edited by the publisher, but the unaltered manuscript version was well known. We do not know how many copies were made and only three copies have survived. The oldest and the one considered to have been most faithful to the original is the copy made by Marino De Raphaeli in 1475.

In it, Cotrugli is pious and declares his faith many times. He is also a realist, willing to argue against the tenets of the established church when he perceived it misguided and ill informed, most prominently on the subject of usury: the charging of interest on amounts lent or overdue. To redress this injustice, he provides his readers with the necessary learned sources to cite should they ever need to defend themselves against accusations of this 'crime'. He also addressed the church's stance on 'just price',[7] which he defined as one that is no more than 50 percent above cost, presumably the accepted view at the time; and he offers some ethical advice, advising against selling illegal goods, goods bought for their own use or goods received as gifts. On other aspects of morality, he devotes many pages while leaving the reader with the overwhelming impression that 15th century mercantile society was largely bereft of honesty and ethical values.

In his introduction, Cotrugli establishes the importance of merchants and commerce to society, describing it as "vital to human operations . . . the noblest activity . . . [and] more goes into the making of a merchant than a High Court judge" (Carraro & Favero, 2017, p. 25). Later, he describes the benefits that merchants bring to society (Cotrugli, 1458, c. 60v-61r):

> The utility, the comfort and the health of the Republic owes much to the great merchants . . . whose hard work and trade brings food and supplies to where it is not produced, bringing an abundance in

money, jewels, gold, silver and all kinds of metal; providing work for various arts and professions in the city and the country; cultivating the lands, breeding the livestock, and causing incomes and revenues to flourish; they support the poor to live through their efforts; . . . [and] through their constant importing and exporting, they enrich the public and communal exchequers, increasing the tax yields and excise duties of rulers and republics.

On merchants, he acknowledged that the public perception was that merchants were honest and trustworthy (Cotrugli, 1458, c. 61v):

dignity is served to the merchant with respect to trust, which is held as much in him by others as it is by him of others. For his part, because he keeps the deposits of others faithfully and pays his debts, as we see continuously; commonly it is said that trust only remains in merchants and men-at-arms. And, on the other side, faith and credit is placed upon them to an extent that neither kings, nor princes, nor prelates, nor any other men enjoy.

But, their public persona notwithstanding, Cotrugli does not have a good opinion of his former mercantile colleagues, describing them in terms that make it very clear that he viewed merchants as an uneducated rabble incapable of doing the job well. He believed that most lacked the appropriate upbringing and education and that their work ethic and their moral values were deficient and inappropriate for someone striving to make a career as a merchant.

His manual is his attempt to address this and, as the earlier quote illustrates, he clearly viewed doing so as important for society. However, as will be described later, his own moral values reflect those of the guilds: he is extremely intolerant and prejudiced, using profiling based on color and appearance, gender, homophobia and astrology—one of his clearest messages is that a merchant should learn whether or not to trust someone based on their appearance. He adds to this by advising the importance of knowing under which sign of the zodiac someone is born, saying that great care is needed to counteract those natural urges that those unfortunate enough to be 'born under a bad sign' may have. In other words, do not trust anyone who does not look 'right', nor anyone born in the wrong cycle of the moon. To those criteria, he adds many more.

He not only sets criteria for trust, he lists categories of people who should not be merchants irrespective of how they appear, presumably because they did not conform to his image of the perfect merchant. After listing those prohibited from doing so by law—royalty, nobles and anyone of noble birth, knights and gentlemen—he adds others, some of which are to be expected, such as those in holy orders, young people and the insane;

but he also invokes a class-based exclusion of peasants and servants. To these he adds wastrels, the uneducated, thieves, footpads, counterfeiters, alchemists and others of similar type, and women. His view of women, at a time when there was no sense of gender equality, was summed up in his advice that husbands should beat their wives if they have disobeyed them, but only as a last resort (Carraro & Favero, 2017). On servants, he advocated treating them humanely, giving rewards based on merit and educating them "as if they were your own children, and if you fail to do this, you commit a sin", though they should be worked hard and beaten if they disobey (Carraro & Favero, 2017, p. 167).

He believed that the best merchants are sons of merchants because, while growing-up, they learn "the gestures, manners, habits and speeches of merchants and display fluency and sober dignity in every action" and discipline (Carraro & Favero, 2017, p. 37). However, he cautions against anyone becoming a merchant, even sons of merchants, unless they are lively, not idle, well-turned-out, honorable, profit-seeking and physically fit, willing to endure hardship and long hours, while maintaining a body that is "tender and delicate" (Carraro & Favero, 2017, p. 39). To this he adds that merchants must maintain their reputation by not engaging in gambling, extravagance, alchemy, jousting, smuggling, use of false weights or measures; and only moderate eating and drinking, avoiding controversy and bad company.

In sum, a merchant had to be a paragon of virtue.

9.1 Coping With a Lack of Morality in Business

The emphasis in the text indicates that Cotrugli believed that trade at that time was a perilous venture, for both merchant and customer, with charlatans and unscrupulous merchants very much the rule rather than the exception, equivalent to the modern stereotype of the used car salesman or the backstreet money lender. He dismisses entire cities and regions as bad places to trade because the merchants could not be trusted: Calabria, Sicily and Valencia were places to avoid (Carraro & Favero, 2017); and he advocates using barter as the means of trade when trading somewhere like that, citing the example of doing so in Sicily, the place he condemns most, because barter avoids the risk of not being paid amounts due (Carraro & Favero, 2017).

Continuing on this vein, he offers advice on how to reduce the risks inherent in this mercantile environment. In his opinion, merchants had to be extremely careful about selecting, not just whom to trade with, but where to trade. For example, acknowledging that it may not always be obvious when somewhere would be a poor choice to live or trade, he recommends living and trading where merchants have succeeded in accumulating the greatest wealth, where peace reigns but, paradoxically, where business is not too successful because that attracts the unscrupulous.

Even the law was not above reproach, and not just the laws of the church concerning usury. He emphasizes the importance of only trading where (Cotrugli, 1458, c. 13r):

> trade is governed by mercantile law and not according to the Code of Justinian, because the disputes of the jurists, which in all things are hostile to a merchant's profits, are no small problem for the merchant. Mercantile practice needs brevity and speed, which is entirely contrary to the ways of the jurists.

On who to trade with and whom to offer credit, he is particularly narrow and discriminatory in his focus: merchants should avoid "the lame, the cross-eyed, the crooked-mouthed, the red-haired and suchlike, and above all those who when talking to you will not meet your eye . . . [and, avoid men] whose [family] name suggests iniquity" (Carraro & Favero, 2017, p. 48). Above all, "do your business then with men whom nature has created with pleasing proportions" (Carraro & Favero, 2017, p. 49).

Moving past the purely physical, he believed that the way in which a man is dressed revealed a lot about his character, particularly how he wore his hat. A well-positioned hat was a sign of virtue (Cotrugli, 1458, c. 72r):

> those who wear their hat or hood drawn over their eyes are haughty and irascible; those who appear in front of men and leave their hoods down, are vain men or in love; those who wear their hat to one side are fantastical, lightweight, very weak-brained, quarrelsome, presumptuous, boastful and bestial, and the multitude of words they speak are full of the sound of the vain; those who wear their hat well-placed, equalized, like a crown, they are good men, of sound mind and full of authority and modesty, 'for virtue is a habit of choice in the midst of all' Aristotle, II.º *Ethicorum*.

Continuing on the theme of clothing, Cotrugli was a great believer in adhering to appropriate moral values. One on which he dwelt was what he viewed as the immorality of dressing inappropriately, in finery and without modesty: "[it is] against all morality and good practice, since a man in his sober and civil dealings should never exceed the moderation appropriate to our nature" (Carraro & Favero, 2017, p. 148). He declares that merchants, many of whom dressed-up in furs and silks on holidays, should not wear anything that is considered clothing suitable for a woman: "it is not seemly" (Carraro & Favero, 2017, p. 150); nor should they use makeup or die their hair: "if you have the misfortune to come across a man who makes up his face or hair such as I have seen, avoid him like a demon from hell: he might have all the wisdom of Solomon, but he will prove be an idiot none the less" (Carraro & Favero, 2017, p. 152).

9.2 The Perfect Ethical Merchant

Cotrugli covers many aspects of what contributes to making the perfect ethically driven merchant, some he views as moral virtues, some he views as simply essential.

- The importance of studying moral philosophy (Cotrugli, 1458, c. 63v):

   [A merchant should] not work on unknown or unnecessary or obscure things, neglecting things pertinent and necessary to us; as if, for example, we ignored moral philosophy and, instead, chose to learn geometry or astrology.

- A merchant should be prudent (Cotrugli, 1458, c. 63v):

   He must be circumspect and beware of contrary vices, while preserving utility. Also cautious in discerning the good from the evil, the white from the black and the useful from the damaged, the true from the false and illusion from the truth and, beneath the manner of the good and the useful, to not be deceived, as the Greeks with their horse deceived the Trojans, pretending it as a gift to Minerva. And yet you who are prudent and cautious, beware of those who seem good, upright, holy and come 'in sheep's clothing but inwardly are ravenous wolves,' as said by Saint Paul: 'Such men are asps, deaf and walk with twisted necks.'

- A merchant's integrity (Carraro & Favero, 2017, p. 123):

   He should be a man of equable temperament, upright and reliable, so that his word can be trusted and the currency of his promises undoubted and never fall short. In fact, he should be especially punctilious in respecting his promises and any financial engagements he has entered into and hold to his agreements.

- A merchant should be unforgiving (Carraro & Favero, 2017, p. 124):

   One should never extend one's trust or credit to bankrupts, least of all those who have failed through iniquity, because 'whoever has been wicked on one occasion, one can presume to be wicked always'.

- A merchant should show exemplary diligence and dispatch, which are the progenitors of wealth (Carraro & Favero, 2017).

- Application should be an attribute of the interior man, from which all mercantile aptitude stems (Carraro & Favero, 2017).

- A merchant should be shrewd, virtuous, innocent and pure of heart (Carraro & Favero, 2017, pp. 126–127):

The shrewdness of a merchant, or his cunning, must be employed in moderation: he should neither hurt others nor allow himself to be got the better of, but manage to intuit where deceit and falsity lurk. And if a man is credulous or lacking in reasoning, he should not take up trade, because in this profession nowadays there are a thousand snares, frauds and deceits. And this guile, which is linked to fraud, should not be used even to a good end . . . [and] within himself the merchant must always be virtuous, innocent and pure in heart, without even contemplating trickery, still less practicing it.

- On money (Carraro & Favero, 2017, p. 127): "a merchant should be urbane, moderate in regard to money with country, friends, children, parents, wife or servants, in fact, to each according to his position, and to the time and place, but also not denying himself his due."

- On fairness, judgement, and truth (Carraro & Favero, 2017, p. 128):

Fairness, according to St Augustine, is rendering to each what is his, and this is a virtue that embraces many others. Therefore, a merchant should always be concerned to render to each his due. . . . A merchant's sense of fair play requires that he . . . uphold fairness towards others, not only in obvious matters, but also in concealed ones . . . [and] you must be fair not only in managing money but also in delivering judgements, because it usually falls to merchants to be arbitrators . . . resolving disputes simply and to general agreement, without the brouhaha and formality of a full trial, but respecting the essence of the truth.

- On doing favors (Carraro & Favero, 2017, p. 131):

And be sure that the favor you do to one does nor entail doing harm to another, because what favors one person whereas harming another, is not a favor but fawning. And therefore, as Seneca says, 'One should try to practice a liberality that benefits many but harms no-one', not like that great multitude of merchants who engage in all kinds of usury and then build churches and hospitals.

- A merchant should excel in modesty and personal honesty (Carraro & Favero, 2017).

- A merchant should be flexible and able to get along with (Carraro & Favero, 2017, p. 135):

He should be a sociable man and adroit in conversation . . . amiable and benevolent, fashioned pleasingly of human clay . . . agreeable with all, and, especially when buying and selling, cheerful and good-humored. He must be chaste . . . regular in his gait . . . morally solid and mature . . . [and] able to get on with every sort of person . . . and conversely, he must not be irascible, vindictive, arrogant, argumentative, fickle, a buffoon, empty, spendthrift, without substance, a drunkard or a glutton.

- A merchant and his friends, borrowing and lending (Carraro & Favero, 2017, p. 139):

    The merchant therefore should have many acquaintances and few friends, even if the term 'friend' is one we use too freely, because one finds very few true friends. . . . Try not to accept others' money as security, or to make loans: it is better to blush once than blanch a hundred times.

- Being the perfect and complete merchant (Cotrugli, 1458, c. 64r&v):

    The merchant not only . . . must be a good writer, mathematician, bookkeeper, etc. but, must be literate and a good rhetorician, and this is necessary to him, because command of grammar and language makes the intelligent man understand a contract well and the merchant makes contracts every day. . . . Rhetoric is necessary because not only does the art of rhetoric make man eloquent in the Latin language, but also convincing in the vernacular, which part is a fine ornament of the person of the merchant. It lets him know how to write letters elegantly and address lords and great masters and, when in need, to know how to begin formal correspondence in an appropriate manner.

Overall, what Cotrugli sought was an ethically driven mercantile class that behaved in a way that was superior in all respects and avoided what he perceived as the poor ethical and moral values of many who, at that time, were engaged in trade. Adopting a mirrored view, he is telling his readers that most merchants were not ethical in their business practices and that anyone engaged in trade, merchant or consumer, needed to be aware of the pitfalls of doing business with the wrong people. Given that he had spent many years as an international merchant, this assessment of the mercantile class is surely more likely to be based on what he himself had witnessed than on imagination and paranoia.

As merchants comprised the vast majority of 15th-century bookkeepers, it appears that the account books of many merchants may not have been consistently maintained ethically. Whether they were or not, merchant courts existed in major centers of trade to deal with disputes. To guide them, Juristic law placed an emphasis upon accuracy and completeness in determining which set of account books to trust when amounts recorded were challenged (Minaud, 2011, p. 800):

> medieval jurists analyzed the possibilities for account books to be elements of proof in case of dispute. Each accounting entry must relate to only one transaction of which it gives details of the date, amount, and cause. . . . The accounting entry is not a means of constituting an obligation, the accounting entry provokes a presumption of obligation. . . . Medieval jurists weighed the legal scope of each record in an account book by taking from it all the irrefutable proof.

These elements being proven, it follows that the debit written in such an account book is judged sound (Minaud, 2011, p. 808):

> [they] . . . targeted the material aspect of the accounts as their interior presentation or the drafting of each record, without forgetting the arithmetic links existing between the debits and the credits. According to them, compliance with all the recommended rules gave to an account book its full authority and legal value, especially in the event of a dispute brought before a court or an arbitrator.

Pacioli (1494) was more specific about bookkeeping, telling merchants how they should maintain their account books and records if they were to be considerable trustworthy, truthful and honest. In doing so, he reveals many of the practices that were lacking in ethics and offers advice on how to avoid them.

10. Pacioli on Merchants, Bookkeepers, and Ethics

In his twenty-seven-page manual of double entry bookkeeping,[8] Pacioli (1494) offered several ethical suggestions concerning how to maintain account books, including not having two sets of books and obtaining permission from debtors before you entered anything in their account. He begins the manual by highlighting the importance of a merchant's honor if he is to be successful:

> It has happened that many without capital of their own but whose credit was good carried on big transactions and by means of their credit, which they faithfully kept, became very wealthy. We became acquainted with many of these throughout Italy. In the great republics nothing was considered superior to the word of the good merchant, and oaths were taken on the word of a good merchant (Pacioli, 1494, Chapter 1).

10.1 Trust

To protect a merchant's honor and maintain the trust of those with whom he deals, Pacioli (1494) emphasizes,

1. The importance of keeping well maintained account books:

    > There are three things needed by anyone who wishes to carry on business carefully . . . cash and any other substantial resources . . . being a good and quick mathematician . . . **and recording all his affairs systematically so that information may be had quickly concerning each of them, as to their debit and their credit, because there is no greater need in trade.** (Pacioli, 1494, Chapter 1, bold emphasis added and original translation amended)

2. Acting both lawfully and without avarice: "the purpose of every merchant is to make a lawful and reasonable profit so as to keep up his business" (Pacioli, 1494, Chapter 2).
3. Keeping a full record of everything: "[everything must be described] in proper order . . . with all marks, names, surnames—as far as possible—for things are never too clear to a merchant on account of the different things that may happen in business" (Pacioli, 1494, Chapter 4).
4. Because of the infinite range of possible situations in commerce, being at all times alert: "the merchant must have a much better understanding of things than a butcher" (Pacioli, 1494, Chapter 17). "[The proverb says:] if you are in business and do not know all about it, your money will go like flies" (Pacioli, 1494, Chapter 23).

   Right is the proverb which says: More bridges are necessary to make a good merchant than a lawyer can make. . . . the merchant is like a rooster, which of all the animals (*animale*) is the most alert and in winter and summer keeps his night vigils and never rests . . . the head of the merchant has a hundred eyes, and still they are not sufficient for all he has to say or to do. . . . The law helps those that are awake, not those that sleep." (Pacioli, 1494, Chapter 4)

5. To ensure that his account books will be trusted, a merchant should take his account books to an appropriate authority and:

   state that those are the books in which you intend to write down, or somebody else write down for you, all your transactions in an orderly way; and also state in what kind of money the transactions therein should be entered. . . . The good merchant should put down these things always on the first page of his book. . . . The clerk should mention all this in the records of the said officer . . . [and] the said clerk shall write down on the first page of your books, in his own handwriting, the name of the said officer, and will attest to the truth of everything and shall attach the seal of that office to make the books authentic for any case in court when they might be produced. (Pacioli, 1494, Chapter 7)

6. Just as a merchant must do everything to protect his honor and maintain other people's trust, so he must make sure that what his books contain can be trusted: "you must state in your daybook with precision the way that you have made the purchase, or have somebody else do it for you, and you will do well" (Pacioli, 1494, Chapter 9).
7. Also, trust all his employees to keep a record of transactions:

   At times . . . only the servants or the women who, perhaps, can barely write [remain at home]. These latter, in order not to send customers away, must sell, collect or buy, according to the orders left by the boss or owner, and they, as well as they can, must enter every transaction in this daybook, naming simply the money and weights which they know; they should note the various kinds of money that they may collect or take in or that they may give in exchange. (Pacioli, 1494, Chapter 6)

10.2 Fraud

Pacioli (1494) first mentions fraud when he emphasizes the need to number all pages in account books:

> As we have seen, for many of the bigger merchants, not one, but several pages have to be used in one day. If someone would wish to do something crooked, he could tear out one of the pages and this fraud could not be discovered, as far as the dates are concerned, for the days would follow properly one after the other. . . . Therefore, for this and other reasons, it is always good to number and mark each single page in all the books of the merchants; the books kept in the house or kept in the store.
> (Pacioli, 1494, Chapter 6)

He adds:

> This custom ought to be greatly commended; also, the places where the custom is followed. Many keep their books in duplicate. They show one to the buyer and one to the seller, and this is very bad, because in this way they commit perjury. By presenting books to the said officer, one cannot easily lie or defraud.
> (Pacioli, 1494, Chapter 7)

Pacioli (1494, Chapter 28) focuses on avoiding any bookkeeping act that might be deemed fraudulent or imply fraud:

> When an account has been filled out, either in the debit or In the credit, and you cannot make any more entries in the space reserved for such an account, you must at once carry this account forward to a page after all your other accounts, so that there is no space left in the Ledger between this transferred account and the last of the other accounts. Otherwise it would be considered a fraud. . . . Accounts should be opened in the order in which they originate in such place and at such time, so that nobody can speak evil of you.

10.3 Conforming to Custom and Law

In Venice, the journal was recognized as the primary book to be consulted in the event of any dispute (Antinori, 2004). Not surprisingly, Pacioli (1494, Chapter 10) emphasizes that the journal must be kept neatly; and advises using terms and signs "used by the other merchants, so that it will not look as if you would deviate from the usual mercantile custom" (Pacioli, 1494, Chapter 12).

Merchants could not simply record that someone owed them payment, nor that they had particular unconfirmed rights with a creditor. Doing so violated the integrity of their books and their reputation: "you can never enter in your books as a debtor any person without his knowing it, nor put him as a creditor under certain conditions without his consent. If you should do these things, it would not be right and your books would be considered wrong" (Pacioli, 1494, Chapter 23).

> You cannot add terms or conditions to a credit without permission and consent of the creditor. If you should, that statement would be untrue. . . . If a new account should be opened, you must use a new page and must not go back even if there was room enough to place the new account. You should not write backward, but always forward—that is, go forward as the days go, which never come back. If you do otherwise, the book would be untrue.
> (Pacioli, 1494, Chapter 36)

According to Pacioli, merchants could place their trust in the books of the Venetian State revenue officers, whose books were subject to oversight and audit by State officials. But they could not rely on the records of the Office of Public Loans whose clerks, Pacioli tells us, changed often and had a reputation for adopting new methods of record keeping that made verification of transactions made with their predecessors difficult. To counter this, merchants needed to maintain detailed records of any transactions made with them, if possible, in the hand of the clerk with whom they dealt.

10.4 Dealing With Bad Faith in the Financial Market

In Chapter 24, Pacioli states that the banking system and the system of international money transfers suffered from bad faith. He counsels taking the trouble to record everything with due diligence and taking many other precautions, including

- in dealing with banks, obtaining receipts for deposits and withdrawals; and keep separate accounts when dealing with a bank on behalf of others;
- when asked by a creditor to transfer an amount from their account to the account of someone else, record it in the journal;
- noting all details of bills of exchange, always obtaining a proper receipt and obtain and destroy all copies of bills issued in the merchant's own hand after they have been honored.

10.5 Being Honorable to Those With Whom a Merchant Trades

In Chapter 30, Pacioli focuses on the importance of statements of account and the need to prepare them with great care so that disputes do not arise:

> you must know how to make an abstract or a statement of an account if your debtor requests it . . . back to the time from which he desires to have his statement . . . and you should do this willingly. . . . But before these statements are delivered, they ought to be compared carefully with each entry in the Ledger, Journal and Day Book, or with any other paper relative thereto, so that no mistake could be made between the parties. But if you should act for others as an agent or commissioner, then you will make out a statement for your employer. . . . Your employer will then go through this statement, compare it with his own book, and if he finds it correct, he will like you better and trust you more. . . . If you are the employer, you may have your managers or commissioners make out these statements for you.

10.6 The Merchant Bookkeeper

In Chapter 32, Pacioli (1494) identified the closure of a ledger as an opportunity to ensure it has been correctly maintained. The audit procedures he described and the closure process itself were to be applied "with great diligence and order". The entries in the daybook were checked against the entries in the journal and the entries in the journal were checked against the entries in the ledger. In doing so, he confirms that merchants were often their own bookkeepers:

> after you have finished checking off the Journal, if you find in the Ledger some account or entry which has not been checked off in debit or credit, this would indicate that there has been some mistake in the Ledger. That is, that that entry is superfluous, whether in the debit or credit. . . . A good bookkeeper should always mention why such differences arise, so that the books are above suspicion. . . . Thus the good bookkeeper must act so that [his] mercantile reputation be [maintained].

Then, in Chapter 34 when Pacioli (1494) describes the process of closing the ledger, he concludes by again confirming the merchant's role as bookkeeper: "if you are not a good bookkeeper in your business, you will go on groping like a blind man and may meet great losses. Therefore, take good care and make all efforts to be a good bookkeeper".

11. Conclusion

Medieval Europe was a time and place of continuous change. It took 500 years for the transition from rural economy to the town, city, fair and port-based international trading commercial environment it had become by the 15th century (North & Thomas, 1973). Merchants, crafts and professions began establishing guilds in the 11th century, which led to a shift of power away from the nobility. By the 13th century, Italian merchants dominated trade and finance; and merchants controlled the city-states of Italy (Byrne, 2004). As both Cotrugli and Pacioli (1494) make clear, their common code gave them a reputation of being trustworthy—their word was their bond. This is evident in how they conducted business, for example, treating promissory notes from other merchants as if they were legally binding:

> A merchant's promissory note can be exchanged without problem whereas those of others only with difficulty and where accepted they circulate at a much higher rate of interest whoever takes them on; and the merchant's clear and simple handwritten receipt is accepted at face value, whereas those of lords and other categories of person are not creditworthy without solid legal backing and restrictions.
> (Carraro & Favero, 2017, p. 115)

Yet, from an ethical perspective, many merchants took advantage of their position and took advantage of those less informed or less equipped. The monopolistic rights they enjoyed restricted markets and opportunity for others. Honoring credit was a slow and sometimes unproductive process and many suffered as a result, from the three largest international Italian merchant banking firms of the 14th century, to the smallest firm. Sometimes, whole cities and regions gained a reputation for defaulting on payment, but only among merchants sufficiently experienced to know.

Whereas Pacioli (1494) tells us that debts could not be recorded in a ledger without the debtor's permission, and merchants appeared to have had the right to inspect their accounts in other merchants' ledgers (Edler, 1934). Some countered this by maintaining duplicate ledgers for their debtors. At a time when a merchant's account book had the status of a notarized document, the only defense for those abused in this way was to record everything, which is what Pacioli (1494) went to great lengths to emphasize.

Some of the measures taken to avoid trading with the 'wrong' person advocated by Cotrugli appear strange and unethical to us today and some undoubtedly were irrespective of the more than five centuries that have passed: discriminating on the basis of color, religion, physical deformity and gender. Yet, by definition, Cotrugli's perfect, homegrown-and-raised merchant would have passed all the tests, including these, because he advocated a closed mercantile community from which outsiders were excluded. Above all, he would have looked the part, both in appearance and manner and in education. There would always be exceptions but, if we consider our own modern stereotypes of loan sharks, second-hand car dealers and shady businessmen, it is not difficult to see the point Cotrugli was making: these stereotypes do not dress immaculately and conduct themselves in an upright, morally sound and dignified way.

Bookkeepers who, in the largest firms, did perform many of the activities of a modern accountant—preparing financial reports and auditing the account books—were largely drawn from this community of merchants. So also were the agents who enabled the switch by Italian international merchants from an itinerant to a sedentary lifestyle in the 13th century. These merchant-bookkeepers were the people Cotrugli and Pacioli were writing about. Some were paragons of virtue, but most were not. Yet, in their bookkeeping, aside from those who fraudulently falsified their books, most undoubtedly recognized the perils of not maintaining their account books and supporting evidence to the highest possible standards. Their business ethics may have been suspect, but their bookkeeping was not.

Bookkeepers knew the boundaries and they knew the need to comply with law and custom. The 'red flags' in double entry bookkeeping were obvious to those that used it—Pacioli wrote about them when he described how to use the space in the ledger, always moving forwards in time, never going back. But the greatest problem was that, just as merchants tended to be from families of merchants, so double entry bookkeeping was only known to those who acquired it during their apprenticeships. Anyone else seeking to be a merchant faced the same problem as those who tried to be carpenters but could not join the guild: they were excluded from access to secrets of trade, including double entry, because they had not served an apprenticeship with a merchant who had that knowledge.

This lack of the most comprehensive and legally recognized method of bookkeeping left those merchants at risk from the unscrupulous. By publishing the method of double entry in print, Pacioli enfranchised those small merchants and gave them the tools to protect themselves from the predators with whom they traded; and he established an approach to organizing education in the method of double entry and accounting that others built on and extended. The publication of his manual marked a pivotal and highly ethical moment in accounting education. Whether subsequent generations of authors of double entry manuals and teachers of bookkeeping and accounting placed the same emphasis on ethical bookkeeping and accounting practice is for others to discover, but Pacioli certainly led them in the right direction.

Notes

1. For example, see the discussion of differences between Florentine double entry and Venetian double entry in Edler (1934).
2. For example, in 1481 when Lorenzo di Matteo Morelli needed to update his financial records, he had no choice but to use the information extracted from his account with his bank, even though he did not agree with it: the double entry bank ledger was recognized by the courts as legal evidence (Goldthwaite, 2009).
3. Accounting—"the system of recording and summarizing business and financial transactions and analyzing, verifying, and reporting the results" (Merriam Webster)—existed in two main aspects in Medieval Italy: double entry was used to record transactions and the book closure process provided the ability to determine how much profit had been earned. However, book closure was something only Tuscan partnerships tended to do, unless a ledger was full. For Venetian merchants engaged in voyages, preparing a profit and loss account to identify their overall profit or loss was generally pointless due to the inherent uncertainty of their trade (Lane, 1977).
4. These records were inspected on several occasions by the author between 2011 and 2019 in the *Archivio di Stato di Prato*, and subsequent analysis of images made of the pages in the account books. The description that follows is based on observations made during those activities.
5. There are contrasting views about this monopolistic position enjoyed by the guilds. Some, such as Dessi and Piccolo (2016), argue that society was no worse off than if the State had collected its own taxes. However, there was a significant difference in opportunity and wealth of members of guilds compared to those who were not; and the guilds, supported by the States, ensured that it was maintained.
6. The text of this book and an extensive introduction about Pegolotti (c. 1340) and his text in English are available in Evans, A. (1936) *Francesco Balducci Pegolotti, La Pratica della Mercatura*. Retrieved December 29th, 2019, from https://cdn.ymaws.com/www.medievalacademy.org/resource/resmgr/maa_books_online/evans_0024.htm.
7. For a full explanation of 'just price', see De Roover (1958).
8. All quotations from Pacioli's manual are from Geijsbeek's translation (1914). The term, 'memorandum' has been replaced throughout with, 'daybook'.

References

Antinori, C. (1959). *"Taxationes" dell'arte dei falegnami di Parma per il campo di Padova (1388–89)*. Parma: Tip. Editrice "La Nazionale".

Antinori, C. (2004). La contabilità pratica prima di Luca Pacioli: origine della partita doppia. *De Computis: Revista Española de Historia de la Contabilidad*, 1, 4–22.

Barnard, J. (1972). Trade and finance in the middle ages: 900–1500. In C. M. Cipolla (Ed.), *The Fontana economic history of Europe: Vol. 1. the middle ages* (pp. 274–338). Glasgow: Collins/Fontana.

Black, R. (2007). *Education and society in Florentine Tuscany: Teachers, pupils and schools, c. 1250–1500*. Leiden: Brill.

Braudel, F. (1972). *The Mediterranean and the Mediterranean world in the age of Philip II* (Vol. 1). 1995 reprint. Berkley & Los Angeles: University of California Press.

Braudel, F. (2002). *The perspective of the world*. London: Phoenix Press.

Byrne, J. P. (2004). Guilds. In C. Kleinhenz (Ed.), *Medieval Italy: Vol. 1, an encyclopedia* (pp. 476–479). New York: Routledge.

Carraro, C., & Favero, G. (2017). *Benedetto Cotrugli: The book of the art of trade*. Cham: Palgrave Macmillan.

Casanova, A. (1558). *Specchio lucidissimo nel quale si vedeno essere diffinito tatti i modi . . . che si deve menare nelle negotiamenti della Mercantia*. Venice: Comin da Trino.

Cherubini, P. (1996). Frammenti di quaderni di scuola d'area umbra alla fine del secolo XV. *Quellen und Forschungen aus italienischen Archiven und Bibliotheken, 76*, 219–252.

Cipolla, C. M. (1956). *Money, prices and civilization in the Mediterranean world*. Princeton: Princeton University Press.

Cotrugli, B. (1458). Libro de Larte dela Mercatura, manuscript copy of 1475. Reprinted in facsimile. In A. Sangster (Ed.) (2014), *Libr. XV: Cotrugli and de Raphaeli on business and bookkeeping in the renaissance* (pp. 25–220). Stirling: Lomax Press.

Davids, K. (2004). The bookkeeper's tale: Learning merchant skills in the Northern Netherlands in the sixteenth century. In K. Goudriaan, J. van Moolenbroek, & A. Tervoort (Eds.), *Education and learning in the Netherlands, 1400–1600* (pp. 235–251). Leiden: Brill.

de Roover, R. (1954). New interpretations of the history of banking. *Journal of World History, 2*, 38–76.

de Roover, R. (1958). The concept of the just price: Theory and economic policy. *The Journal of Economic History, 18*(4), 418–434.

de Roover, R. (1963). The organization of trade. In M. M. Postan, E. E. Rich & E. Miller (Eds.), *The Cambridge economic history of Europe from the decline of the Roman Empire: Vol. 3, economic organisation and policies in the Middle Ages* (pp. 42–118). Cambridge: Cambridge University Press.

Dessi, R., & Piccolo, S. (2016). Merchant guilds, taxation and social capital. *European Economic Review, 83*, 90–110.

Edler, F. (1934). *Glossary of mediaeval terms of business*. Cambridge, MA: The Mediaeval Academy of America.

Fazzini, M., Fici, L., Montrone, A., & Terzani, S. (2016). A modern look at the Banco De'Medici: Governance and accountability systems. *International Business & Economics Research Journal (IBER), 15*(6), 271–286.

Flori, L. (1636). *Trattato Del Modo Di Tenere Il Libro Doppio Domestico Col Suo Esemplare*. Reprinted 1677. Roma: Lazzari Varese.

Geijsbeek, J. B. (1914). *Ancient double-entry bookkeeping*. Denver, USA: J. B. Geijsbeek.

Goldthwaite R. A. (1972). Schools and teachers of commercial arithmetic in Renaissance Florence. *The Journal of European Economic History, 1*, 418–433.

Goldthwaite, R. A. (1985). Local banking in Renaissance Florence. *Journal of European Economic History, 14*(1), 5–55.

Goldthwaite, R. A. (2009). *The economy of Renaissance Florence*. Baltimore: Johns Hopkins University Press.

Goldthwaite, R. A. (2015). The practice and culture of accounting in Renaissance Florence. *Enterprise & Society, 16*, 611–647.

Grendler, P. F. (1989). *Schooling in Renaissance Italy: Literacy and learning, 1300–1600*. Baltimore: Johns Hopkins University Press.

Grendler, P. F. (1990). Schooling in Western Europe. *Renaissance Quarterly*, 43(4), 775–787.
Grendler, P. F. (2002). *The universities of the Italian Renaissance*. Baltimore: Johns Hopkins University Press.
Jeannin, P. (1991). L'*lmpresa. Industria, commercio, banca (xiii-xviii secolo)*, Istituto internazionale di storia economica. In Anon. (Ed.) *Atti delle Settimane di studi*, 22 (pp. 243–259). Florence. F. Datini: Prato.
Kuter, M., Gurskaya, M., Andreenkova, A., & Bagdasaryan, R. (2018). Asset impairment and depreciation before the 15th century. *Accounting Historians Journal*, 45(1), 29–44.
Lane, F. C. (1977). Doubles entry bookkeeping and resident merchants. *Journal of European Economic History*, 6, 177–191.
Lee, G. A. (1977). The coming of age of double entry: The Giovanni Farolfi ledger of 1299–1300. *Abacus*, 4(2), 79–95.
Marino, J. A. (2002). Economic encounters and the first stages of a world economy. In G. Ruggiero (Ed.), *A companion to the worlds of the Renaissance* (pp. 279–295). Oxford: Blackwell.
Marshall, R. K. (1999). *The local merchants of Prato: Small entrepreneurs in the late medieval economy*. Baltimore: Johns Hopkins University Press.
Martinelli, A. (1974). *The origination and evolution of double entry bookkeeping to 1440* (Doctoral dissertation, North Texas State University). Retrieved from https://digital.library.unt.edu/ark:/67531/metadc504552/m2/1/high_res_d/1002777549-Martinelli.pdf
Minaud, G. (2011). Les juristes médiévaux italiens et la comptabilité commerciale avant sa formalisation en partie double de 1494. *Revue Historique*, 660, 781–810.
Molmenti, P. G. (1880). *La storia di Venezia nella vita privata dalle origini alia caduta della repubblica*. Totino: Roux et Favele.
Mueller, R. C. (1997). *The Venetian Money Market: Banks, panics, and the public debt, 1200–1500*. Baltimore: Johns Hopkins University Press.
Munro, J. H. (2003). The medieval origins of the financial revolution: Usury, rentes, and negotiability. *The International History Review*, 25(3), 505–562.
North, D. C., & Thomas, P. (1973). *The rise of the western world*. Cambridge: Cambridge University Press.
Ogilvie, S., & Dessi, R. (2003). *Social capital and collusion: The case of merchant guilds* (CESifo Working Paper Series No. 1037). Retrieved June 27, 2020, from https://ssrn.com/abstract=449263
Pacioli, L. (1494). *Summa de Arithmetica Geometria Proportioni et Proportionalita*. Venice: Paganino de Paganini.
Postan, M. (1973). *Medieval trade and finance*. Cambridge: Cambridge University Press.
Rosen, M. (2008). The republic at work: S. Marco's reliefs of the Venetian trades. *The Art Bulletin*, 90(1), 54–75.
Sangster, A. (2014). *Libr. XV: Cotrugli and de Raphaeli on business and bookkeeping in the renaissance*. Stirling: Lomax Press.
Sangster, A. (2015). The earliest known treatise on double entry bookkeeping by Marino de Raphaeli. *Accounting Historians Journal*, 42(2), 1–33.
Sangster, A. (2016). The genesis of double entry bookkeeping. *The Accounting Review*, 91(1), 299–315.

Sangster, A. (2018a). Pacioli's lens: God, humanism, Euclid, and the rhetoric of double entry. *The Accounting Review*, *93*(2), 299–314.

Sangster, A. (2018b). *De Raphaeli: Venetian double entry bookkeeping in 1475*. Stirling: Lomax Press.

Sangster, A., & Rossi, F. (2018). Benedetto Cotrugli on double entry bookkeeping. *De Computis: Revista Española de Historia de la Contabilidad*, *15*(2), 22–38.

Sangster, A., Stoner, G. N., & McCarthy, P. (2008). The market for Luca Pacioli's Summa Arithmetica. *Accounting Historians Journal*, *35*(1), 111–134.

Smith, F. (2008). The influence of Amatino Manucci and Luca Pacioli. *BSHM Bulletin: Journal of the British Society for the History of Mathematics*, *23*(3), 143–156.

Spufford, P. (2006). From Antwerp and Amsterdam to London: The decline of financial centres in Europe. *De Economist*, *154*, 143–175.

Van Egmond, W. (1981). *Practical mathematics in the Italian Renaissance: A catalog of Italian abbacus manuscripts and printed books to 1600*. Firenze: Editrice Giunti Barbèra.

2 The Long Strange Trip
A Reflection on the Historical Relativity of Accounting Ethics

Timothy J. Fogarty

1. The Tenor of Our Times

Modernism is a convenient way to describe a host of attitudinal and institutional circumstances that most of us accept as essential or commonsensical. This includes a secular state that is accountable to the public, professions that serve the public interest and capitalism as a dominant economic system that provides useful incentives and resultant allocations of resources. Bolstered by an expansive scientific method, modernism has prevailed over earlier world orders based on religion, kinship and primitive technical knowledge.

Through a steadfast belief in an objective reality and the ultimate triumph of reason, modernism elevated the inevitability of progress to a canon of faith. This was done in various ways in different contexts, with businesses leaning heavily upon 'tools' like cost/benefit analysis and mantras that expressed the equivalence of measurement and management. The world that was build tended to be totalizing in its effects, even threatening to subsume that which was irreducibly human or joyfully idiosyncratic. The core problem of modernity was the coordination of the complex relationships among people with largely impersonal means and methods not very sensitive to differing values (Ray & Reed, 2002). Within this arrangement, elite groups gained the bulk of rewards but were charged with the responsibility of manufacturing the consent of the governed (van Dijk, 1993). Whereas these societal conditions do not directly condition accounting ethics and the research of such, they formed the environment and background for every sustained inquiry.

To believe that modernity is a continuous era would not be erroneous. Efforts consistent with this worldview and beliefs persist in most domains. Rather than the dawning of a new age, there is the progressive identification of contradictions and inconsistencies with the current one. This might be represented as late modernity, even if such a term leaves unspecified the timing of its ultimate replacement.

At the most fundamental level, new ideas have developed about the nature of knowledge itself. Our ability to completely assert its objectivity is weakening. This crisis of faith is the combined result of the identification of previously under recognized contingencies in what we know and the recognition of altogether new dimensions.

The mildest challenge to modernity is posed by the recognition that 'nationality' is not value-free but instead has been, and continues to be, a tipping of the scales in one systematic way. The sorting of those who benefit and those that do not is far from an accident or an incidental byproduct. The purpose of scholarship is to make historical choices more visible (Willmott, 1992). In other words, the dark side of success needs to be exposed and this often results in voice given to the losers (Gilligan, 1993).

The processes of modernity need to be evaluated with consequences in the foreground. 'Tools' have a moral dimension in such a light. Rationality is not bottomless and must be revisited prior to its more complete penetration of the lifeworld of people.

Another deviation from the modernist narrative is a broader recognition of contingency. Cultural forces push for fragmentation, diversity and possibly disorder (Ray & Reed, 2002). Conventional universal truths become more nuanced to the point of being recast so that if anything is invariably true, it is permeated by context to the point of reconfiguration in application (Hanks, 1993).

The rationalization of the world that so distinctly marked modernity classified and categorized domains such that operating rules for each area could be more clearly discerned. However, there has been a general recognition that subtle connections exist between institutions and fields. Here, the work is linked to the organizations and the people that do it and efforts to separate and isolate are rather arbitrary in their essence. Strategies and decisions within them have collateral consequences and 'second order' implications in distant realms (Sunstein & Ullmann-Margalit, 1999). Greater awareness of these interdependencies makes special allowances and privileges less acceptable, if for no other reason, an inability to tolerate what might be collateral damage.

We also begin to recognize that the objective truth that we use to put exclusive faith upon does not exist apart from the discourses that surround it. More returns to the achieved truth of that which is believed in, focusing attention to the process whereby people achieve that result. Only with great difficulty is the rhetoric that surrounded modernity dismantled (Burrell, 1993). However, the mere fact that attention is paid to ideology and its communication constitutes a severe departure from the faith that modernity once commanded.

Late modernity may require us to re-conceptualize the nature of self-interest. Marxist thought notwithstanding, modernity made self-interest mostly invisible even if it made just about all private sector activity possible. An exception existed when fraud trigged by excessive greed was present. As modernity aged, the notion that any activity or institution was not permeated by the pursuit of economic gain became more fanciful.

Rather than a perversion that can be safely quarantined and effectively ignored, self-interest has become an important element of any analysis.

Ironically enough, the broadening recognition of self-interest occurs in conjunction with the decline of economic hegemony. Pure economics approximated a grand theory for the explanation of life in modernity but has been recently discovered as flawed and quite partial. The absence of good data and rigorous causality in practice renders managerial effectiveness somewhat fictitious (MacIntyre, 2013). A residual human element, diminished by the mathematics of economics, now is ascendant as the new promise of the discipline.

2. Ethics and Its Study in Late Modernity

Ethics needs to follow the trend that has dethroned economies as the privileged worldview of modernity. To declare behavior that does not fit these models as irrational, essentially by not questioning the model, must be stopped before any progress is made (Fuller, 2002). To recognize a hidden morality in economics essentially accomplishes this result (Wolfe, 1989). The journal in this direction may have begun with the juxtaposition of economics and psychology, but this has to be recognized as a preliminary movement.

Baker (1999) illustrates how the study of accounting ethics can be approached in a variety of ways and with the help of several different disciplines. Unlike the economics modestly informed by psychology that has gained some traction, some of these approaches involve deemphasizing the scientific method. Mayper, Hoops, Pavur and Merino (2000) argue that we should remember that the scientific method is a tool and not a religion when studying ethics. Perhaps the first and most important step theoretically is our liberation from bad theory. Although theory provides structure and priority, we should also identify its tendency to constrain. Although we might desire the status, we can derive from emulating the theory we find in nature and other supposedly rigorous fields, enslaving ourselves to it might prove too high a cost.

The case that the study of ethics requires a unique approach not derived from elsewhere can be made. This would recommend that we abandon weak form measures like ethical orientation and ethical sensitivity (e.g., Shaub, Finn & Munter, 1993). The elicitation by force of perceptions that mean little amounts to little. Observation would be a better objective than the simulation of attitudes that may otherwise have no existence. Here, ethics would be that which is read into agent action, perhaps illustrating a preference for the deliberate over the prescriptive. This would provide ethics with the agenda that we need to appreciate people's place in their actual world.

Later modernity's refinement of self-interest and its role in consequential action would seem to demand that we disassociate a group and its ethics. For example, we should not look to accountants to socialize recruits into ethical ways of behavior. The profession and its artifacts such as ethical codes must be heavily discounted as definitive expressions of anything other than the furtherance of self-interest.

In sum, we may have to study ethics without a unifying theory to which we all ascribe. As a prelude to progress, we have to abandon the theoretical boundaries that previously had shackled us. Bad theory is worse than no theory.

In the absence of grand theory, we must soldier on. Although Thomas Kuhn (1962) might be a modernist cheerleader in his faith that new paradigms are on the horizon, we still can take from his work the notion that 'normal science' proceeds in the interim. The belief that the accumulation of such work will identify anomalies that can only be resolved by breakthrough progress does not have to be subscribed to by those positioned to comment upon the potential of various avenues of inquiry to lead to somewhere worthwhile.

Although this chapter takes the position that the study of ethics is in many ways unique, such exceptionalism does not immunize it from false starts and 'dry holes', many of which continue. A long record of published work that has still left most wondering what we really know has been produced. One such line was that which posited a linear ethical development from pre-conventional to post-conventional thinking. This work benefited from easy to administer measures that did not have to be questioned and could be correlated with any other difference in subjects. However, when the development scale collapsed under the weight of mild scrutiny, this work mostly came to an end. Somewhat more resilient is the research typically done in educational settings where an ethical treatment is introduced and a change in ethical position can be documented (e.g., Wright & Jones, 2014). Whereas the most immediate problems with this work may be its demand effects or its permanency, a more basic problem might be the apparently overwhelming need of researchers to reduce the field to that of hypothesis testing. Perhaps even worse, the persistence of the obviously illegal and deviant acts of a few as ethical instruction for the multitudes is a tact taken up by both practitioners and academics. That there can be lessons to be learned from these detailed accounts, sometimes dressed as case studies, gainsays the idiosyncratic nature of fraud and other falls from grace. Guénin-Paracini, Gendron and Morales (2014) argue that such work actually detracts attention from more systemic dimensions. Thus, the persistence of so much work of questionable premise in the ethical area may crowd out the type of work that is more consistent with the contours of late modernism.

The insistence that interdependencies are not important and that domains can be held separate may explain why we have not fully incorporated context in ethical study. Whether or not people will also do the right thing can only be evaluated when surrounded by all the temptation that the world creates to do the wrong thing. Thus, in practice the economic advantages of cutting corners and yielding to pressure must not be suppressed (see Reiter, 1998). Our tendency to discount the political must also be resisted if we are to produce ethical work that resonates with the world that we know. If we are working with students, we cannot be indifferent to the environment of greed and self-interest that is perpetuated by other courses.

Ethical research implicitly holds out some operationalization of the public interest or of the collective welfare as the target that decision makers are supposed to prefer as indicative of high ethical states (e.g., Sack, 1991). Perhaps, this result has achieved an undeserved taken-for-granted status. Do people share a reasonably clear idea of what is a good society? Where does this idea come from? We should entertain the prospect that such an outcome is, if not mythical, a strawman without practical referents.

By introducing more ideology and self-interest, the foundations of ethical research can be shaken. Rather than just assuming that professions like accounting have a 'social contract' with the laity, they may be engaging in a game-theoretic negotiation of their rights and responsibilities (Gaa, 1990). That which we take as truth may be an institutionalized façade that is only loosely coupled to processes that we, as outsiders, cannot fully appreciate (Wexler, 2017). These perspectives have great consequence for the design of the ethics research we might do, because reality itself may be at best pluralistic (Harvey, 1989).

Ironically, certain aspects of ethics (as approached by those that study this state) are not even sufficiently modern. In that modernity is associated with a secular condition, we often assume that it has moved past religion. Conceptions of God were effaced and essentially replaced by belief in the boundless possibilities of people themselves and that their finest creations would bring redemptive progress (see Harari, 2016).

Confined to conceptions of correct behavior, the study of ethics ponders antecedents and causality. This brings many to parental influence, a part of which is instruction in organized religion. The failure of subsequent life's experiences to induce ethical action is then attributed to deficiencies in early life, including the proper religious education. A code word for religion in the study of ethics is virtue. With the origins of virtue purposefully obscured and other institutions more or less disqualified from such, religion fills the vacuum of how people learn to be good. Virtue in accounting has been contrasted with the rule of law (Pincus, 2000) and generally proposed as the true endpoint of education (Mintz, 1995, 2006). Religious fidelity also underlies the power of honor codes (McCabe & Trevino, 2002). Religion will probably persist as an undercurrent of ethics research. In addition to its logical isomorphism in righteous behavior, religion has the advantage of not needing to disassociate from modernity because it never had a home therein.

In many ways, capitalism is the necessary economic system of modernity. Private ownership of the means of production fuels the conversion of technical and organizational innovation into goods and services, which in turn feeds further cycles of progress. Capitalism is strong and self-sustaining and with no real alternatives on the horizon, is likely to persist through late modernity. Ethics research must contend with the nature of this economic system.

Some point out that the problem with capitalism is that it functions too well. Much research has documented how it has permeated other institutions, changing them into its likeness (e.g., Slaughter & Leslie, 1997). People themselves are not immune, being seen and seeing themselves as commodified units of labor markets (Tinker & Koutsoumadi, 1997). Public accounting firms, despite their distance from being paragons of propriety, view ethics as a specialized product line (Neimark, 1995). As the scope of the market expands, the case that any activity should operate in non-market ways becomes more difficult to make.

Those writers such as Adam Smith who originally extolled the virtues of the marketplace and its coordination through self-interest, always contemplated that government would possess sufficient power to check the abuses and excesses that would inevitably emerge. More and more evidence exist that insufficient regulatory counterbalance is being exerted. Making arguments on behalf of an independent and sustaining public interest, apart from any private interest, becomes increasingly difficult. The exploitation of incomplete prohibitions has never been as rampant, as celebrated and as lightly sanctioned as now. The business school is partly at fault here with its elevation of financial success to the top of the esteem ladder (Balachandran, 2009).

To some extent, we have rationalized the privatization of regulation through our excessive belief in such processes as corporate governance and self-regulation. The literature is dominated by agency theory, which normalizes bad behavior (agency's moral hazard) and suggests that restoration can occur through the structure of proper incentives (agency costs). The manner and the morals of the marketplace thus accepted do not leave much conceptual space for ethical reasoning.

The external audit and the companies that provide it would like to portray it as part of the solution. But this product and its sellers are also part of the market and therefore not immune from its dictates. As such, the audit will only possess the quality for which its purchasers are willing to pay. Unless reputational losses are threatened, the audit will not achieve the quality that other parties would like to see. In other words, ethics have been cost/benefited by the market.

The power of capitalism without governmental oversight will be sufficient to force us to wonder if ethics research will attain sufficient oxygen to survive. The market generates its own rationales for consistent behavior and doing the right thing often is poorly aligned with that.

Professionalism is a third institution created in modernity and continuing into its maturity. Professions are prized by society because of the power they are supposed to exert over their clients, pushing them toward proactive prosocial behaviors. To do so, professionals eschew unabashed client advocacy in the exercise of their specialized skill. This is done in ways that cannot be fully captured by codes or rules and therefore is rather dependent upon professionals possessing the right values and being very concerned for their ongoing reputation. Professionals are privy to many aspects of client behavior that require correction in pursuit of desired long-run sustainability.

The breakdown of professionalism as an ethically positive force when the delicate balance between client and societal interested are tipped in favor the former. Professionals are also subsumed by the markets that value the services that they bring to others. One market lure is the expanding line of services wherein professionals start to believe that their social duties are confined to a core, around which profitable peripheries can flourish. To sustain a commercialized profession, a new discourse emerges. Here values espoused and value enacted become loosely coupled (Windsor, 2000).

In accounting, the tensions run particularly high since the safeguarding of constituents is a primary purpose of the profession. Because the profession has never been receptive to a bifurcation of client advocacy and public interest guardian roles (see Gaa, 1997), some pseudo-constraints must be developed. The failure of such to bring about a suitably ethical position may be indicted by the observed cycle of failure, promised reform and gradual return to the conditions threatening a new failure. Professions, like businesses, also have a growth imperative wherein they gravitate toward swallowing other bodies of expertise notwithstanding potential conflicts (Greenwood & Suddaby, 2006).

Whereas it might be tempting to declare professionalism either dead or neutered, one should not underestimate its ongoing rhetorical power. Professionalism is believed in and therefore will continue to be true, albeit in a postmodern sense. That occupational groups possess ethical codes and believe themselves special for ethical purposes will be also observed in the literature. Academics find the storyline of a social contract between professions and the larger society to be such a compelling narrative that they also will extend its life. We shall continue to see ethical research based on what can only be called romantic thinking about a mostly mythical past.

3. Morality, Agency and the Search for Truth

3.1 *Some Basic Choices*

If modernity tells us that a truth about accounting ethics is out there to be discovered, perhaps we should begin to express our doubts about the premise rather than accept these marching orders. These doubts do not necessitate a singular reaction, but instead open multiple possibilities.

The lack of a consensus truth about ethics has led some to reduce their research ambitions. Rather than aspire to construct unassailable empirical findings that they hope will gradually accumulate, some researchers establish the objective of creating awareness of ethical dimensions. Others get to the same place by asserting the need to establish an ethical context for action or decisions. Leaning heavily upon the blurry line that seems to exist in late modernity, these researchers see their job as storytelling (e.g., Reiter, 1997). Whereas these fallback positions reflect the growing distrust of conventionally modernist work in the ethics area, they may overestimate the willingness of practitioners to value what is being offered, because it does not articulate the impossibility of the more conventional 'ethics be damned' position. Given the tendency toward less sophisticated reasoning in the accounting field (Mintchik & Farmer, 2009), academics should not assume too much.

A more pervasive cynicism is displayed by those that go further down this path. Rather than just question whether ethical action can be reduced to measurable variables, some problematize the possibility of any meaningful ethical action by accountants. This follows the idea that the real has been effectively replaced by simulacra (Poster & Mourrain, 2002). Accounting ethics lacks substance because what accountants do exist only as signs, a second-handed derivative whose value depends upon convincingly substituting for the real. Work on accounting ethics therefore prioritizes the establishment and propagation of myth. Institutional theory focuses our attention on symbols that are central to the semi-permanent façades that allow unobserved self-interest in buffered cores to thrive. This line of thought works only because of a certain level of disengagement that can be documented throughout the socialization cycle (e.g., Cory & Treviño, 2017).

The success of capitalism at the end of modernity also needs to be recognized as a template for ethical research. The bottom line on ethics is the faith that capitalism can be reformed or at least tempered by the systematic ideation of sustainability. The pursuit of self-interest is both the engine of action and the ultimate condition of its downfall. We have overwhelming evidence of the thesis that advantage should be pursued ruthlessly. That is the rock-bottom hidden premise of accounting education. Ethical obligation and constraint are positioned at best in premodernity and therefore are always fighting a rearguard battle. The commodification of knowledge has mostly aligned against any meaningful ethical antithesis because that would necessitate its own commodification. Ideas are now judged on their performativity (Lyotard, 1984). Progressively, we see a hardening of an advocacy culture and the lessening of remorse for the role of self-interest, with the former advanced in the name of democracy and the latter striking a blow for honesty. So much for the moral high ground!

3.2 Is This a Bad Time to Be Holding the Ethics Bag?

Ethics research may be unique in its straddle between normative prescription and empirical detachment. In science, the association between a certain condition and a resultant event can be observed with a high degree of confidence that the researchers' opinion about what association is preferable is not a major element. Unfortunately, the existence of a singular virtuous state that is established *a priori* pervades the accounting ethics literature. That the researcher has a preferred outcome is often very clear and unbalanced in its articulation. Although we appreciate the conflict that this creates with the norms of science, we excuse ourselves based on the obvious importance and correctness of our positions.

Accepting that moral indignation might produce the passion necessary to motivate work we still cannot conclude that it is likely to produce good work. Believing to the contrary requires one to open the question about why any work is done. If one lacks the spirit rendered by evildoers that must get their comeuppance, will the work necessarily be inferior? The idea that one result is necessary and its opposite is flawed is a dangerous precipice.

Confidence about what is right not only might be a source of bias, but also essentially arbitrary. Many things are wrong, but we choose to react to only some of them. Every organization does things that may not be great offenses but are bad enough so that they need to be not publicized beyond its boundaries. Every profession has similar 'dirty little secrets' that enable corners to be cut and deviations from the letter of righteous behavior to occur. Collectively we agree to look the other way essentially extending a belief that the efficiencies that are gained offset the harm that may be caused. Additionally, the advantages earned by moderate forms of deviance are necessary to the incentives of key participants. Joining the club essentially entails a slight but important redrawing of the line between right and wrong, for researchers as well as practitioners.

Over a period of time, some environmental shift also occurs in our moral sense. That which used to be considered wrong does not become right. However, that which used to be wrong gradually steps into a moral neutrality. Acts that used to be condemned, and therefore avoided by most, lose their strict and universal sanction. The reputational damage that used to be inevitable becomes less of a problem to endure or less certain to happen. The loss of stigma is an interesting conclusion in that it expresses the uncertainty that we feel about an act. While before the circumstances were irrelevant as the reputational loss was automatic, we now enter a new place where we make consequences more conditional on the specifics. The willingness to excuse tempts some to offset their behavior with exculpatory rhetoric that is occasionally successful. In fact, that which was once misbehavior of a grievous nature now becomes the basics for notoriety if not celebrity.

Our disgust about moral underpinnings extends to those we nominate as heroes, as well as those we choose to vilify. Whereas more that deserved vilification through moral approbation have escaped in the modern era, we have changed the nature of those that we celebrate. The rise of the CEO as modern cultural icon suggests a shift toward success as the ultimate exemption. We celebrate not those that deserved to do well, but those that did well even if it means overlooking some of the means that were used in the process. Business leaders who succeeded in capturing market share and bringing us products/services that enhanced our life as consumers are allowed to immiserate workers and despoil communities. On the other hand, we can barely tolerate whistle blowers. Within professions, those who are held up for admiration are those that sacrificed the most for the client. Those that took principled stands against clients are only admired if doing so proved to save the firm the reputational costs with association.

Our growing ambivalence about moral right has great consequence for ethics research. The need to demonstrate the value of ethics, rather than establish that as a maintained hypothesis, turns us away from concern over the nature of ethics. We move from dependent to independent variable when we feel compelled to associate certain levels of ethics with other outcomes for whom there is more of an indigenous appetite.

3.3 Letting Go of the Illusion of Control

Academic research is the effort to exert control over a phenomenon in the effort to describe it and to study its effect on another phenomenon over which a similar degree of control is claimed or demanded. Since the journey through modernity could be described as the growing confidence of such control and the beginning of a questioning of such power, consequences for the study of accounting ethics are likely.

A possible fundamental tension exists between economics, as the dominant social sciences discipline of the age and ethical analysis. Economics presumes selfish behavior and has great difficulties explaining the existence of altruism. The prospect of behavior aligned with a moral compass exists only a 'noise' in economic analysis. Accordingly, ethical behavior exists outside the tight world of reactions to incentives and to signals. For the most part, ethical research can be seen as the effort to find the regularities that would move the effort into that which can be explained or predicted. Ironically, economics works well only without a moral logic, but the study of ethics wants to be more like economics.

If we were to relax the assumption that control was possible, the effort to understand accounting ethics could be repositioned. Ethics could have more free-standing existence because it no longer had to serve the superior rationality of the organization, the belief of which may be unfounded (Reed, 1993). Accounting itself presents boundaries that are difficult to defend (Cooper, Taylor, Smith & Catchpole, 2002). If accounting ethics are no longer subservient to totalities with cross-purposes, a clearer view is possible. At that point, when causality is abandoned, we can at least create space to see whose interests are being served.

Just as auditing's existence depends upon making things auditable (Power, 1996), ethics existence in modernity is largely dependent upon a reproduction process that has skewed the meaning of ethical behavior. Accounting ethics has been captured by the accounting establishment whereas pretending to be the result of a scientific process (see Bjorkegren, 1993). Dominant groups sustain their position by naturalizing the status quo and deflecting attention from the problematic. We must resist the study of accounting ethics that have been made all too consistent with organizational interests. To do so, we must be emancipated from our own vocabularies.

Speaking of liberation, our progression into late modernity also should renew our appreciation for the role of choice in ethical action. Modernity built a proverbial iron cage for people in that it prioritized organizational dictates and scientific regularities. So too accounting ethics research was imprisoned in rigid ideas about how it should be conducted and what questions it should address. Choice always existed, but it was increasingly painted as a Hobson one, tinged as it was by an industrial morality.

As accounting ethics scholarship slowly realizes that it is in late modernity, a renewed agency will be given to free will. The power of organizations and progressions to socialize individuals will be understood as much more contingent and circumstantial. Their diminishment as omnipotent agendas will be partly attributable to the growing awareness of their purposeful efforts and their self-interest.

Left with the individual, what will research do? Perhaps explore the intuitive ideas about the contours of the good society. Here a fine line exists between that which is an unarticulated natural state and that which is a rationalization of consequences. Research must recast responsibility if we believe in free will, lessening that which we now attribute to 'systems' or to the vagaries of psychology. Perhaps all we can hope for is localized logic and individualized solutions. In a world where we should not presume that individuals cannot compute the rational thing to do, the expectation that universal laws exist to be discovered seems fanciful. When the literal is losing to the symbolic, ethical research needs to first find and then go with the flow.

References

Baker, R. (1999). Theoretical approaches to research on accounting ethics. *Research on Accounting Ethics*, 5, 115–134.
Balachandran, B. (2009). *Education or Indoctrination? Accounting Education in the UK*. Unpublished paper, London: South Bank University.
Bjorkegren, D. (1993). What can organization and management theory learn from art. In J. Hassard & M. Parker (Eds.), *Postmodernism and organizations* (pp. 101–113). London: Sage.
Burrell, G. (1993). Eco and the bunnymen. In J. Hassard & M. Parker (Eds.), *Postmodernism and organizations* (pp. 71–82). London: Sage.
Cooper, C., Taylor, P., Smith, N., & Catchpole, L. (2002). The social creation of the disciplined graduate—social accounting with a twist. *Research Seminar Series, Glasgow Caledonian University*.

Cory, S. N., & Treviño, M. R. (2017). An exploratory study: Moral disengagement levels in accounting majors. *Southern Journal of Business & Ethics*, 9, 135–143.

Fuller, S. (2002). *Social epistemology*. Bloomington: Indiana University Press.

Gaa, J. C. (1990). A game-theoretic analysis of professional rights and responsibilities. *Journal of Business Ethics*, 9(3), 159–169.

Gaa, J. C. (1997). *The moral syndromes of the public accounting profession*. Unpublished paper, Document de travail. University of Alberta.

Gilligan, C. (1993). *In a different voice*. Cambridge, MA: Harvard University Press.

Greenwood, R., & Suddaby, R. (2006). Institutional entrepreneurship in mature fields: The big five accounting firms. *Academy of Management Journal*, 49(1), 27–48.

Guénin-Paracini, H., Gendron, Y., & Morales, J. (2014). Neoliberalism, crises and accusations of fraud: A vicious circle of reinforcing influences? *Qualitative Research in Accounting & Management*, 11(4), 317–356.

Hanks, W. F. (1993). Notes on semantics in linguistic practice. In C. Calhoun, E. Lipuma, & M. Postone (Eds.), *Bourdieu: Critical perspectives* (pp. 139–155). Chicago, USA: University of Chicago Press.

Harari, Y. N. (2016). *Homo Deus: A brief history of tomorrow*. New York: Random House.

Harvey, D. (1989). *The condition of postmodernity*. Oxford, UK: Blackwell.

Kuhn, T. S. (1962). *The structure of scientific revolutions*. Chicago: University of Chicago Press.

Lyotard, J. F. (1984). *The postmodern condition: A report on knowledge*. Minneapolis: University of Minnesota Press.

MacIntyre, A. (2013). *After virtue*. Notre Dame, IN: University of Notre Dame Press.

Mayper, A. G., Hoops, W., Pavur, R., & Merino, B. (2000). Accounting: A moral discipline? *Proceedings of the Interdisciplinary Perspective on Accounting Conference*, Adelaide, South Australia.

McCabe, D., & Trevino, L. K. (2002). Honesty and honor codes. *Academe*, 88(1), 37.

Mintchik, N. M., & Farmer, T. A. (2009). Associations between epistemological beliefs and moral reasoning: Evidence from accounting. *Journal of Business Ethics*, 84(2), 259–275.

Mintz, S. M. (1995). Virtue ethics and accounting education. *Issues in Accounting Education*, 10, 247–268.

Mintz, S. M. (2006). Accounting ethics education: Integrating reflective learning and virtue ethics. *Journal of Accounting Education*, 24(2–3), 97–117.

Neimark, M. (1995). The selling of ethics: The ethics of business meets the business of ethics. *Accounting, Auditing & Accountability Journal*, 8(3), 81–96.

Pincus, K. (2000). The role of rules in accounting. *Research on Accounting Ethics*, 6, 243–258.

Poster, M., & Mourrain, J. (2002). *Jean Baudrillard: Selected writings*. Stanford: Stanford University Press.

Power, M. (1996). Making things auditable. *Accounting, Organizations and Society*, 21(2–3), 289–315.

Ray, L. J., & Reed, M. (2002). Max Weber and the dilemmas of modernity. In L. Ray & M. Reed (Eds.), *Organizing modernity* (pp. 165–204). London, UK: Routledge.

Reed, M. (1993). Organizations and modernity: Continuity and discontinuity in organization theory. In J. Hassard, & M. Parker (Eds.), *Postmodernism and organizations* (pp. 163–182). London, UK: Sage.

Reiter, S. A. (1997). Storytelling and ethics in financial economics. *Critical Perspectives on Accounting, 8*(6), 605–632.

Reiter, S. A. (1998). *Expanding the focus of research on accounting ethics: Lessons from business ethics research.* Working paper, Binghamton University.

Sack, R. (1991). Integrating ethics into the accounting curriculum. *Journal of Accountancy, 172*(4), 43–44.

Shaub, M. K., Finn, D. W., & Munter, P. (1993). The effects of auditors' ethical orientation on commitment and ethical sensitivity. *Behavioral Research in Accounting, 5*(1), 145–169.

Slaughter, S., & Leslie, L. L. (1997). *Academic capitalism: Politics, policies, and the entrepreneurial university.* Baltimore: Johns Hopkins University Press.

Sunstein, C. R., & Ullmann-Margalit, E. (1999). Second-order decisions. *Ethics, 110*(1), 5–31.

Tinker, T., & Koutsoumadi, A. (1997). A mind is a wonderful thing to waste: 'Think like a commodity', become a CPA. *Accounting, Auditing & Accountability Journal, 10*(3), 454–467.

van Dijk, T. A. (1993). *Elite discourse and racism.* Newbury Park, CA: Sage.

Wexler, P. (2017). *Social analysis of education: After the new sociology.* London: Routledge.

Willmott, H. (1992). *Critical theory and accounting ethics.* Paper presented at the Ethics and Independence Meeting of the American Accounting Association, Washington DC, August.

Windsor, C. (2000). *Do professional values influence multinational accounting firms' cultural values? An exploration of cultural dissonance.* Paper presented at the Annual meeting of the American Accounting Association, Philadelphia, August.

Wolfe, A. (1989). *Whose keeper?: Social science and moral obligation.* Berkeley, CA: University of California Press.

Wright, M., & Jones, S. (2014). *How teaching ethics affects accounting students: Ethical position and ethical judgment.* Paper presented at the Ethics and Independence Meeting of the American Accounting Association, Atlanta, August.

3 Accounting Ethics Education Research
A Historical Review of the Literature

Lan Anh Nguyen and Steven Dellaportas

1. Introduction

The business ethics literature is littered with examples of corporate collapses, scandals, corruption and audit failures impacting negatively on society's belief that accountants possess the ethical commitment to protect the public interest. The response from regulators and the profession has been multifaceted, including regulatory intervention (Sarbanes-Oxley Act in the United States; and the Corporate Law Economic Reform Program (CLERP) 9 Act in Australia); soft law enhancement with the promulgation of principles and guidelines on governance and ethics in codes of conduct; and calls for ethics education interventions in university accounting education and professional development programs. The present study is focused on examining research in the latter. Increased calls for an expanded ethics coverage in the accounting curriculum stem from a belief that ethics education can enhance professionalism among accountants in which the pressure to compromise personal and professional values is ever present (AICPA, 1988; Albrecht & Sack, 2000). The call for ethics interventions in the accounting curriculum is reinforced by accrediting bodies, by revising education standards to include ethics coverage. Responding to these calls entrenched ethics education firmly in the accounting curriculum (Blanthorne, Kovar & Fisher, 2007; Dellaportas, Kanapathippillai, Khan & Leung, 2014). This was followed a burgeoning body of research to understand and improve the impact of ethics interventions in accounting education. The present study will examine publications in academic research journals on accounting ethics education to capture and summarize what has been learned in four decades of research.

Since the first article on accounting ethics education was published by Loeb and Bedingfield (1972), this body of research has evolved to represent a significant stream of inquiry underpinned by a dedicated group of accounting and business scholars. Despite the decades-long scholarly work on ethics education in accounting, producing a substantial amount of research from diverse perspectives and approaches, a comprehensive review of accounting ethics education research is scant.

The purpose of this study is to synthesize the research on accounting ethics education by identifying and exploring trends and key themes of accounting ethics education research. The data in this study is comprised of published manuscripts in academic research journals to provide a profile on accounting ethics education research. Profiling occurs from the extrapolation of characteristics of published manuscripts such as the topic themes to draw inferences about the body of research on accounting ethics education. The analysis will facilitate a comprehensive review of contemporary research on accounting ethics education to provide a full overview of research on this very important topic. The information gained from this review will help identify and assess the nature of ethics education to assist educators in the development of pedagogy on accounting ethics as well as provide valuable guidance for future scholars in this area of research. The present study will complement this body of research by endeavoring to provide structure to accounting ethics education from the perspective of research.

Drawing from a key word search of major publication databases, the sample frame consists of 256 published articles on accounting ethics education. A detailed examination of published manuscripts will help us understand the role of research in producing knowledge on accounting ethics education and provide an opportunity to examine how journals have contributed to this body of research. Whereas accounting ethics education research is represented by a vast number of published articles, two studies have undertaken a systematic review of the relevant literature (Bernardi, Bean & Melton, 2008; Loeb, 2006). Loeb (2006) conducted a review of the literature, addressing ethics education in the accounting curriculum over a period of eighteen years from 1988 to 2006. Loeb (2006) characterized issues on ethics education including the factors influencing the level of teaching ethics and the need for ethics education, and explored the debate on who should teach ethics: ethicists or business faculty. This was followed by Bernardi et al. (2008), who summarized academic research on accounting ethics education research in the top forty journals in North America. Bernardi et al. (2008) analyzed trends based on the number of publications, number of ethics authors, institutions affiliated with ethics publications and the approach to addressing ethics in the curriculum between 1986 and 2005. Bernardi et al. (2008) argued that the number of publications was evidence of growing expertise and engagement among accounting faculty, enhancing contributions to the teaching of ethics in accounting education. The present study will not only update the literature in this area of research but also examine the characteristics of research on ethics education including key topic themes and the purpose and motivation for ethics education research in accounting. This is an important subject, not only for accounting researchers and educators but also for academics in diverse disciplines who may be contemplating an extension or intervention of ethics education in their respective fields.

The remainder of this chapter is structured as follows. In the second section, the typology and the rationale for article selection is outlined. The third section gives an overview of accounting ethics education spanning five decades of research. Key themes are presented and described in the fourth section, and conclusions are presented in the fifth.

2. Data Collection

Data is collected by collating the details of published articles to develop a profile of accounting ethics education research. Profiling relies on the methodological tool of 'research profiling' proposed by Porter, Kongthon and Lu (2002). Research profiling aims to map research by scanning publications to address questions such as the following: What are the major topics studied within a particular field? How is the research informed? How has the research evolved? The present study is primarily focused on analyzing publication descriptors at the level of the manuscript to help construct a comprehensive picture of accounting ethics education research. This will be achieved by identifying and analyzing trends and key research themes inherent in the underlying characteristics of published research on accounting ethics education. The findings provide insight on how accounting ethics education research has evolved from literature distribution patterns over five decades of research.

Profiling in this study relies on the collection and analysis of descriptor variables appearing in published articles as control words to construct and represent themes. Prominent university library databases were scanned to develop a preliminary list of manuscripts on accounting ethics education: Google Scholar and databases (ACER), Inform Global (Proquest), EBSCOHost Web Research Databases (EBSCO), PsycINFO (ProQuest), Science Direct and SCOPUS (Elsevier). The search criteria for published articles relied on the following keywords and phrases: ethics education in accounting, accounting ethics education, ethics in accounting and ethics education. To minimize the risk of missing compatible published research, the databases were scanned without restriction on the year of publication to develop a full repertoire of research on 'accounting ethics education'. In addition to the keyword search, specific journals that were expected to include research on ethics education were also examined: *Journal of Business Ethics; Journal of Accounting Education; Issues in Accounting Education; Accounting Education;*[1] *Managerial Auditing Journal; Research on Professional Responsibility and Ethics in Accounting; Business and Professional Ethics Journal; Critical Perspectives on Accounting* and *Journal of Business Ethics Education.*

This process resulted in the collection of 320 articles. Most importantly, 'ethics education', 'accounting students' or 'accounting curriculum' were essential criteria in building the sample frame. Published articles on 'business' ethics education, rather than accounting ethics education, were not included in the sample frame unless the research comprised sub-samples inclusive of accounting students. Furthermore, the term 'accounting students' for the purpose of data collection was defined liberally to include undergraduate students, postgraduate students and practicing accountants undertaking continuous professional education (CPE). The sample frame also includes research on instructors, lecturers and faculty members who had interacted in the delivery of accounting ethics education courses. Articles excluded from the sample include unpublished manuscripts (e.g., papers presented in conference proceedings) as well as articles exclusively or predominantly concerned with business ethics or students but not addressing accounting ethics or accounting students. The titles of these articles were scanned to remove duplicate articles and abstracts were examined to remove articles that did not meet the selection criteria. This process resulted in the removal of sixty-five articles leaving a total sample of 256 articles for data analyses ranging from 1972 to the end of 2018.

Data collection relies on inspecting and recording the details of each published article to gain a picture of ethics education research in accounting and infer generalizations about accounting ethics education research. Frequency counts were used to rank-order descriptor variables to help gain a picture of occurrence and regularity. The data was examined by undertaking a schematic categorization of the published articles to uncover trends, topics and other categorical themes and relationships to understand the research fields investigated by researchers. Categorization is an iterative process of investigating and tallying the characteristics of published articles to signify important and dominant artefacts. The categorization of qualitative characteristics such as topic themes occurred in two iterative stages. In stage one, data was collected by examining key words nominated by authors in their publications and information contained in the abstract. Where this was unclear, the researchers delved deeper by reading the articles to obtain the relevant data. In stage two, the descriptors were assessed and classified into subject group domains to identify basic categories.

The findings are presented in two sections, the first section examines key trends through five decades of accounting ethics education research and section two delves deeper into the reasons and rationale for accounting ethics research illustrating the importance and benefits of accounting ethics education. The citations appearing in the following discussion are not intended to be exhaustive but, rather, representative of the assertions presented, so as to bring to the readers' attention a path to key readings.

3. Trends in Research on Ethics Education in Accounting

A total of 256 manuscripts from 88 journals were published during five decades of research (see Table 3.1). A large proportion of articles (110 manuscripts) were published in only three journals accounting for

Table 3.1 Articles per journal

No.	Journal title	1970s	1980s	1990s	2000s	2010s	Total
1	Journal of Business Ethics			20	20	17	57
2	Journal of Accounting Education		2	15	8	9	34
3	Issues in Accounting Education		3	4	9	3	19
4	Accounting Education: An International Journal				2	5	7
5	Managerial Auditing Journal				4	3	7
6	Research on Professional Responsibility and Ethics in Accounting			1	4	2	7
7	Business and Professional Ethics Journal			6			6
8	Critical Perspectives on Accounting			2	3	1	6
9	Journal of Education for Business				3	3	6
10	Teaching Business Ethics				4	1	5
11	Business Ethics: A European Review				3	1	4
12	Journal of Business Ethics Education				2	2	4
13	Journal of Leadership, Accountability and Ethics				1	2	3
14	Journal of Academic Ethics				2	1	3
15	Malaysian Accounting Review				2	1	3
16	Social Responsibility Journal				3		3
17	Academy of Educational Leadership Journal					2	2
18	American Journal of Business Education					2	2
19	Asian Social Science					2	2
20	Global Perspectives on Accounting Education				1	1	2
21	International Journal of Ethics Education					2	2
22	Journal of Accounting and Management Information Systems					2	2
23	Meditari Accountancy Research					2	2
24	South African Journal of Accounting Research				1	1	2
25	The Accounting Educators' Journal		1			1	2
26	The CPA Journal				2		2
27	Abacus					1	1
28	Academic Journal of Economic Studies					1	1
29	Academy of Accounting and Financial Studies				1		1

No.	Journal title	1970s	1980s	1990s	2000s	2010s	Total
30	Academy of Management Learning & Education					1	1
31	Accounting & Finance			1			1
32	Accounting and The Public Interest					1	1
33	Accounting Horizons			1			1
34	Accounting Perspectives					1	1
35	Accounting Research Journal				1		1
36	African Journal of Business Ethics					1	1
37	Asian Academy of Management Journal					1	1
38	Asian Journal of Business Ethics					1	1
39	Asian Review of Accounting					1	1
40	Australian Accounting Review				1		1
41	Business and Society Review					1	1
42	College Student Journal		1				1
43	DLSU Business & Economics Review					1	1
44	Ethics & Behavior			1			1
45	Etikk I Praksis-Nordic Journal of Applied Ethics					1	1
46	European Accounting Review				1		1
47	European Integration—Realities and Perspectives					1	1
48	General and Professional Education					1	1
49	Indian Journal of Accounting					1	1
50	International Journal of Economics & Finance Research & Applications					1	1
51	International Journal of Education Research					1	1
52	International Review of Business Research Papers				1		1
53	Journal of Accounting and Finance					1	1
54	Journal of Accounting and Organizational Change					1	1
55	Journal of Asia Business Studies					1	1
56	Journal of Business and Accounting					1	1
57	Journal of Business and Educational Leadership					1	1
58	Journal of Business Disciplines				1		1
59	Journal of College Teaching and Learning				1		1
60	Journal of Economics and Management				1		1
61	Journal of Financial Reporting and Accounting					1	1

(Continued)

Table 3.1 (Continued)

No.	Journal title	1970s	1980s	1990s	2000s	2010s	Total
62	Journal of Global Business Issues					1	1
63	Journal of International Business Disciplines					1	1
64	Journal of Legal, Ethical and Regulatory Issues					1	1
65	Journal of Moral Education				1		1
66	Journal of Religion and Business Ethics					1	1
67	Journal of Teaching in International Business				1		1
68	Journal of The Academy of Business Education					1	1
69	Malaysia Journal of Society and Space					1	1
70	Management Accounting Research			1			1
71	Management Accounting Quarterly					1	1
72	Management and Service Science					1	1
73	Management Decision			1			1
74	Management Research News				1		1
75	Ohio CPA Journal				1		1
76	Pacific Accounting Review					1	1
77	Procedia Social and Behavioral Sciences					1	1
78	Research in Accounting in Emerging Economies					1	1
79	Social Behavior and Personality				1		1
80	Southern Business Review					1	1
81	Sustainability					1	1
82	Technical Journal of Engineering and Applied Sciences					1	1
83	The Accounting Review	1					1
84	The British Accounting Review				1		1
85	The International Journal of Educational Management				1		1
86	The International Journal of Organizational Innovation					1	1
87	The Journal of International Social Research					1	1
88	World of Accounting Science					1	1
	Total	1	6	52	91	106	256

43 percent of total publications. The *Journal of Business Ethics* ranks highest with a total of fifty-seven published articles, more than 60 percent higher than the second-ranked journal, the *Journal of Accounting Education* with thirty-four published articles; and a little over 100 percent higher than the third-ranked journal, *Issues in Accounting Education* with nineteen published articles. The remaining articles were spread across 85 journals. Interestingly, the combined output of accounting education articles published in journals dedicated to the dissemination of research in 'accounting' (119 manuscripts) is less than the combined output of published articles in journals in the broader discipline of 'business' (137 manuscripts). Furthermore, the manuscripts published in accounting or business journals outnumber the manuscripts published in education journals, suggesting that authors favor non-education journals as their outlet for accounting ethics education research. The diversity of accounting and non-accounting journals in which accounting ethics education research is published raises the question of whether a journal dedicated to accounting ethics education is warranted.

Evidence of accounting education research first appeared in the 1970s with a publication by Loeb and Bedingfield (1972) in *The Accounting Review*. This article examines the importance of teaching ethics and how colleges and universities organize their ethics teaching. A small increase in publications occurred during the 1980s with six articles suggesting that accounting ethics education research is emergent in this period. The research content of published manuscripts in the 1980s did not change greatly from the work published by Loeb and Bedingfield (1972) focusing on the importance of accounting ethics education and investigating the nature and content of ethics education. Published research in this period emanated from the United States and discussed in detail, educational issues such as teaching methods (Scribner & Dillaway, 1989) and the integration of ethics into accounting courses (Cohen & Pant, 1989; Langenderfer & Rockness, 1989). Research in the 1980s also highlighted a need for more ethics education either through additional courses in accounting ethics or additional ethics subject matter in existing accounting courses (Cohen & Pant, 1989; Karnes & Sterner, 1988; Loeb, 1988; Scribner & Dillaway, 1989). The need to improve the impact of ethics education was raised by Scribner and Dillaway (1989), who claim that case discussion on ethics can contribute greatly to the accounting curriculum which at the time, was lacking in accounting ethics instruction. During this period, ethics education was predominantly restricted to auditing courses focusing on the code of ethics and issues associated with auditor independence (Cohen & Pant, 1989).

Loeb (1991) noted an increased effort by universities and business colleges to engage with ethics education, including organizing accounting ethics education conferences and developing materials for teaching ethics. The activities and investment in accounting ethics in the 1980s benefited the academic community by increasing published articles by fifty-two in the 1990s. Research in the 1990s can be grouped into three broad categories: teaching accounting ethics; cognitive moral development and perceptions on the relationship between ethics education and other factors (for example, culture, religion, whistleblowing and cheating). In teaching, research examines different areas of accounting ethics education such as the curriculum content (see for example Sisaye & Lackman, 1994); teaching methods (see for example Awasthi & Staehelin, 1995; Kerr & Smith, 1995; Leung & Cooper, 1994); discussion on whether ethics should be integrated throughout many courses or taught in a stand-alone course (see for example Hiltebeitel & Jones, 1992; Pizzolatto & Bevill, 1996); and issues related to the delivery of ethics education (see for example McDonald & Donleavy, 1995; McNair & Milam, 1993). In the second category, research examines whether ethics interventions enhanced student's moral development relying predominantly on Kohlbergs's theory of cognitive moral development (see for example Eynon, Hill, Stevens & Clarke, 1996; Shaub, 1994b; Wright, 1995) and other measures of ethical awareness and judgment (Ameen, Guffey & McMillan, 1996a). Research in the third category is focused on eliciting the views or perceptions of accounting ethics education impacted or influenced by culture and religion (see for example Whipple & Swords, 1992), gender (see for example Ameen, Guffey & McMillan, 1996b; Davis & Welton, 1991) and whistleblowing and cheating (see for example Ameen et al., 1996a; Brody & Bowman, 1998).

The number of manuscripts increased markedly in the two decades that followed with ninety-one articles published during the 2000s and 106 articles published in the nine-year period between 2010 and 2018. With the volume of published works in this period increasing, this might reasonably be considered the highpoint of accounting ethics education research. The significant increase in the latter two decades could be the result of an investment or accumulation of intellectual capital in accounting ethics from previous decades combined with or enticed by the presence of corporate scandals that occurred in this period. Although not included as part of the sample frame of this study, it is worth noting that PhD programs and doctoral students investigating accounting ethics education emerged within this decade (Buell, Cavico, Mujtaba & Rentfro, 2009; Cannon, 2001; Galla, 2007). A growing number of doctoral students on accounting ethics education research is not only expected to enhance research output on accounting ethics education but will also propagate further research when doctoral candidates become faculty and guide others in the pursuit of accounting ethics education research.

The wave of corporate scandals in the late 1980s (for example Bankers Trust, ESM Government Securities, MiniScribe scandal in United States, Barlow Clowes scandal in United Kingdom; and Bond Corporation and Christopher Quintex in Australia) shone a spotlight on ethics in business and the accounting profession and raised the call for ethics interventions in the accounting curricula. It was at this point we see an increase in the number of articles published on accounting ethics education, particularly in the 1990s. The corporate scandals of the 1980s reoccurred in the early years of the 2000s with the collapse of major corporations such as Enron and WorldCom (in the US), Parmalat (in Europe), Satyam Computers (in India) and HIH Insurance (in Australia); and the implosion of the global accounting firm Arthur Andersen. This spate of corporate collapses once again provided faculty with the impetus and opportunity to conduct research in accounting ethics education, appearing as published outputs in the 1990s and 2000s.

Similar to the 1990s, research in the 2000s continued to focus on teaching related matters in accounting ethics education including the importance of ethics education and ethical decision-making among students (Chan & Leung, 2006; Elias, 2006) and the impact of ethics education on students' ethical perceptions (Chan & Leung, 2006; Elias, 2006; Larres & Mulgrew, 2009; O'Leary & Mohamad, 2008). Research in the 1990s and 2000s extended the research from the 1980s by examining the impact of ethics education in specific contexts such as whistleblowing (see for example Liyanarachchi & Newdick, 2009; O'Leary & Radich, 2001; O'Leary & Cotter, 2000), bribe acceptance (O'Leary & Cotter, 2000) and exam cheating (O'Leary & Radich, 2001; O'Leary & Cotter, 2000). Among this research, two key themes emerged and were demonstrated in the highest number of published articles during this period. The first theme is centered on approaches to teaching ethics by comparing stand-alone ethics courses with a pervasive approach to teaching ethics where ethics is integrated across all or many required courses (see for example Cooper, Leung, Dellaportas, Jackling & Wong, 2008; O'Leary & Mohamad, 2008; Shawver, 2009). The second theme is focused on the importance of ethics education and how ethics education may impact the ethical behavior of the future accountants (Abdolmohammadi, 2008; Cooper et al., 2008; Gonzalo & Garvey, 2005; Rahman, 2003).

In addition to matters relating to ethics education, research during the 2000s found that ethics education in the accounting curricula, especially in undergraduate degree programs, had increased significantly. It was also during this period that new topics emerged with researchers' investigating the relationship between ethics and religion (Auyeung, Dagwell, Ng & Sands, 2006; Burks & Sellani, 2008; Levy & Mitschow, 2008). The international spread of accounting ethics education research occurred in this decade with the study of ethics education in developing countries appearing in published research, including Malaysia (O'Leary & Mohamad, 2006, 2008; Rahman, 2003), Turkey (Tunca Caliyurt & Crowther, 2006), China (Chan & Leung, 2006) and South Africa (Naudé, 2008).

The nine years from 2010 to 2018 displayed the highest number of publications resulting in the peak period for published research on accounting ethics education. While research in this period built on the work carried out in previous decades, the location of such research extended to developing countries, increasing markedly the number of publications from non-Western locations. In the 2000s, six articles were published in four different countries, whereas in the 2010s, twenty-eight manuscripts were published in fifteen different countries. In the period from 1990 to 2018, there were thirty-five manuscripts published in fifteen developing countries, displaying the spread of this research across the globe, potentially reflecting the reach of accounting ethics education or the response to local and international business scandals. Research publications on developing or non-Western countries include Malaysia (8), Turkey (5), South Africa (4), China and Iran (3), Ghana and India (2) and one publication each in Albania, Indonesia, Nigeria, Mexico, Philippines, Romania, Tunisia and Zimbabwe. The majority of studies aimed to evaluate the importance and impact of ethics education in countries including Ghana (Singh & Vasudeva, 2006), Iran (Chafi, 2013; Royaee, Ahmadi & Jari, 2013), Malaysia (Graham, 2012; Koumbiadis & Pandit, 2014; Mohd Ghazali, 2015; Saat, Porter & Woodbine, 2010a, 2012), South Africa (Fourie & Contogiannis, 2014), Nigeria (Salami, Sanni & Uthman, 2018) and Turkey (ŞENGÜR, 2017; Uyar & GÜNGÖRMÜŞ, 2013). Three studies in particular diverged from mainstream ethics education research to examine the implications of ethics education from a cultural perspective by examining ethics education using a non-Western lens. Chang, Davis and Kauffman (2012) examined the framework and process of Buddhist ethics education in India; Mahdavikhou and Khotanlou (2012) examined Islamic ethics in accounting education by developing ethical thinking among students; Hakan Özkan (2013) examined the constraint on accounting ethics education in Turkey among student diverse religious orientations.

Whereas the research was undertaken in diverse cultural contexts, the nature of the research did not vary greatly from previous decades. Han (2011) examined ethics education in China by investigating the approaches to improve the effectiveness of ethics education in relation to curriculum, course content and the teaching methods. Billiot, Daniel, Glandon and Glandon (2012) examined the effect of education on measures of ethical sensitivity and levels of moral reasoning among accounting students in Mexico. Arfaoui, Damak-Ayadi, Ghram and Bouchekoua (2016) similarly examined the influence of ethics intervention on accounting students' level of moral development in Tunisia. Manalo (2013) explored the teaching strategies for a business ethics course in the accounting curriculum in the Philippines. In South Africa, Taylor (2013) investigated ethics training for accounting students and Nathan (2015) examined how ethics education influences final year accounting students in attempting to raise ethical consciousness and responses to ethical situations. These two studies examine how societal and circumstantial factors impact the ethical attitudes of prospective accountants in South Africa. Finally, Warinda (2013) studied faculty views on three areas: the importance of ethics, the importance of goals of accounting ethics education and methods of teaching ethics (such as integration of ethics in cores accounting courses or teach ethics as a stand-alone course) in Zimbabwe.

In addition to the research in developing countries, further issues were investigated: the benefits of teaching ethics (see for example Arfaoui et al., 2016; Singh & Vasudeva, 2006), the extent of teaching ethics and ethics subject matter incorporated in the curriculum (Ahmad, 2017; Marzuki, Subramaniam, Cooper & Dellaportas, 2017; Onumah, Antwi-Gyamfi, Djin & Adomako, 2012; ŞENGÜR, 2017; Simpson, Onumah & Oppong-Nkrumah, 2016; Win, Ismail & Hamid, 2014), the influence of ethics education on students' ethical attitude (including awareness, judgment, behavior) (Fourie & Contogiannis, 2014; Mohd Ghazali, 2015; Saat et al., 2010a, 2012) and the relationship between ethics and accounting education to demonstrate that education is a valuable tool to improve ethics (Chafi, 2013). Win et al. (2014) examined the accounting educator's perceptions on ethics education curriculum, and Ahmad (2017) and Marzuki et al. (2017) studied the integration of ethics into accounting curriculum. In this period, a large focus of research remained on teaching methods but extended to include alternative pedagogies such as presentations (Canarutto, Smith & Smith, 2010; Faello, 2017), case studies (Manalo, 2013; Shawver, 2011), role plays, film/video (Manalo, 2013) and web-based, multimedia-orientated teaching modules (McManus, Subramaniam & James, 2012).

4. Topic Themes on Research in Ethics Education in Accounting

The topics of accounting ethics education research capture the key themes from 1972 to 2018, which reflect an appreciation and understanding of the importance and benefits of teaching ethics to accounting students (see Table 3.2). The topic themes are identified by mining each manuscript using the keywords provided by the submitting authors and by examining the research aims and rationale of each manuscript. Key topic themes were collated, categorized and recategorized based on cognitive overlap to arrive at a list of main categories. Overall, the top six most frequently occurring themes accounted for 64 percent of published research on accounting ethics education between 1972 and 2018. Notably, the purpose and rationale for accounting ethics education research remained constant throughout the five decades of research. The most frequently occurring theme is concerned with the 'methods of teaching ethics', accounting for 12.55 percent of the total manuscripts. The second most frequent theme deals in the 'importance of accounting ethics education', representing 11.37 percent of total publications. The next two most frequent themes, 'ethical

Table 3.2 Research themes

Rank	Research themes	%	Total
1	Methods of teaching accounting ethics education	12.89%	33
2	Important and the effectiveness of accounting ethics education	11.33%	29
=3	Ethical decision-making	10.94%	28
=3	Integrate ethics into the accounting curriculum or stand-alone course	10.94%	28
4	Moral development, moral capability, moral intensity, moral reasoning	10.16%	26
5	Accounting ethics education curriculum	8.20%	21
	Other	35.54%	91

decision-making' and the 'integration of ethics into the accounting curriculum', were ranked equally in third position, with each theme accounting for 10.98 percent of the total sample population. Issues associated with 'moral and ethical development', examined in terms of moral capability, moral intensity and moral reasoning, are ranked fourth with only two fewer manuscripts than the themes ranked in third position, accounting for 10.2 percent of the total publications. The fifth theme relates to topics dealing with the 'accounting curriculum' accounting for 8.24 percent of overall publications. The remaining themes account for 36 percent of the total publications, dealing in diverse and scattered topics. The following findings present a synthesis of accounting ethics education research for the period 1972 to 2018 based on the six major topic themes. The length of the discussion appearing in each section should be interpreted as reflective not of the quantity of research produced but of the diversity of topics within each broad category.

4.1 Methods of Teaching Ethics

The methods utilized in the classroom to teach ethics provides a significant motivation for research when new and innovative pedagogies have the potential to support students' learning as well as assist educators to deliver classes using more stimulating formats. This research stems from a desire to understand the impact of different pedagogies on ethics education. Several authors examine both inductively and empirically the pros and cons of diverse teaching methods, including case problems (real or imaginary), film/video, role playing, ethical games, small group discussion, educational novels and published journal articles, the lecture method, group and collaborative learning through ethical discussion, exposure to alternative viewpoints, personal value journals, guest speakers and practitioner participation, service-learning, e-learning, written assignments identifying personal heroes and a review of the AAA Casebook (Kerr &

Smith, 1995; Naudé, 2008; Faello, 2017; Manalo, 2013; Scribner & Dillaway, 1989; Shawver, 2011; Ocampo-Gómez & Ortega-Guerrero, 2013; Apostolou & Apostolou, 1997; Gunz & McCutcheon, 1998). In early research, Gunz and McCutcheon (1998) identify an absence of case studies in accounting ethics education stemming from the lack of interest in embedding ethics in the accounting curriculum. Manalo (2013) found that the ethical discussion and collaborative learning were teaching strategies most preferred by students whereas technology-enhanced learning or e-learning strategies were least preferred. Written vignettes were deemed by McNair and Milam (1993) to be the most effective of all methods but were not favored among faculty for teaching ethics, as only 48 percent applied this method. McDonald and Donleavy (1995) engaged in this debate by challenging the resistance and misconceptions of the limitations of ethics education to enhance and encourage faculty understanding of effective ethics education.

Whereas many authors advocate pedagogical diversity, the lecture is the most commonly used method to teach ethics (Loeb & Bedingfield, 1972; McNair & Milam, 1993). McNair and Milam (1993) find the reason behind the popularity of the lecture method to be the relative ease in adding ethics dimensions to discussion across a wide variety of accounting classes. Furthermore, lectures can be delivered with minimal preparation or grading time compared to case or vignette assignments. However, Han (2011) strongly argued that the lecture method is unsuitable for teaching ethics. Whereas the lecture method is easy to practice and enables students to learn knowledge in a passive, non-threatening way in a short time, students tend to find this method tedious and ineffective (Han, 2011). An active learning approach to ethics education is advocated by many researchers over conventional methods of teaching (Armstrong, 1987; Han, 2011; Loeb, 2006; Massey & Van Hise, 2009). With this in mind, a number of authors link pedagogy with experiential learning such as individual journals/diaries and project reports to better understand ethics in accounting (Loeb, 2015; Naudé, 2008). Kuhn (1998) advocates pedagogy in real-world situations to encourage students to confront diversity, ambiguity, market failures and systemic injustices. Taplin, Singh, Kerr and Lee (2018) are motivated by role-plays because they help students develop ethical awareness and prepare them for dealing with ethical dilemmas in the workplace. Deno and Flynn (2018) invested in authentic classroom exercises by familiarizing students with audited financial statements and internal control shortcomings. Stephenson (2017) introduced a Reflective Ethical Decision Model, offering a hands-on pedagogical approach to decision-making. Kuhn (1998) supports games and simulations to accompany deeper probing of ethical theory. Taplin et al. (2018) reported how short 10-minute role-plays can be used as an effective tool for ethics education. This stream of research is based on the premise that real-world experiences enhance the critical thinking abilities of the participating students.

Research on the methods of teaching is driven by the belief that pedagogy in accounting ethics education contributes to enhancing the ethics of future accounting professionals. Understanding and developing teaching effectiveness is prompted by the question of how ethics can be taught so that effective learning takes place (Armstrong, 1990, 1993; Christensen & Woodland, 2018; Frank, Ofobike & Gradisher, 2009; Geary & Sims, 1994; Taylor, 2013). Many authors call for moral growth through ethics interventions, however, the need for ethics education is dependent upon whether or not such teaching would prove effective. In general, the ethics education interventions with diverse teaching methods produce conflicting results. O'Leary and Stewart (2013) examined the interaction between learning styles and found that some teaching methodologies in an auditing course had a greater impact on active learners than on passive learners. Shawver (2011) explored the effectiveness of five components (cases, participation, textbook readings, a research paper and exams) of teaching ethics in an Advanced Financial Accounting course. Both Scribner and Dillaway (1989) and Awasthi and Staehelin (1995) suggest that the case study approach to teaching and effective ethics education have positive influence on students.

4.2 Importance of Ethics Education

Research on ethics education in accounting stems from attempting to understand its importance to the development of future accounting professionals (Abdolmohammadi, 2008; Maruszewska, 2011; Tunca Caliyurt & Crowther, 2006; Uyar & GÜNGÖRMÜŞ, 2013; Warinda, 2013). This body of literature addresses the importance of ethics education in terms of its goals but also evaluates potential problems and issues in the delivery of accounting ethics education. The media attention and subsequent investigations into corporate collapses left commentators questioning the ethics of the accounting profession resulting in an upsurge of accounting ethics education, inspiring research on the reasons and benefits of accounting ethics education (Bean & Bernardi, 2005; Costa, Pinheiro & Ribeiro, 2016; Ferguson, Collison, Power & Stevenson, 2011; Fisher, Swanson & Schmidt, 2007; Fourie & Contogiannis, 2014; Gordon, 2011; Halbesleben, Wheeler & Buckley, 2005; Koumbiadis & Okpara, 2008; Loeb, 2006; McManus & Subramaniam, 2009; Misiewicz, 2007; Mohd Ghazali, 2015; Saat et al., 2010a; ŞENGÜR, 2017; Sugahara & Boland, 2011; Van Hise & Massey, 2010; Win et al., 2014). Corporate scandals involving the accounting profession have thus become a major catalyst for accounting ethics education research (e.g., Canarutto et al., 2010; Jackling, Cooper, Leung & Dellaportas, 2007; Jennings, 2004; Wilson, Strong & Mooney, 2016). The rationale was prompted initially by the fraudulent activities of companies such as Enron, WorldCom, HealthSouth and others and the devastating effects on financial markets and investors, creating public concern toward accountants (Bean & Bernardi, 2005).

One stream of research attributes accounting frauds to the failure of educators to implement adequate ethics training in accounting education programs (Brown-Liburd & Porco, 2011; Ferguson et al., 2011; Miller & Shawver, 2018). Some authors suggest that the education system should bear some of the responsibility for the apparent low moral standards of the accounting profession, highlighting the need to reexamine the level and type of ethics education (McPhail, 1999; Shawver, 2009). The implicit rationale calling for ethics education is to reduce the level of fraud in business by integrating ethics into accounting education programs (Uyar & GÜNGÖRMÜŞ, 2013). Support for critics who challenge the ability of the accounting profession to hold corporations to account embed their claims in evidence questioning the ethicality of accounting students. For example, O'Leary and Cotter (2000) discovered a willingness among accounting students to accept a bribe and/or cheat in an exam. Ameen et al. (1996a) similarly investigated students' perceptions of questionable academic practices and their propensity to cheat. Elias and Farag (2010) considered the psychological variable 'the love of money' in determining how accounting students view cheating actions inside and outside the classroom and (Burns, Tackett & Wolf, 2015) examined the effect of ethics education on the incidence of student plagiarism in a college writing assignment.

The relationship between recruiting aspiring accountants and accounting ethics education was also the aim of a small quantity of articles. From the viewpoint of the recruiter, Ahadiat and Mackie (1993) identified the relative importance of ethical behavior compared with the more traditional personal characteristics utilized by public accounting firms during their recruiting process. Breaux, Chiasson, Mauldin and Whitney (2009) explored ethical coverage in accounting programs as an important factor affecting recruiting decisions for entry-level accounting positions. Research on CPE and members of the profession eventually turned to professional accounting bodies and their perceptions of ethical training. Jackling et al. (2007) sought the viewpoint of professional accounting bodies on the likelihood of ethical issues arising in different types of organizations, the perceived causes of ethical failure and their role in ethics education. Fleming (1996) also discussed the factors preventing professional accounting bodies from successfully integrating an effective ethics education into their assessment schemes for prospective members.

The viewpoint of accounting faculty on the importance of ethics education was sought and compared with that of accounting students to identify differences in the way the two cohorts perceive the goals and benefits of accounting ethics education (Adkins & Radtke, 2004). This stream of research finds that students embrace the importance of accounting ethics education and value their experience in ethics education (Cooper et al., 2008; Gonzalo & Garvey, 2005; Rahman, 2003). Blanthorne et al. (2007) provided faculty opinions on whether ethics should be included in the accounting curriculum, who should teach ethics and how and where in the curriculum ethics should be taught. Miller and Shawver (2018) similarly examined faculty perceptions on what is being taught and how much time is dedicated to ethics training. The authors suggest that ethics training is insufficient and had not changed a great deal in two decades. Hurtt and Thomas (2008) found support from educators on the implementation of a course in ethics as a prerequisite requirement for CPA examination candidates. Evidence suggests that faculty give credence to the importance of ethics education and call for the integration of ethics throughout required accounting courses (Loeb, 1988; Milam & McNair, 1992). Smith, Smith and Mulig (2005) found that students accept the importance of ethics education and called on educators to encourage students to learn how to do the 'right thing' within ethics education.

Cultural issues in the globalization of business and accounting expanded the debate on accounting ethics education to draw attention to the importance of cross-cultural factors in the ethics of accountants. Tweedie, Dyball, Hazelton and Wright (2013) emphasize that ethical beliefs are highly diverse and often deeply held, especially when intertwined with local cultural or religious practices. Understanding guanxi is popular in the relational society of China in which loyalty to one's superior tends to take precedence over one's commitment to professional and ethical obligations (Yang & Wu, 2009). Singh and Vasudeva (2006) and Tunca Caliyurt and Crowther (2006) identify important shortcomings in the ethics education imparted to future accounting professionals in India. Ramirez (2017) examined the impact of the financial corruption in Spain on the accounting curriculum and the development of ethical competencies among students. Research analysis moved from cultural issues and ethics in accounting to the ethics of individual students in diverse cultural settings (Auyeung et al., 2006; Ge & Thomas, 2008; Ho & Lin, 2008; Waldmann, 2000). For example, Irsyadillah and Lasyoud (2018) examined the ethical development of accounting students in Indonesia. Further research compares the ethical perceptions of students from different nations and ethnicities: the United States and Ireland (Eynon et al., 1996); English-Canada and the United States (Thorne, 1999); Canada and China (Ge & Thomas, 2008); Anglo-Australian, Chinese and Muslim, (Auyeung et al., 2006); Malaysia, Australia and Ireland, (O'Leary & Mohamad, 2006); the United States and the United Kingdom (Whipple & Swords, 1992); the United States and Taiwan (Ho & Lin, 2008; Su, Kan & Yang, 2010). This stream of research tends to rely on the cultural dimensions developed by Hofstede and Bond (1984) in describing the effects of society's culture on the values and behavior of its members.

4.3 Ethical Decision-Making

The impact of education on students' ethical decision-making was the focus of several studies stemming from a belief that education and decision-making are key to reducing unethical behavior (Gray, Bebbington & McPhail, 1994; Leitsch, 2004; Singh & Vasudeva, 2006; Sweeney & Costello, 2009; Williams & Elson, 2010a). Sweeney and Costello (2009) demonstrate a relationship between the students' moral intensity and their ethical decision-making. Christensen and Woodland (2018) found that ethics education is positively and significantly associated with moral judgment and ethical decision-making. Ramirez (2017) provides students with the tools to make ethical decision when facing prohibited acts. O'Leary and Pangemanan (2007) analyzed the effect of group decision-making on ethical issues and find that the group approach is not conducive to optimal or complex ethical decisions. Whereas the majority of research on ethical decision-making infers improved ethical behavior, some studies focus on the behavioral choices of specific issues such as whistleblowing to help root out fraud (Brody & Bowman, 1998; Shawver, 2011). This research is aimed at examining the relationship between accounting ethics education and whistleblowing when faced with a serious wrongdoing. Liyanarachchi and Newdick (2009) found that the strength of retaliation and participants' level of moral reasoning is positively associated with the propensity to blow the whistle. McManus et al. (2012) found that students exposed to a web-based ethics instruction module are more likely to blow the whistle than were students exposed to traditional in-class textbook ethics instruction. Elias (2008) investigated students' perceptions of internal and external whistleblowing and found that senior students demonstrated a commitment to the profession and were more likely to blow the whistle on illegal management actions.

Much of the work on ethics education and ethical decision-making stems from the theoretical framework of Rest's (1986) four-component model in which ethical decision-making is the result of four interlinking components: ethical sensitivity, ethical judgment, ethical intention and ethical behavior. Developing students' ethical sensitivity, representing the first component of Rest's (1986) model, is considered important because ethical conflicts occur when accountants perceive their duties differently between stakeholder groups or when self-interest is central. Several studies refer to enhancing ethical sensitivity so that students are better able to recognize issues in accounting and, by implication, change students' behavior (Armstrong, 1993; O'Leary, 2009; Welton, Lagrone & Davis, 1994; Wright, Dyball, Byers & Radich, 2012). Developing ethical awareness and sensitivity is critically important when ethical violations result from ignorance rather than from deliberate action (Williams & Elson, 2010b). Shawver and Sennetti (2009) examined diverse measures of ethical sensitivity, moving discussion on measurement away from the well-established Defining Issues Test, such as multidimensional ethical scale (MES), to measure the effects of undergraduate accounting ethics education.

On the second component of Rest's model, Koumbiadis and Pandit (2014) examined the influence of ethics instruction on the moral judgment of two groups of accountants: graduates of programs with 120-credits and graduates of programs with 150-credits. The results found no significant difference in the domains of self-interest, efficiency, social responsibility or legal compliance between the two groups. Saat et al. (2012) found that a moral education program was able to enhance the levels of moral judgement and that practical training contributed significantly to the observed improvement. Dellaportas (2006) similarly found that a dedicated course on ethics had a positive effect on students' moral judgement. Koumbiadis and Okpara (2008) and Coate and Frey (2000) tested the third and fourth components of Rest's model and evaluated how accounting ethics education impacts students' behavioral intent and ethical behavior. Koumbiadis and Okpara (2008) revealed that accounting students were more likely to be aware of the importance of ethical behavior as a result of the demise of large corporations and the ripple effect of these catastrophes on the economy. Miller, Becker, and Pernsteiner (2014) studied the impact of a course on accounting ethics incorporating a formal 'Ethics Education Framework and associated Toolkit', on students' ethical development, moral sensitivity/awareness and the intent to take ethical actions. Miller et al. (2014) find that accounting ethics education has a positive impact on the four stages of Rest's framework: ethical awareness, judgment, intention and behavior.

One stream of research aims to facilitate structured decision-making by socializing students in accepting and adhering to the principles of the code of professional ethics and integrate the principles of the code into students' personal ethical code and behavior (Loeb, 1994; McCarthy, 1997; Persons, 2009). With this rationale, McCarthy (1997) examined students' affinity with the code of ethics and found no significant difference between beginning- and advanced-level accounting students, or students who had or had not taken the ethics course. The results indicate that ethical orientation does not significantly improve with exposure to the AICPA Code of Conduct in collegiate courses in accounting. Persons (2009) examined the factors related to the code of ethics that could potentially influence students' ethicality and found that gender, academic major, work experience and the number of work placements providing ethics training had a positive influence on students' ethicality measured in terms of the code of ethics. A similar stream of research among accounting professionals examined their commitment to the code of ethics, acting as a barometer of the quality of work carried out with honesty and integrity. This research emphasizes the importance of character, integrity and responsibility in accounting education, augmenting the need for instruction on the code of ethics (Haas, 2005) combined with a more general discussion of ethical behavior (Larres & Mulgrew, 2009). Research evidence suggests that training in codes of ethics allows organizations to improve employees' conduct by working through and increasing employees' perceptions of their immediate ethical context (Valentine & Fleischman, 2004).

4.4 Moral Reasoning, Development and Capability

Moral reasoning, development and capability is ranked fourth in the list of key topic themes and is implicit in ethical decision-making and behavior and therefore discussed following the discussion on ethical decision-making. Research on moral development among accounting students relies predominantly on Kohlberg's (1981) theory of moral reasoning and development to understand and measure improvements in student's ethical reasoning (Arfaoui et al., 2016; Dellaportas, 2006; Irsyadillah & Lasyoud, 2018; Shaub, 1994a; Thorne, 1999). Whereas research on ethical decision-making relies on Rest's (1986) four-component model, Kohlberg's (1981) theory is the most widely used to explain elevations in moral and ethical reasoning, following an ethics intervention in accounting education. This research is motivated in part by empirical evidence suggesting that accounting students lack moral reasoning skills compared with students in other disciplines such as medicine or law (e.g., Liu, Yao & Hu, 2012). The impact of ethics education on student's moral capability is mixed (Tweedie et al., 2013). Whereas many studies find accounting ethics education contributes to students' moral thinking and behavior (e.g., Dellaportas, 2006; Melé, 2005; Thorne, 2001; Williams & Elson, 2010a), additional studies find that ethics education does not have significant influence on students' ethical attitude (Low, Davey & Hooper, 2008; Ponemon, 1993). Ponemon (1993) find that ethics interventions had no effect on accounting students' level of ethical reasoning and did not curtail students' free-riding behavior. Whereas Low et al. (2008) found that students did not believe that ethics education would a have significant influence on their ethical attitude, the authors continue to advocate for an ethics course deeming it an essential component of learning for future accounting professionals. Research has also found that the gains in students' moral reasoning from an ethics intervention are transitory and do not persist after graduation (LaGrone, Welton & Davis, 1996; Welton & Guffey, 2009). Overall, the research findings are inconsistent.

The factors elevating moral reasoning and development have drawn attention from many researchers (Billiot et al., 2012; Brown-Liburd & Porco, 2011; Fleming, Lightner & Romanus, 2009; Fourie & Contogiannis, 2014). Both Shaub (1994b) and Thorne (1999) evaluate the relationship between demographic variables and student's moral reasoning and development. Whereas Shaub (1994b) debated potential weaknesses in implementing ethics in the classroom, Thorne (1999) found that the moral development among a sample of Canadian accounting students is associated with years of education and gender but is not associated with age or audit experience. Research also evaluates the perception of ethical behavior and moral development of accounting students to examine the effectiveness of ethics education (Saat, Porter & Woodbine, 2010b) or by the individual factors (gender, age, work experience and attendance of a course on ethics) (Costa et al., 2016). These studies also indicate that ethics education significantly influences ethical conduct and moral development (Gonzalo & Garvey, 2005; Rahman, 2003; Saat et al., 2010b), whereas Costa et al. (2016) found that gender, age and work experience influences students' initiative, obedience and integrity. In spite of the positive findings, authors continue to claim a need for a more ethics education by business schools and accounting programs and future accountants (Abdolmohammadi, 2008).

4.5 Extent of Ethics in the Accounting Curriculum

In order to assess the adequacy of ethics instruction in accounting programs, one stream of research (ranked third in the list of key themes) investigates the extent of ethics coverage in the accounting curriculum (Dellaportas et al., 2014; Fleming et al., 2009; Low et al., 2008; Marzuki et al., 2017; Massey & Van Hise, 2009; Williams & Elson, 2010a). Research evidence suggests that the integration of ethics education in accounting programs has grown steadily (Massey & Van Hise, 2009), however, there is a widely held perception among accounting faculty that more needs to be done to improve the quality of ethics education (Farnsworth & Kleiner, 2003). Research findings indicate that accounting ethics education is not covered in a significant way in university education (Armstrong & Mintz, 1989; Cohen & Pant, 1989; Karnes & Sterner, 1988). Frank et al. (2009) similarly argue that ethics coverage has not yet reached the point of supporting students effectively in developing their moral attitudes. Additional evidence suggests that accounting education lacks ethics 'subject matter' (Borkowski & Ugras, 1992; Rahman, 2003) or provides little ethics training to accounting students (Cowton & Cummins, 2003; Hiltebeitel & Jones, 1992; Loeb, 1988). In the US, Miller and Becker (2011) found that the average level of coverage of all ethics topics in a course was approximately 3.4 hours in total (9 percent of the course). Their findings were similar to 3.18 hours reported by McNair and Milam (1993) and 4 hours reported by Fisher et al. (2007). Whereas the level of ethics coverage through both required and elective offerings had increased between 2003 and 2016, it remained quite low overall (Miller & Shawver, 2018). This research is premised on improving ethics coverage in accounting education by calling for an increase of ethics education in the accounting curriculum, which appears inadequately addressed (Cohen & Pant, 1989; Haas, 2005; Marzuki et al., 2017; Miller & Becker, 2011; Cohen & Pant, 1989; Loeb & Rockness, 1992).

When researchers accept the premise that ethics education should be enhanced, research turns to the question of whether ethics should be integrated throughout required accounting courses or taught as a stand-alone course. For example, Abdolmohammadi (2008) encourages discussion on the implications of ethics education between stand-alone and integrated ethics courses. Ellis (2013) presents the advantages of a stand-alone accounting ethics course addressing specific ethics applications across the curriculum, and Tunca Caliyurt and Crowther (2006) call upon accounting academics to revise course materials to educate students on ethics by integrating ethics subject matter into diverse accounting courses. A large amount of literature supports the integration of ethics education in the accounting curriculum (see for example Blanthorne et al., 2007; Burns et al., 2015; Chen, Chen & Chenoweth, 2013; Jackling et al., 2007; Langenderfer & Rockness, 1989; Levy & Mitschow, 2008; Mintchik & Farmer, 2009; Simpson et al., 2016; Sisaye & Lackman, 1994; Thomas, 2004; West & Buckby, 2018). Bampton and Cowton (2002) argue that integration provides an opportunity to expose students to a variety of ethical issues as well as reflect on broader ethical scenarios that accounting students may face in real life. Research suggests that accounting faculty support the inclusion of ethics subject matter in several accounting courses rather than a stand-alone course (Blanthorne et al., 2007; Milam & McNair, 1992). However, there are a number of factors at play that limit the integration of ethics in the accounting curriculum: lack of training or faculty specialized in ethics; lack of teaching materials; lack of time and space to prepare for student for working environment on ethical issues; lack of motivated or qualified accounting faculty to teach ethics; and minimizing of the importance of ethics course (Adkins & Radtke, 2004; Bampton & Cowton, 2002; Dellaportas, 2014; Langenderfer & Rockness, 1989; Naudé, 2008). The integration of ethics into the curriculum requires all accounting faculty to have a basic understanding of what is taught on ethics and would require them to link ethical insights to their areas of expertise (Naudé, 2008).

The alternative to integrating ethics into courses in accounting is the development of a stand-alone course dedicated to ethics instruction. Proponents claim that a stand-alone course is superior because it offers a clearer focus to students on accounting ethics and provides a more profound rationale for ethics training and preparation for the workplace (Bean & Bernardi, 2005; Graham, 2012; Jackling et al., 2007; O'Leary, 2009; Williams & Elson, 2010b). Graham (2012) found that students favored stand-alone courses over integration because it enabled the study of a wide range of issues in one place, enhancing students' awareness of ethical problems and how to solve them. However, a stand-alone course on ethics has been criticized when the ethical issues are limited to one area of practice, creating a narrow impression of ethics in accounting (Low et al., 2008). A single course in ethics education is inadequate if it is too brief, lacks depth and would not have a lasting effect on students' ethical sensitivity (Hiltebeitel & Jones, 1991; Karnes & Sterner, 1988).

Armstrong (1993) in particular calls for both integration and separation by advocating a 'sandwich approach' for teaching business ethics in which students are exposed to a general business ethics course, a strong ethics component in other accounting classes and a dedicated capstone course on accounting ethics.

4.6 Curriculum Issues

The subject matter of ethics education is the final key topic theme in Table 3.2, raising considerable discussion among researchers. Kidwell, Fisher, Braun and Swanson (2013) highlight a lack of rigorous discussion on curriculum content, particularly the core-knowledge learning objectives in accounting ethics education. Critics of accounting education claim that the curriculum has become so technical that it fails to produce more liberally educated accountants (Levy & Mitschow, 2008). Gray et al. (1994) advocate the acquisition of moral expertise, particularly when the accounting curricula is focused on the technical aspects of accounting, squeezing out softer topics such as ethical behavior. However, when discipline-specific knowledge pertinent to the accounting curriculum is considered fixed by faculty, it is unlikely to be replaced with requests to include ethics subject matter (Madison & Schmidt, 2006; Miller & Becker, 2011). In spite of this claim, proponents of ethics education continue to call for specific topics to be incorporated into the curriculum, for example, accounting manipulations and earnings management (Fiolleau & Kaplan, 2017; Fischer & Rosenzweig, 1995; Tormo-Carbó, Seguí-Mas & Oltra, 2016). However, beyond topics, some authors call for conceptual underpinnings in ethics education such as Kohlberg's theory of cognitive moral development to enhance students' abilities to recognize ethical issues (Cooper et al., 2008; Dellaportas, Jackling, Leung & Cooper, 2011; Han, 2011; Miller et al., 2014). Miller et al. (2014) argue that the application of ethical theory in more complex ethical scenarios over an extended period of time enhances the ability to recognize ethical components in a given scenario and the intention to do the right thing. Kidwell et al. (2013) proposed a comprehensive framework based on six areas: codes of ethical conduct, corporate governance, the accounting profession, moral development, classical ethics theories and decision models. Han (2011) proposed an ethical decision-making model to deepen relevant ethical requirements and sharpen professional skills to encourage students to undergo self-questioning in accordance with the profession's code of ethics. Research in the latter stages of the sample period emphasize the inclusion of issues on corporate social responsibility and sustainability (Jorge, Andrades Pena & Muriel de los Reyes, 2015; Sisaye, 2011; Tormo-Carbó, Seguí-Mas & Oltra, 2018). Sisaye (2011) examined the development in sustainability management for ethics integration in the accounting and business curriculum. The social sustainability approach to accounting education is considered crucial by proponents to improve the effectiveness of business ethics and corporate social responsibility helping to improve business students' awareness of ethical issues (Tormo-Carbó et al., 2018).

The intellectual debate on what should be taught in ethics education was paralleled by one about who should teach ethics. This research raises the question of whether accounting faculty possess the embedded expertise to teach accounting ethics (Bernardi et al., 2008). Cohen and Pant (1989) conducted a survey of accounting department chairpersons and find that accounting faculty were well qualified to teach ethics. Blanthorne et al. (2007) suggest that faculty are well equipped to teach ethical dilemmas in accounting, whereas Williams and Elson (2010a) argue that accounting faculty lack the necessary training and interest to teach ethics. Dellaportas et al. (2014) analyzed the barriers to enhancing ethics education highlighting a shortage of qualified staff teaching ethics education in accounting. The alternative to accounting faculty teaching ethics is to have courses led by philosophers who are better equipped to teach theories of moral reasoning to students. However, overly theoretical applications of knowledge may lack relevance to the discipline of accounting (Loeb, 1988; Williams & Elson, 2010a; Langenderfer and Rockness (1989). Other solutions include co-lecturing or team teaching (Williams & Elson, 2010a).

5. Conclusion

Overall, the present study reviewed and profiled published research on accounting ethics education during the period 1972 to 2018. This study contributes to the current state of accounting ethics education research by providing insight into the field's strengths and weaknesses. Strengths include the development of increasingly more complex methods of teaching ethics, the enhancement of students' ethical decision-making and ethical behavior (such as cheating, whistleblowing). Major weaknesses include a lack of theoretical grounding or a specific tool to measure the effectiveness of ethics education, particularly when research ventures beyond experimental methods of research. This study highlights the impact and educational response immediately following the prevalence of illegal and unethical corporate behavior, which fueled skepticism and uncertainty about the role of ethics in modern business and accounting practice. The analysis in this study provides a level of comfort to stakeholder groups with increasing attention on accounting ethics education, evidenced by the growing published research on this topic. It is our hope that the present study will stimulate additional research in this important area.

The findings were presented in two major sections. The first section highlighted the trends of accounting ethics education over five decades of research from 1972 to 2018. Whereas major themes do not vary greatly between the decades, the depth, rigor and quantum of research was enhanced over time. Early research on accounting ethics education relied on interpretive analysis, whereas research in the latter period relied on complex or sophisticated models of analysis such as regressions, experiment, ground theory and meta-analysis. Early research tends to question the value and extent of ethics education (Hiltebeitel & Jones, 1991; Levy & Mitschow, 2008; Loeb, 1988; Ponemon, 1993; Smith et al., 2005), whereas later research tends to focus on the ethics of the individual and ethical decision-making (Costa et al., 2016; Faello, 2017; Fiolleau & Kaplan, 2017; Mohd Ghazali, 2015; Ramirez, 2017; Waldron & Fisher, 2017), as well as perspectives on ethics education from the practicing profession (Caglio & Cameran, 2017; Loeb, 2012; Rockness & Rockness, 2010; Wilson et al., 2016) and from educators and instructors (Jones & Spraakman, 2011; Liu et al., 2012; Miller & Shawver, 2018). Similarly, teaching pedagogies changed over time to include case studies, role-plays, games, video presentations and novels, influenced in part by the introduction of learning technology platforms such as a web-based multimedia-orientated teaching module (McManus et al., 2012). The number of publications in developing countries also increased overtime, peaking during the 2010s, implying a recognition of the importance of ethics education by faculty in developing and non-Western countries. The trends in accounting ethics education research and the number of publications is in part reflective of the number of corporate scandals appearing in the media, which increased over time. The research trends shifted from a discussion of the need for having ethics in accounting education to how accounting ethics education can educate students to support ethical decision-making and moral development. This shift in trends contributed greatly to the ethics development of future accountants.

The second section on findings highlighted six key topic themes of accounting ethics education research and their components occurring over five decades of research: teaching methods, the importance of ethics education, ethical decision-making, moral development the integration of ethics into accounting courses and curriculum issues. Discussion on the key themes was not intended to be exhaustive, particularly when each theme comprises many sub-categories, but, rather, illustrative of the research appearing in academic journals under these broad headings. Research on accounting ethics education, for the most part, is motivated by a narrow frame of thinking based on whether ethics education has an impact on students' moral or ethical sensitivity and decision-making and how can ethics be taught so that it makes a difference. Numerous issues were raised in this body of research and can be categorized into two broad groups: (1) the ethics of the individual in which moral cognition and sensitivity are central and (2) pedagogical issues to help elevate moral cognition and sensitivity with an ultimate to improve ethical decision-making.

The process involved in identifying major trends and the categorization of key themes is not a precise science, introducing an element of subjectivity in categorizing and frequency counts, which may not be replicated precisely by other researchers. However, the discussion in this study is general and unlikely to differ significantly from different methods of data collection and analysis. Further research could delve more deeply into particular issues and rely on more sophisticated methods of analysis. Furthermore, the cognitive overlap between business ethics and accounting ethics suggests that the issues raised in 'ethics education research' are applicable to all business disciplines. Critical issues raised in the non-accounting literatures could have been overlooked in the present study, suggesting that future research could expand the search criteria to include all business ethics education research. While the analysis in the present study provides a broad overview of accounting ethics education research, author co-citation and journal co-citation analysis would give an indication of the attention authors give to accounting ethics education and the impact of individual authors and manuscripts.

Note

1. Formerly known as *Accounting Education: An International Journal*.

References

Abdolmohammadi, M. (2008). Who should teach ethics courses in business and accounting programs? In C. Jeffrey (Ed.), *Research on professional responsibility and ethics in accounting* (pp. 113–134). Bingley, UK: Emerald Group Publishing Limited.

Adkins, N., & Radtke, R. R. (2004). Students' and faculty members' perceptions of the importance of business ethics and accounting ethics education: Is there an expectations gap? *Journal of Business Ethics, 51*(3), 279–300.

Ahadiat, N., & Mackie, J. J. (1993). Ethics education in accounting: An investigation of the importance of ethics as a factor in the recruiting decisions of public accounting firms. *Journal of Accounting Education, 11*(2), 243–257.

Ahmad, N. L. (2017). Integrating ethics into accounting curriculum: Overview from Malaysian accounting educators. *Geografia-Malaysian Journal of Society and Space, 11*(6).

Albrecht, W. S., & Sack, R. J. (2000). *Accounting education: Charting the course through a perilous future* (Vol. 16). Sarasota, FL: American Accounting Association.

Ameen, E. C., Guffey, D. M., & McMillan, J. J. (1996a). Accounting students' perceptions of questionable academic practices and factors affecting their propensity to cheat. *Accounting Education, 5*(3), 191–205.

Ameen, E. C., Guffey, D. M., & McMillan, J. J. (1996b). Gender differences in determining the ethical sensitivity of future accounting professionals. *Journal of Business Ethics, 15*(5), 591–597.

American Institute of Certified Public Accountants (AICPA). (1988). *Code of professional conduct*. New York: AICPA.

Apostolou, B., & Apostolou, N. (1997). Heroes as a context for teaching ethics. *Journal of Education for Business, 73*(2), 121–125.

Arfaoui, F., Damak-Ayadi, S., Ghram, R., & Bouchekoua, A. (2016). Ethics education and accounting students' level of moral development: Experimental design in Tunisian audit context. *Journal of Business Ethics*, 138(1), 161–173.

Armstrong, M. B. (1987). Moral development and accounting education. *Journal of Accounting Education*, 5(1), 27–43.

Armstrong, M. B. (1990). Professional ethics and accounting education: A critique of the 8-step method. *Business and Professional Ethics Journal*, 9(1/2), 181–191.

Armstrong, M. B. (1993). Ethics and professionalism in accounting education: A sample course. *Journal of Accounting Education*, 11(1), 77–92.

Armstrong, M. B., & Mintz, S. M. (1989). Ethics education in accounting: Present status and policy implications. *Association of Government Accountants Journal*, 38(2), 70–76.

Auyeung, P. K., Dagwell, R., Ng, C., & Sands, J. (2006). Educators' epistemological beliefs of accounting ethics teaching: A cross-cultural study. *Accounting Research Journal*, 19(2), 122–138.

Awasthi, V. N., & Staehelin, E. (1995). Ethics and management accounting: Teaching note for a video case, 'the order: A progressive disclosure vignette'. *Journal of Accounting Education*, 13(1), 87–98.

Bampton, R., & Cowton, C. J. (2002). The teaching of ethics in management accounting: Progress and prospects. *Business Ethics: A European Review*, 11(1), 52–61.

Bean, D. F., & Bernardi, R. A. (2005). Accounting ethics courses: A professional necessity. *The CPA Journal*, 75(12), 64.

Bernardi, R. A., Bean, D. F., & Melton, M. R. (2008). Do accounting academics have the expertise to teach a discipline specific ethics course?. In C. Jeffrey (Ed.), *Research on professional responsibility and ethics in accounting* (pp. 155–177). Bingley, UK: Emerald Group Publishing Limited.

Billiot, M. J., Daniel, D., Glandon, S., & Glandon, T. (2012). Educational context: Preparing accounting students to identify ethical dilemmas. *American Journal of Business Education*, 5(3), 277–286.

Blanthorne, C., Kovar, S. E., & Fisher, D. G. (2007). Accounting educators' opinions about ethics in the curriculum: An extensive view. *Issues in Accounting Education*, 22(3), 355–390.

Borkowski, S. C., & Ugras, Y. J. (1992). The ethical attitudes of students as a function of age, sex and experience. *Journal of Business Ethics*, 11(12), 961–979.

Breaux, K., Chiasson, M., Mauldin, S., & Whitney, T. (2009). Ethics education in accounting curricula: Does it influence recruiters' hiring decisions of entry-level accountants? *Journal of Education for Business*, 85(1), 1–6.

Brody, R., & Bowman, L. (1998). Accounting and psychology students' perceptions of. *College Student Journal*, 32(2), 162–166.

Brown-Liburd, H. L., & Porco, B. M. (2011). It's what's outside that counts: Do extracurricular experiences affect the cognitive moral development of undergraduate accounting students? *Issues in Accounting Education*, 26(2), 439–454.

Buell, E. K., Cavico, F., Mujtaba, B. G., & Rentfro, R. (2009). The relationship of ethics education to the moral development of accounting students. In *International Handbook of Academic Research and Teaching*, Vol. 6 (p. 87). Dallas, TX: Intellectbase International Consortium (IIC) Conference Committee.

Burks, B. D., & Sellani, R. J. (2008). Ethics, religiosity, and moral development of business students. *Journal of Leadership, Accountability and Ethics, 49*.

Burns, D. J., Tackett, J. A., & Wolf, F. (2015). The effectiveness of instruction in accounting ethics education: Another look. In C. Jeffrey (Ed.), *Research on professional responsibility and ethics in accounting* (pp. 149–180). Bingley, UK: Emerald Group Publishing Limited.

Caglio, A., & Cameran, M. (2017). Is it shameful to be an accountant? GenMe perception (s) of accountants' ethics. *Abacus, 53*(1), 1–27.

Canarutto, G., Smith, K. T., & Smith, L. M. (2010). Impact of an ethics presentation used in the USA and adapted for Italy. *Accounting Education: An International Journal, 19*(3), 309–322.

Cannon, C. (2001). *Does moral education increase moral development: A reexamination of the moral reasoning abilities of working adult learners* (PhD thesis). Nova Southeastern University, Florida.

Chafi, R. (2013). The effect of accounting education on occupational ethics. *Technical Journal of Engineering and Applied Sciences, 3*(23), 3468–3474. Retrieved October 2019, from http://tjeas.com/wp-content/uploads/2013/10/3468-3474.pdf

Chan, S. Y., & Leung, P. (2006). The effects of accounting students' ethical reasoning and personal factors on their ethical sensitivity. *Managerial Auditing Journal, 21*(4), 436–457.

Chang, O. H., Davis, S. W., & Kauffman, K. D. (2012). Accounting ethics education: A comparison with Buddhist ethics education framework. *Journal of Religion and Business Ethics, 3*(1), 4.

Chen, M.-L., Chen, R. D., & Chenoweth, T. (2013). Stand-alone college accounting ethics course and insight for accounting ethics modules. *International Journal of Education Research, 8*(1).

Christensen, A. L., & Woodland, A. (2018). An investigation of the relationships among Volunteer Income Tax Assistance (VITA) participation and ethical judgment and decision making. *Journal of Business Ethics, 147*(3), 529–543.

Coate, C. J., & Frey, K. J. (2000). Some evidence on the ethical disposition of accounting students: Context and gender implications. *Teaching Business Ethics, 4*(4), 379–404.

Cohen, J. R., & Pant, L. W. (1989). Accounting educators' perceptions of ethics in the curriculum. *Issues in Accounting Education, 4*(1), 70–81.

Cooper, B. J., Leung, P., Dellaportas, S., Jackling, B., & Wong, G. (2008). Ethics education for accounting students: A toolkit approach. *Accounting Education: An International Journal, 17*(4), 405–430.

Costa, A. J., Pinheiro, M. M., & Ribeiro, M. S. (2016). Ethical perceptions of accounting students in a Portuguese university: The influence of individual factors and personal traits. *Accounting Education, 25*(4), 327–348.

Cowton, C. J., & Cummins, J. (2003). Teaching business ethics in UK higher education: Progress and prospects. *Teaching Business Ethics, 7*(1), 37–54.

Davis, J. R., & Welton, R. E. (1991). Professional ethics: Business students' perceptions. *Journal of Business Ethics, 10*(6), 451–463.

Dellaportas, S. (2006). Making a difference with a discrete course on accounting ethics. *Journal of Business Ethics, 65*(4), 391–404.

Dellaportas, S., Jackling, B., Leung, P., & Cooper, B. J. (2011). Developing an ethics education framework for accounting. *Journal of Business Ethics Education, 8*(1), 63–82.

Dellaportas, S., Kanapathippillai, S., Khan, A., & Leung, P. (2014). Ethics education in the Australian accounting curriculum: A longitudinal study examining barriers and enablers. *Accounting Education*, *23*(4), 362–382.

Deno, C. F., & Flynn, L. (2018). Ethical standards for accounting students: A classroom exercise on internal controls. *Journal of Business and Educational Leadership*, *7*(1), 4–13.

Elias, R. Z. (2006). The impact of professional commitment and anticipatory socialization on accounting students' ethical orientation. *Journal of Business Ethics*, *68*(1), 83–90.

Elias, R. Z. (2008). Auditing students' professional commitment and anticipatory socialization and their relationship to whistleblowing. *Managerial Auditing Journal*, *23*(3), 283–294.

Elias, R. Z., & Farag, M. (2010). The relationship between accounting students' love of money and their ethical perception. *Managerial Auditing Journal*, *25*(3), 269–281.

Ellis, J. L. (2013). Accounting ethics education: Proposed pedagogy applying cognitive moral development. *Journal of Business and Accounting*, *6*(1), 65.

Eynon, G., Hill, N. T., Stevens, K. T., & Clarke, P. (1996). An international comparison of ethical reasoning abilities: Accounting students from Ireland and the United States. *Journal of Accounting Education*, *14*(4), 477–492.

Faello, J. (2017). The use of a non-fiction fraud-related book as a method for teaching accounting ethics. *Journal of Leadership, Accountability and Ethics*, *14*(3).

Ferguson, J., Collison, D., Power, D., & Stevenson, L. (2011). Accounting education, socialisation and the ethics of business. *Business Ethics: A European Review*, *20*(1), 12–29.

Farnsworth, J. R., & Kleiner, B. H. (2003). Trends in ethics education at US colleges and universities. *Management Research News*, *26*(2/3/4), 130–140.

Fiolleau, K., & Kaplan, S. E. (2017). Recognizing ethical issues: An examination of practicing industry accountants and accounting students. *Journal of Business Ethics*, *142*(2), 259–276.

Fischer, M., & Rosenzweig, K. (1995). Attitudes of students and accounting practitioners concerning the ethical acceptability of earnings management. *Journal of Business Ethics*, *14*(6), 433–444.

Fisher, D. G., Swanson, D. L., & Schmidt, J. J. (2007). Accounting education lags CPE ethics requirements: Implications for the profession and a call to action. *Accounting Education: An International Journal*, *16*(4), 345–363.

Fleming, A. I. (1996). Ethics and accounting education in the UK: A professional approach? *Accounting Education*, *5*(3), 207–217.

Fleming, D. M., Lightner, S. M., & Romanus, R. N. (2009). The effect of professional context on accounting students' moral reasoning. *Issues in Accounting Education*, *24*(1), 13–30.

Fourie, S., & Contogiannis, E. (2014). The impact of business ethics education on attitudes toward corporate ethics of BCom: Accounting students at the University of Zululand. *South African Journal of Accounting Research*, *28*(1), 1–23.

Frank, G., Ofobike, E., & Gradisher, S. (2009). Teaching business ethics: A quandary for accounting educators. *Journal of Education for Business*, *85*(3), 132–138.

Galla, D. (2007). *Moral reasoning of finance and accounting professionals: An ethical and cognitive moral development examination*. College Ave, FL: Nova Southeastern University.

Ge, L., & Thomas, S. (2008). A cross-cultural comparison of the deliberative reasoning of Canadian and Chinese accounting students. *Journal of Business Ethics*, 82(1), 189–211.

Geary, W. T., & Sims, R. R. (1994). Can ethics be learned? *Accounting Education*, 3(1), 3–18.

Gonzalo, J. A., & Garvey, A. M. (2005). In the aftermath of crisis: The post-Enron implications for Spanish University Accounting Educators. *European Accounting Review*, 14(2), 429–439.

Gordon, I. M. (2011). Lessons to be learned: An examination of Canadian and US financial accounting and auditing textbooks for ethics/governance coverage. *Journal of Business Ethics*, 101(1), 29–47.

Graham, A. (2012). The teaching of ethics in undergraduate accounting programmes: The students' perspective. *Accounting Education*, 21(6), 599–613.

Gray, R., Bebbington, J., & McPhail, K. (1994). Teaching ethics in accounting and the ethics of accounting teaching: Educating for immorality and a possible case for social and environmental accounting education. *Accounting Education*, 3(1), 51–75.

Gunz, S., & McCutcheon, J. (1998). Are academics committed to accounting ethics education? *Journal of Business Ethics*, 17(11), 1145–1154.

Haas, A. (2005). Now is the time for ethics in education. *The CPA Journal*, 75(6), 66.

Hakan Özkan, A. (2013). Regional differences on the cognition as a constraint on accounting ethics education. *Journal of Global Business Issues*, 7(2).

Halbesleben, J. R., Wheeler, A. R., & Buckley, M. R. (2005). Everybody else is doing it, so why can't we? Pluralistic ignorance and business ethics education. *Journal of Business Ethics*, 56(4), 385–398.

Han, X. (2011). *Education and teaching of accountancy ethics in universities*. Paper presented at the 2011 International Conference on Management and Service Science, Bangkok, Thailand.

Hiltebeitel, K. M., & Jones, S. K. (1991). Initial evidence on the impact of integrating ethics into accounting education. *Issues in Accounting Education*, 6(2), 262–275.

Hiltebeitel, K. M., & Jones, S. K. (1992). An assessment of ethics instruction in accounting education. *Journal of Business Ethics*, 11(1), 37–46.

Ho, Y.-H., & Lin, C.-Y. (2008). Cultural values and cognitive moral development of accounting ethics: A cross-cultural study. *Social Behavior and Personality: An International Journal*, 36(7), 883–892.

Hofstede, G., & Bond, M. H. (1984). Hofstede's culture dimensions: An independent validation using Rokeach's value survey. *Journal of Cross-Cultural Psychology*, 15(4), 417–433.

Hurtt, R. K., & Thomas, C. W. (2008). Implementing a required ethics class for students in accounting: The Texas experience. *Issues in Accounting Education*, 23(1), 31–51.

Irsyadillah, I., & Lasyoud, A. A. (2018). Does accounting education develop ethical maturity? Evidence from Indonesia. *Accounting and Management Information Systems*, 17(3), 462–483.

Jackling, B., Cooper, B. J., Leung, P., & Dellaportas, S. (2007). Professional accounting bodies' perceptions of ethical issues, causes of ethical failure and ethics education. *Managerial Auditing Journal*, 22(9), 928–944.

Jennings, M. M. (2004). Incorporating ethics and professionalism into accounting education and research: A discussion of the voids and advocacy for training in seminal works in business ethics. *Issues in Accounting Education*, 19(1), 7–26.

Jones, J., & Spraakman, G. (2011). A case of academic misconduct: Does self-interest rule? *Accounting Perspectives*, 10(1), 1–22.

Jorge, L. M., Andrades Pena, F. J., & Muriel de los Reyes, M. J. (2015). Factors influencing the presence of ethics and CSR stand-alone courses in the accounting masters curricula: An international study. *Accounting Education*, 24(5), 361–382.

Karnes, A., & Sterner, J. (1988). The role of ethics in accounting education. *The Accounting Educators' Journal*, 1(Fall), 18–31.

Kerr, D. S., & Smith, L. M. (1995). Importance of and approaches to incorporating ethics into the accounting classroom. *Journal of Business Ethics*, 14(12), 987–995.

Kidwell, L. A., Fisher, D. G., Braun, R. L., & Swanson, D. L. (2013). Developing learning objectives for accounting ethics using Bloom's taxonomy. *Accounting Education*, 22(1), 44–65.

Kohlberg, L. (1981). *The meaning and measurement of moral development*. Worcester, MA: Clark University Press.

Koumbiadis, N., & Okpara, J. O. (2008). Ethics and accounting profession: An exploratory study of accounting students in post secondary institutions. *International Review of Business Research Papers*, 4(5), 147–156.

Koumbiadis, N., & Pandit, M. G. (2014). Has the AICPA changed the accounting profession for better or worse? The case of educational change. *Journal of Accounting & Organizational Change*, 10(2), 190–215.

Kuhn, J. W. (1998). Emotion as well as reason: Getting students beyond 'interpersonal accountability'. *Journal of Business Ethics*, 17(3), 295–308.

LaGrone, R. M., Welton, R. E., & Davis, J. R. (1996). Are the effects of accounting ethics interventions transitory or persistent? *Journal of Accounting Education*, 14(3), 259–276.

Langenderfer, H. Q., & Rockness, J. W. (1989). Integrating ethics into the accounting curriculum: Issues, problems and solutions. *Issues in Accounting Education*, 4(1), 58–69.

Larres, P. M., & Mulgrew, M. (2009). A review of an initiative to introduce a short ethics component into a non-ethics course at a UK university. *Journal of Business Ethics Education*, 6, 5–23.

Leitsch, D. L. (2004). Differences in the perceptions of moral intensity in the moral decision process: An empirical examination of accounting students. *Journal of Business Ethics*, 53(3), 313–323.

Leung, P., & Cooper, B. (1994). Ethics in accountancy: A classroom experience. *Accounting Education*, 3(1), 19–33.

Levy, D., & Mitschow, M. (2008). Accounting ethics education. In C. Jeffrey (Ed.), *Research on professional responsibility and ethics in accounting* (pp. 135–154). Bingley, UK: Emerald Group Publishing Limited.

Liu, C., Yao, L. J., & Hu, N. (2012). Improving ethics education in accounting: Lessons from medicine and law. *Issues in Accounting Education*, 27(3), 671–690.

Liyanarachchi, G., & Newdick, C. (2009). The impact of moral reasoning and retaliation on whistle-blowing: New Zealand evidence. *Journal of Business Ethics*, 89(1), 37–57.

Loeb, S. E. (1988). Teaching students accounting ethics: Some crucial issues. *Issues in Accounting Education*, 3(2), 316–329.
Loeb, S. E. (1991). The evaluation of 'outcomes' of accounting ethics education. *Journal of Business Ethics*, 10(2), 77–84.
Loeb, S. E. (1994). Accounting academic ethics: A code is needed. *Issues in Accounting Education*, 9(1), 191.
Loeb, S. E. (2006). Issues relating to teaching accounting ethics. In C. Jeffrey (Ed.), *Research on professional responsibility and ethics in accounting* (pp. 1–30). Bingley, UK: Emerald Group Publishing Limited.
Loeb, S. E. (2012). Education in accountancy and social control: Questions and comments. *Issues in Accounting Education*, 27(4), 1059–1069.
Loeb, S. E. (2015). Active learning: An advantageous yet challenging approach to accounting ethics instruction. *Journal of Business Ethics*, 127(1), 221–230.
Loeb, S. E., & Bedingfield, J. P. (1972). Teaching accounting ethics. *The Accounting Review*, 47(4), 811–813.
Loeb, S. E., & Rockness, J. (1992). Accounting ethics and education: A response. *Journal of Business Ethics*, 11(7), 485–490.
Low, M., Davey, H., & Hooper, K. (2008). Accounting scandals, ethical dilemmas and educational challenges. *Critical Perspectives on Accounting*, 19(2), 222–254.
Madison, R. L., & Schmidt, J. J. (2006). Survey of time devoted to ethics in accountancy programs in North American colleges and universities. *Issues in Accounting Education*, 21(2), 99–109.
Mahdavikhou, M., & Khotanlou, M. (2012). New approach to teaching of ethics in accounting 'introducing Islamic ethics into accounting education'. *Procedia-Social and Behavioral Sciences*, 46, 1318–1322.
Manalo, M. V. (2013). Teaching strategies for business ethics courses in the undergraduate accountancy curriculum. *DLSU Business & Economics Review*, 22(2).
Maruszewska, E. W. (2011). Ethical education of accounting students in Poland. *General and Professional Education*, 2011(1), 26–30.
Marzuki, M., Subramaniam, N., Cooper, B. J., & Dellaportas, S. (2017). Accounting academics' teaching self-efficacy and ethics integration in accounting courses: A Malaysian study. *Asian Review of Accounting*, 25(1), 148–170.
Massey, D. W., & Van Hise, J. (2009). Walking the walk: Integrating lessons from multiple perspectives in the development of an accounting ethics course. *Issues in Accounting Education*, 24(4), 481–510.
McCarthy, I. N. (1997). Professional ethics code conflict situations: Ethical and value orientation of collegiate accounting students. In M. Fleckenstein, M. Maury, L. Pincus, & P. Primeaux (Eds.), *From the universities to the marketplace: The business ethics journey* (pp. 257–263). Dordrecht, Netherlands: Springer.
McDonald, G. M., & Donleavy, G. D. (1995). Objections to the teaching of business ethics. *Journal of Business Ethics*, 14(10), 839–853.
McManus, L., & Subramaniam, N. (2009). Ethical evaluations and behavioural intentions of early career accountants: The impact of mentors, peers and individual attributes. *Accounting & Finance*, 49(3), 619–643.
McManus, L., Subramaniam, N., & James, W. (2012). A comparative study of the effect of web-based versus in-class textbook ethics instruction on accounting

students' propensity to whistle-blow. *Journal of Education for Business, 87*(6), 333–342.

McNair, F., & Milam, E. E. (1993). Ethics in accounting education: What is really being done. *Journal of Business Ethics, 12*(10), 797–809.

McPhail, K. (1999). The threat of ethical accountants: An application of Foucault's concept of ethics to accounting education and some thoughts on ethically educating for the other. *Critical Perspectives on Accounting, 10*(6), 833–866.

Melé, D. (2005). Ethical education in accounting: Integrating rules, values and virtues. *Journal of Business Ethics, 57*(1), 97–109.

Milam, E., & McNair, F. (1992). An examination of accounting faculty perceptions of the importance of ethics coverage in accounting courses. *Business and Professional Ethics Journal, 11*(2), 57–71.

Miller, W. F., & Becker, D. A. A. (2011). Ethics in the accounting curriculum: What is really being covered? *American Journal of Business Education, 4*(10), 1–10.

Miller, W. F., Becker, D., & Pernsteiner, A. (2014). The accounting ethics course reconsidered. *Global Perspectives on Accounting Education, 11*, 77–98.

Miller, W. F., & Shawver, T. J. (2018). An exploration of the state of ethics in UK accounting education. *Journal of Business Ethics, 153*(4), 1109–1120.

Mintchik, N. M., & Farmer, T. A. (2009). Associations between epistemological beliefs and moral reasoning: Evidence from accounting. *Journal of Business Ethics, 84*(2), 259–275.

Misiewicz, K. M. (2007). The normative impact of CPA firms, professional organizations, and state boards on accounting ethics education. *Journal of Business Ethics, 70*(1), 15–21.

Mohd Ghazali, N. A. (2015). The influence of a business ethics course on ethical judgments of Malaysian accountants. *Journal of Asia Business Studies, 9*(2), 147–161.

Nathan, D. (2015). How South African societal and circumstantial influences affect the ethical standards of prospective South African Chartered Accountants. *African Journal of Business Ethics, 9*(1).

Naudé, P. (2008). Ethics education in accounting: An outsider perspective. *South African Journal of Accounting Research, 22*(1), 1–17.

Ocampo-Gómez, E., & Ortega-Guerrero, J. C. (2013). Expanding the perspective and knowledge of the accounting curriculum and pedagogy in other locations: The case of Mexico. *Critical Perspectives on Accounting, 24*(2), 145–153.

O'Leary, C. (2009). An empirical analysis of the positive impact of ethics teaching on accounting students. *Accounting Education: An International Journal, 18*(4–5), 505–520.

O'Leary, C., & Cotter, D. (2000). The ethics of final year accountancy students: An international comparison. *Managerial Auditing Journal, 15*(3), 108–115.

O'Leary, C., & Mohamad, S. (2006). A tri-national study of accountancy students' ethical attitudes. *Malaysian Accounting Review, 5*(1), 139–157.

O'Leary, C., & Mohamad, S. (2008). The successful influence of teaching ethics on Malaysian accounting students. *Malaysian Accounting Review, 7*(2), 1–16.

O'Leary, C., & Pangemanan, G. (2007). The effect of groupwork on ethical decision-making of accountancy students. *Journal of Business Ethics, 75*(3), 215–228.

O'Leary, C., & Radich, R. (2001). An analysis of Australian final year accountancy students' ethical attitudes. *Teaching Business Ethics, 5*(3), 235–249.

O'Leary, C., & Stewart, J. (2013). The interaction of learning styles and teaching methodologies in accounting ethical instruction. *Journal of Business Ethics, 113*(2), 225–241.

Onumah, J. M., Antwi-Gyamfi, N. Y., Djin, M., & Adomako, D. (2012). Ethics and accounting education in a developing country: Exploratory evidence from the Premier University in Ghana. In V. Tauringana & M. Mangena (Eds.), *Accounting in Africa* (pp. 127–154). Bingley, UK: Emerald Group Publishing Limited.

Persons, O. (2009). Using a corporate code of ethics to assess students' ethicality: Implications for business education. *Journal of Education for Business, 84*(6), 357–366.

Pizzolatto, A. B., & Bevill, S. (1996). Business ethics: A classroom priority? *Journal of Business Ethics, 15*(2), 153–158.

Ponemon, L. A. (1993). Can ethics be taught in accounting? *Journal of Accounting Education, 11*(2), 185–209.

Porter, A., Kongthon, A., & Lu, J.-C. (2002). Research profiling: Improving the literature review. *Scientometrics, 53*(3), 351–370.

Rahman, A. R. A. (2003). Ethics in accounting education: Contribution of the Islamic principle of Maslahah. *International Journal of Economics, Management and Accounting, 11*(1).

Ramirez, R. R. (2017). Teaching ethics through court judgments in finance, accounting, economics and business. *Etikk i praksis-Nordic Journal of Applied Ethics, 1*, 61–87.

Rest, J. R. (1986). *Moral development: Advances in research and theory.* New York: Praeger.

Rockness, H. O., & Rockness, J. W. (2010). Navigating the complex maze of ethics CPE. *Accounting and the Public Interest, 10*(1), 88–104.

Royaee, R., Ahmadi, S. A., & Jari, A. (2013). Students' and faculty members' perceptions of the importance of business ethics and accounting ethics education: Iranian case. *Asian Journal of Business Ethics, 2*(2), 163–171.

Saat, M. M., Porter, S., & Woodbine, G. (2010a). An exploratory study of the impact of Malaysian ethics education on ethical sensitivity. *Journal of Business Ethics Education, 7*, 39–62.

Saat, M. M., Porter, S., & Woodbine, G. (2010b). The effect of ethics courses on the ethical judgement-making ability of Malaysian accounting students. *Journal of Financial Reporting and Accounting, 8*(2), 92–109.

Saat, M. M., Porter, S., & Woodbine, G. (2012). A longitudinal study of accounting students' ethical judgement making ability. *Accounting Education, 21*(3), 215–229.

Salami, A. A., Sanni, M., & Uthman, A. B. (2018). Accounting ethics education in Nigeria: Value-improving or value-deteriorating tool? *Academic Journal of Economic Studies, 4*(4), 116–126.

Scribner, E., & Dillaway, M. P. (1989). Strengthening the ethics content of accounting courses. *Journal of Accounting Education, 7*(1), 41–55.

ŞENGÜR, E. D. (2017). Accounting ethics education in developing countries: The extent of accounting ethics education in Turkey. *Journal of International Social Research, 10*(53).

Shaub, M. K. (1994a). An analysis of the association of traditional demographic variables with the moral reasoning of auditing students and auditors. *Journal of Accounting Education, 12*(1), 1–26.

Shaub, M. K. (1994b). Limits to the effectiveness of accounting ethics education. *Business and Professional Ethics Journal, 13*(1/2), 129–145.

Shawver, T. J. (2009). Can ethics and professional responsibility be taught to accounting students. *Journal of Business Disciplines, 10*(2), 1527–1553.

Shawver, T. J. (2011). Can ethics education impact whistleblowing? *Management Accounting Quarterly, 12*(4), 29.

Shawver, T. J., & Sennetti, J. T. (2009). Measuring ethical sensitivity and evaluation. *Journal of Business Ethics, 88*(4), 663–678.

Simpson, S. N., Onumah, J., & Oppong-Nkrumah, A. (2016). Ethics education and accounting programmes in Ghana: Does university ownership and affiliation status matter? *International Journal of Ethics Education, 1*(1), 43–56.

Singh, A. K., & Vasudeva, S. (2006). Benefits and shortcomings of ethics education: An empirical analysis of perception of accounting students and faculty members in India. *Indian Journal of Accounting, 37*.

Sisaye, S. (2011). The functional-institutional and consequential-conflictual sociological approaches to accounting ethics education: Integrations from sustainability and ecological resources management literature. *Managerial Auditing Journal, 26*(3), 263–294.

Sisaye, S., & Lackman, C. (1994). Ethics in undergraduate accounting education: An empirical study. *Business and Professional Ethics Journal, 13*(1/2), 79–87.

Smith, L. M., Smith, K. T., & Mulig, E. V. (2005). Application and assessment of an ethics presentation for accounting and business classes. *Journal of Business Ethics, 61*(2), 153–164.

Stephenson, S. S. (2017). Reflective ethical decision: A model for ethics in accounting education. *The Accounting Educators' Journal, 26*.

Su, S.-H., Kan, C., & Yang, H.-L. (2010). Cross-cultural difference and accounting ethics: An empirical study for accounting students. *International Journal of Organizational Innovation (Online), 2*(3), 161.

Sugahara, S., & Boland, G. (2011). Faculties' perceptions of ethics in the accounting curriculum: A Japanese study. In C. Jeffrey (Ed.), *Research on professional responsibility and ethics in accounting* (pp. 193–224). Bingley, UK: Emerald Group Publishing Limited.

Sweeney, B., & Costello, F. (2009). Moral intensity and ethical decision-making: An empirical examination of undergraduate accounting and business students. *Accounting Education, 18*(1), 75–97.

Taplin, R., Singh, A., Kerr, R., & Lee, A. (2018). The use of short role-plays for an ethics intervention in university auditing courses. *Accounting Education, 27*(4), 383–402.

Taylor, A. (2013). Ethics training for accountants: Does it add up? *Meditari Accountancy Research, 21*(2), 161–177.

Thomas, C. W. (2004). An inventory of support materials for teaching ethics in the post-Enron era. *Issues in Accounting Education, 19*(1), 27–52.

Thorne, L. (1999). An analysis of the association of demographic variables with the cognitive moral development of Canadian accounting students: An examination of the applicability of American-based findings to the Canadian context. *Journal of Accounting Education, 17*(2–3), 157–174.

Thorne, L. (2001). Refocusing ethics education in accounting: An examination of accounting students' tendency to use their cognitive moral capability. *Journal of Accounting Education, 19*(2), 103–117.

Tormo-Carbó, G., Seguí-Mas, E., & Oltra, V. (2016). Accounting ethics in unfriendly environments: The educational challenge. *Journal of Business Ethics*, *135*(1), 161–175.

Tormo-Carbó, G., Seguí-Mas, E., & Oltra, V. (2018). Business ethics as a sustainability challenge: Higher education implications. *Sustainability*, *10*(8), 2717.

Tunca Caliyurt, K., & Crowther, D. (2006). The necessity of fraud education for accounting students: A research study from Turkey. *Social Responsibility Journal*, *2*(3/4), 321–327.

Tweedie, D., Dyball, M. C., Hazelton, J., & Wright, S. (2013). Teaching global ethical standards: A case and strategy for broadening the accounting ethics curriculum. *Journal of Business Ethics*, *115*(1), 1–15.

Uyar, A., & GÜNGÖRMÜŞ, A. H. (2013). Accounting professionals' perceptions of ethics education: Evidence from Turkey. *Accounting and Management Information Systems*, *12*(1), 61–75.

Valentine, S., & Fleischman, G. (2004). Ethics training and businesspersons' perceptions of organizational ethics. *Journal of Business Ethics*, *52*(4), 391–400.

Van Hise, J., & Massey, D. W. (2010). Applying the Ignatian pedagogical paradigm to the creation of an accounting ethics course. *Journal of Business Ethics*, *96*(3), 453–465.

Waldmann, E. (2000). Teaching ethics in accounting: A discussion of cross-cultural factors with a focus on Confucian and Western philosophy. *Accounting Education*, *9*(1), 23–35.

Waldron, M., & Fisher, R. (2017). Values and ethical judgments: The adequacy of students as surrogates for professional accountants. *Meditari Accountancy Research*, *25*(1), 37–64.

Warinda, T. (2013). Faculty views on the teaching of ethics to accounting students: The Zimbabwean perspective. *Asian Social Science*, *9*(2), 191–202.

Welton, R. E., & Guffey, D. M. (2009). Transitory or persistent? The effects of classroom ethics interventions: A longitudinal study. *Accounting Education: An International Journal*, *18*(3), 273–289.

Welton, R. E., Lagrone, R. M., & Davis, J. R. (1994). Promoting the moral development of accounting graduate students: An instructional design and assessment. *Accounting Education*, *3*(1), 35–50.

West, A., & Buckby, S. (2018). Ethics education in the qualification of professional accountants: Insights from Australia and New Zealand. *Journal of Business Ethics*, 1–20.

Whipple, T. W., & Swords, D. F. (1992). Business ethics judgments: A cross-cultural comparison. *Journal of Business Ethics*, *11*(9), 671–678.

Williams, J., & Elson, R. J. (2010a). The challenges and opportunities of incorporating accounting ethics into the accounting curriculum. *Journal of Legal, Ethical & Regulatory Issues*, *13*(1).

Williams, J., & Elson, R. J. (2010b). Improving ethical education in the accounting program: A conceptual course. *Academy of Educational Leadership Journal*, *14*(4), 107.

Wilson, B., Strong, J., & Mooney, K. (2016). An exploratory investigation of effective accounting ethics CPE. *Journal of International Business Disciplines*, *11*(2).

Win, Y. Y., Ismail, S., & Hamid, F. A. (2014). Malaysian accounting educators' perceptions on ethics education in the accounting curriculum. *Management & Accounting Review (MAR)*, *13*(1), 1–25.

Wright, M. (1995). Can moral judgement and ethical behaviour be learned? A review of the literature. *Management Decision, 33*(10), 17–28.

Wright, S., Dyball, M. C., Byers, P., & Radich, R. (2012). Preparing students for an international career: The case for contextualizing and integrating ethics education.

Yang, H. L., & Wu, W. P. (2009). The effect of moral intensity on ethical decision making in accounting. *Journal of Moral Education, 38*(3), 335–351.

Part 2
Challenges, Opportunities and Developments

4 Industry 4.0
Reimagining Higher Education and Value Transformation

Philomena Leung

1. Background

> Of the many diverse and fascinating challenges, we face today, the most intense and important is how to understand and shape the new technology revolution, which entails nothing less than a transformation of humankind. We are at the beginning of a revolution that is fundamentally changing the way we live, work and relate to one another.
>
> (Schwab, 2016, p. 8)

Fast-developing technologies and their commercialization have expanded opportunities for people around the world. For example, artificial intelligence could generate up to $5 trillion across nearly twenty countries (Chiu et al., 2018) and blockchain could help revolutionize not only finance systems, but also programs for humanitarian relief (Ardittis, 2018). The Fourth Industrial Revolution (4IR) or Industry 4.0 is fundamentally challenging our ideas about the world, our activities and our expectations of externalities. It has the impact of slowly fracturing social cohesion, widening inequality and inexorably transforming everything, globally and individually.

The term 'the Fourth Industrial Revolution' was coined by Schwab (2016), founder and chairman of the World Economic Forum. He referred to such time when new technologies and physical, digital and biological boundaries of our lives became blurred. The Fourth Industrial Revolution (4IR) will impact all disciplines, economies and industries at an unprecedented pace. It was predicted by World Economic Forum data (2018)[1] that by 2025 there will be commercial use of nanomaterials 200 times stronger than steel and a million times thinner than human hair, the first transplant of a 3D printed liver and so on (Schwab & Davis, 2018).

This chapter looks at the impact of 4IR and provides an analysis of possible changes in the nature and extent of higher education in Australia. In the following section, I provide an overview of Industry 4.0's impact on society. This impact includes those with respect to the economy, business and the nature of work. The section identifies not only different employment models, but also how governments and governance systems need to change. The concept of agile governance is introduced at the World Economic Forum, as it is important to consider the changing and far reaching nature of how value and ethics are embedded within the development of technology. I discuss the human-centered approach in addressing ethical issues of technological development. This approach is further elaborated as a relevant methodology in addressing the key features in technological development: these are the unpredictable speed and scale of innovation and disruption, the difference in timing of implementable technology demonstrated by Diana (2015)'s *Valley of Death* and the need to consider values and ethics from a more fundamental transformational process of appreciation and internalization. Fuller (1954)'s business eunomics is introduced to highlight the importance of a flexible approach where both means and ends of systems are assessed with a view to support agile governance. A broader perspective of ethics and value should be integrated in education as a foundation.

In "Mapping the Fourth Industrial Revolution: Global Transformations on 21st Century Education on the context of Sustainable Development", Nordin and Norman (2018) reported that the major areas of impact would include: 1. disruption to job and skills; 2. innovation and productivity; 3. inequality; 4. agile governance; 5. security and conflict; 6. business disruption; 7. fusing technologies; and 8. ethics and identity.[2] A number of topics in education were offered in addressing these themes. However, my concern is whether these more peripheral concepts are sufficient to support an education ecosystem in order to equip learners and educators for such transformation.

For the purpose of this chapter, the Fourth Industrial Revolution (4IR) is understood within the context of Industry 4.0, and the two concepts are used interchangeably.

2. Impact on Society

Schwab (2016) describes the profound systemic changes brought about by 4IR in four categories: the economy, business, that related to national and global environment and that pertaining to society (including individuals). These factors are discussed here.

Whereas it is appreciated that Industry 4.0 has a profound impact on all systems, relations, expectations for individuals, societies and entities, with speed and scale, Schwab (2016) highlighted such impact through the significance of 'empowerment', that is, how an empowered individual relates to others and society. Industry 4.0 disrupts the existing political, economic and social models and contends that empowered individuals will become a part of a distributed network, resulting in more integration and collaboration. Schwab (2016) believes that all conventional economic variables such as the GDP, investment, consumption, employment and other related factors will change. For example, with the higher functionality and quality standards due to innovative goods and services, there will be a disconnect between the delivery (of the new) and measurement systems (of the old). On the other hand, increased efficiency in the on-demand and apps economy may result in some unaccounted value in national statistics due to the lagging of traditional metrics.

With respect to the change in the nature of work, job substitution (or destruction) and automation will shift employment opportunities. Whereas Schwab (2016) recognizes the ability of humans in adaptation, there is a concern about the timing and extent to which the capitalization of innovation supersedes substitution. Based on the ranking of 702 different professions on their susceptibility to the risk of automation (Oxford Martin Programme on Technology and Employment, 2013), Schwab (2016) listed those professions that were most and least prone to automation. It is noted that the more routine and procedurally driven professions such as telemarketers, insurance appraisers, tax preparers, legal secretaries and real estate brokers are mostly prone to automation, whereas professions that require judgement, such as those performed by health workers, systems analysts, engineers and chief executives, are least prone to automation. It can be argued that low-risk jobs will be those that require social and creative skills and decision-making under uncertainty, as well as those that encourage development of new ideas. But it is noteworthy that artificial intelligence such as automated narrative generation, sophisticated algorithms, are developing fast, so that the skills relevant to future employment trends are rapidly evolving.

Further, in the World Inequality Report[3] (Alvaredo, Chancel, Piketty, Saez & Zucman, 2018), the top 1 percent richest individuals in the world has captured twice as much growth as the bottom 50 percent individuals since 1980. Because of the high and growing inequality within countries, the rising wealth has also concentrated in those running technology businesses. In Standing's (2011) book, he described how Western globalization promoted market-led competition above job security. Flexible work becomes the norm, displacing millions without job or income security. 4IR has created inequality never seen before.

For example, the traditional male domination in some professions such as computer science and engineering, coupled with traditionally undervalued roles mostly occupied by females, such as in social work, psychology and healthcare, create further complications in regard to gender inequalities. Further divergence will occur where there is disconnect with inefficient policies and the timing and extent between capitalization of innovation and substitution of jobs. There is a fine balance between the value of capitalization of innovation and the need to develop society and beliefs, both culturally and in terms of skills.

The impact of the changing nature of work also happens globally, with the fast-developing emerging economies in some parts of the world. There are new forms of social and employment contracts that suit the changing workforce, aided by internet connectivity and human cloud platforms, with unlimited mobility. Daniel Callaghan says "You can now get whoever you want, whenever you want, exactly how you want it" (as cited in O'Connor, 2015).[4] In emerging economies like China and South East Asia, talent cultivation is the norm in recruitment and human resources management, although priorities of skills are defined by top management or government. For example, in Systems, Applications, and Products in Data Processing, its slogan is 'Human Revolution' where the old ways of working no longer work for human resources.[5]

Industry 4.0, therefore, has major impacts on how businesses are led, organized and resourced. Schwab (2016) pointed out that the average life span of a corporation listed on the S&P 500 has dropped from around sixty years to only around eighteen. The time it takes new entrants to dominate markets and achieve significant revenue has also dropped. For example, Facebook took six years to reach a revenue of $1 billion, whereas Google took five. New and emerging technologies together with digital capabilities have driven an ever-increasing speed and scale of change for businesses.

The main impacts on business can be seen in customer expectations, data-driven productivity and products, new forms of collaboration and new digital operating models such as blockchain. All of these factors affect how the supply chain of products are resourced and managed, how transparency are expected in all forms of products, how multiple resources are utilized and how businesses are transforming its value from selling to delivering wide range of services, witnessed by examples such as Amazon and Spotify, Uber Eats and so on. Businesses also need to invest in cyber and data systems security. Data-powered business models where valuable information and software intelligence provide and generate business sensitive insights must be safeguarded and intellectual property (IP) maintained. International guidelines with respect to cyber security and IP issues were considered only gradually. Newer jobs such as data scientists, including social scientists for cyber security, professional hackers for attesting security, etc. are examples of an integrated approach to looking at technology. Emerging operating models also mean that talent and culture are considered in light of new skill requirements and the need to attract and retain suitable human capital. The concept of 'talentism' is one of the most important drivers for competitiveness (Schwab, 2016).

With respect to the global landscape, the disruption brought by 4IR is still being felt by all aspects of national and local governments and public institutions. It fundamentally changes the relations of citizens and the private sector with authorities as well as how countries and governments relate to each other. In essence, with the increasing empowerment and greater fragmentation and polarization of populations, governing is made more difficult and less effective. Some of the impacts include the increasing use of digital platforms and integrated data to continuously manage performance and development, strengthen processes, foster greater transparency and providing greater accessibility of information. Better informed individuals and organizations, irrespective of whether they are public officers or not, are capable to exert power and influence. On the other hand, there is increasing means of monitoring and surveillance technologies, rendering parallel structures that will enable ideologies, opinions and other methods of influence to be disseminated with speed and scale. This is witnessed more recently in large-scale protests guided by social media, increasing cyber-attacks and identity thefts, political influences on election and so on. A linear and mechanistic top-down approach of governing and regulation is no longer possible. The erosion of traditional society values such as integrity and public good are seen to be eroded by populism, and ethics and professionalism are less prevalent in gaining support.

Schwab (2016) recommends agile governance principles so that regulators find ways to adapt continuously to a new, fast-changing environment by reinventing themselves to meet the changing needs of society. Agile governance principles consider the balancing of the complexity of on-demand flexibility and data security, decentralization of transactions and payments, addressing the impact of monopolies disrupted by novel intermediaries, balancing the level of surveillance and privacy, the adequate exercising of digital exclusion and addressing asymmetries created by powerful technologies.

Recognizing the nature, speed and scale of the impact of 4IR, how can we provide a stronger foundation for such value transformation?

3. Technology and Ethics

From recent debate about data collection on social media to environmental stewardship and growing inequality and populism, technology has affected human rights and has integrated into societies and economies. The moral role of technologies, such as the values and ethics of such integrated technological development, must be addressed "at this critical moment in history" (Benioff, 2016, p. 2). A failure of a more critical comprehension of technologies and their moral role in society will reduce our ability to make informed decisions and will impact both human and technological capabilities. A human-centered approach is discussed here.

Both Philbeck et al. (2018) and Benioff (2016) advocate a human-centered approach to ethics on technology. They argued it is because technologies shape people and people shape technologies (Philbeck et al, p. 5). Such relationship is crucial as it impacts transaction flows, business models and education systems. In order to provide a foundation for a just and equitable society that is interconnected through technology, the process must start with people, with their logic, ideals, experience, empathy and collaboration (Philbeck, et al. p. 6). Whereas technology generally addresses unmet needs, the process of development must be integrated with the awareness of the objective of human and societal needs in a just and fair way, that is, a co-development approach between technology and humans. Philbeck et al. (p. 6) refer to three complementary strategies: adopting a systems-view of technologies; appreciating and shaping the moral role of technologies; and engaging with a wide spectrum of stakeholders in the process.

Philbeck et al. (p. 6) demonstrated the systemic approach to how values and ethics integrate into technologies and policy creation through the development of the automobile industry. For example, the extent of the focus on gasoline-powered engines at scale at the turn of the 20th century had affected a wide range of interests, visions, advancements, investments, business models and political support. It had resulted in limiting choices, growth and innovation. There was deep economic dependence on oil, with a negative impact on pollution and health. Another more recent example can be seen in the development of energy transformation and how solar energy is being used to respond to environmental concerns and the economic and social debates on the use of coal and fossil fuels. Such scenarios were also due to government actions such as tax incentives and international trade benefits and the considerations for urbanization, building roads and transit ecosystems.

Thus, technologies impact the entire ecosystem that entails economic, social and political values. Philbeck et al. (2018) enlisted a range of *outer* and *inner* factors in the system integration of values and ethics into technological development. The *outer circle* includes external matters such as technical architecture, product design, economic incentive, operational methodologies, decision-making priority, organizational culture, entrepreneurial values, investment, educational curricula and societal resistance. Throughout the development of the technology, different stakeholders should be engaged to evaluate various possibilities or risks of how ethics and values might be affected and addressed. Examples were included in what the authors referred to as the *inner circle*. These are implementation areas such as values by design, embedded ethical research and processes, shareholder value metrics, stakeholder inclusion and common good priority, codes, leadership values, investment capital strategy, skills development and ethics courses and media and political discussions (Philbeck, et al., p. 7).

Further explanations in regard to the moral role of technologies were also demonstrated by the different social layers of the internet. These layers of the internet, including content, security, commerce and access, involve different values and ethics such as access neutrality, freedom of expression, online education, encryption, surveillance, arbitration, affordability, rights of minority and identities. It is important to engage with a wide variety of stakeholders such as civic leaders, consumers, engineers, executives/boards, policy makers and educators, in order to address the social values and ethics throughout the process of development. Philbeck et al. (2018, p. 10) opined that new curricula and programs should be developed to take into consideration of the human-centered approach and the socially situated contexts. There should be a focus on cross-disciplinary competence. For example, instead of the traditional engineering and business studies programs, students should be exposed to philosophy, politics and engineering, with a deep practice of thinking beyond execution and towards social responsibility and outcomes. Instead of focusing narrowly on compliance and procedure, educational programs should instill within students and learners a broader duty to think through the potential societal impact of the implementation of technologies.

4. Transforming Value

In summarizing Philbeck et al. (2018)'s model of a human-centered approach, it is worth noting their guiding definitions of values and ethics. *Values* is used to describe the aspirations that societies hope to realize as priorities to guide actions and choices. Examples are justice, well-being and privacy. *Ethics* on the other hand, refers to the attempt to discern the right action for society as many actions or decisions may involve conflicting values. In technological development, examples include driverless cars, access and development of algorithms where privacy and transparency can be compromised.

In the wake of the advancement of fusion in technologies, policymakers and governments reacted by increasing access to STEM and computer science skills. But at WISE@NY (2018), panelists suggested an alternative scenario for the most demanded skills: philosophy, ethics and morality education.[6] One can immediately think of examples of the need for moral judgement and ethics, including privacy versus security measures, moral machinery such as driverless cars, genetic editing and so on. When engineers and scientists design artificial intelligence machines, should they aim to replace human work? If humans are designing machines to replace humans instead of helping them to get work done, the structure of humanity will change.

Hence, what is the right action or means that produce different ends? As discussed earlier, the human-centered approach can be regarded as a set of foundational principles for a value transformation process, but such an approach may not assist in developing its related educational paradigm.

Magruk (2016, pp. 275–291) analyzes the phenomenon of Industry 4.0 being determined by a cyber marketplace, with smart tools or robots, high connectivity and decentralized efficiency, involving virtual industrialization and resulting in industrial democracy, fast distributed value chains, changing business models developed by niche markets and convergence. He highlighted that *uncertainty* is the cognitive category that manifests itself where decision-making and information become unpredictable and multidimensional.

For Industry 4.0, there are complex scenarios that lead to uncertainties. The universal digitization and speedy communication between and amongst people, devices and machines have made it difficult to respond with the certainty of accuracy and complete information. Constant and quick implementation of disruptive technological innovations affects the abrupt increase of efficiency, resulting in varied levels of effectiveness of the socioeconomic and physical systems. Furthermore, the process and development of advanced artificial intelligence (AI) has gained the ability to autonomous behavior as determined by the creator of the technology. Diana (2015) referred to the patterns of build relationships between the introduction of breakthrough technologies and megatrends (or disruptive scenarios) as the creation of a new potential paradigm in economics. Such breakthrough technologies, in the absence of immediate and fast adaptation, lead to the collapse of existing economic models. For example, while breakthrough technologies such as the internet, social and mobile technologies, cloud-based data, 3D printing, the Internet of Things (IoT), cognitive systems, robotics and nanotechnology, disrupt existing systems, the uptake or efficient adaptation varies in ecosystems. Innovation scenarios such as smart cars, next generation automation and super AI may become a new economic paradigm, resulting in different U-shaped transformation processes, called 'Valley of Death' (Diana, 2015). In essence, the uncertainty is compounded by the relationships between innovation and implementation—the transformation of different speed and scale forms a valley-shaped uptake scenario.

Transforming value is a fundamental process of appreciation and internalization. It is believed that value not only concerns 'the end' but should also be considered holistically by building clarity from uncertainty and by dynamically and continuously assessing impact and consequences and avoiding the compartmentalization of means and ends.

On examining the scope of business ethics studies at universities, typical topics covered include the different theories of ethics such as deontology, teleology, relativism and examples of ethical decision-making models. It is generally difficult to navigate where each of these theories overlap in complicated decisions, actions and policies. Furthermore, ethics is generally taught without the treatment of a multidimensional and holistic approach, where the learners must realize the extent of scale and uncertainty that underlie real-life situations.

5. The Means-Ends Relation

Business ethics education today largely focuses on shareholder and stakeholders' theories to be used for governing corporate or organizational behaviors. Much of corporate governance topics use business ethics as a base topic, using Friedman (1970)'s shareholder theory and Freeman (1984)'s stakeholders' interests to guide learners. For over two decades, the body of literature on business ethics and governance has remained largely unchanged in scope and approach. Ethics and governance are included as part of the higher education professional programs and as managerial development, so that certain 'ends' or goals are instilled in the way corporations and organizations govern and manage operations. This takes into account matters such as 'shareholder value' or 'stakeholders' perceptions' so that business leaders provide a normative approach to business imperatives and conduct. Externalities such as market forces, geopolitical climate, societal needs and, indeed, the impact of 4IR are 'considered' in governance more so as reference rather than as an embedded integral part of business value.

Schneider (2018, pp. 803–848) provided an insightful discussion of Industry 4.0 as the increasing integration between the intelligence of products and systems, their intra-company cross-linking and the convergence between cross-company systems into value creation networks. He used extensive literature review and an online survey with experts including management consultants, those working in industrial enterprises and academics to identify apparent management challenges of Industry 4.0. The six resultant interrelated clusters of managerial challenges were analysis and strategy, planning and implementation, cooperation and networks, business models and human resources. These were discussed with a view to establish a broader base for future research. Meanwhile higher education institutions and MBAs continue to offer programs that address 4IR as 'new areas' about which one needs to learn. Little research has been done to examine if/whether 4IR is fully embedded within the philosophy or paradigm of an educational program and ethics and value has continued to be more prevalent in particular disciplines such as the arts and philosophy. Schneider (2018)'s concepts adhere to a managerial approach of ethics in relation to 4IR.

On the other hand, Melkevik (2019) reactivated the discussion of a branch of ethics pioneered by Fuller (1954, p. 477) on social architecture. Fuller referred it as 'eunomics', the theory or study of good order and workable arrangements. It shifted the debate from the managerial concerns in typical corporate environments to a more complex design in identifying the elements of how a social institution can behave, where there is no divorce between means and ends. The theory espoused by eunomics is that different means produce different ends and each mean or end changes and there cannot be a single superior end or mean that can be used. How should one appraise the impacts of various means and ends when running an organization?

Eunomics is a neglected branch of jurisprudence that was explored by Fuller (1954) in a number of essays, as he was concerned with the interaction between means and ends. It is unfortunate that Fuller never finished his work, though the concept was picked up by Williamson (1996, p. 11) in relation to governance. Business eunomics was reclaimed by Melkevik (2019, p. 294) to broaden the field of business ethics. Melkevik (2019) claims that business eunomics addresses why the economic institution of capitalism should lead to embrace the ethics of governance in a more holistic way. He opposes to the managerial approach of business ethics and the doctrine of infinite pliability of social arrangements. That is, given sufficient agreement to an end, a society or an organization can arrange its means to produce such ends. The question we should rather ask about businesses is whether this institution, in a context of other institutions, create a pattern of living that is satisfying and worthy of man's capacities (Fuller, 1981, p. 55).

In other words, business eunomics does not have to be committed to any specific theory of value, as its real concern is with whatever ends a given society (or scenario) might pursue. With business ethics, one is primarily concerned with the ability to manage organizational dilemmas. These dilemmas are both real and multifaceted, but educational discourse during business ethics classes are typically hypothetically independent of such reality and complexity. Fuller (1954, p. 478) explained that "the primary concern of eunomics is with the means aspect of the means-end relation and its contribution to the clarification of ends will lie in its analysis of the available means for achieving particular ends." Eunomics can be applied to evaluate different extent and availability of capabilities, or means and provide some trade-off with respect to the ends that is most effective, in accordance to some overarching principles such as human-centered approaches, rather than one that is most desirable such as in profitability. Melkevik (2019, p. 295) regards this approach as opposed to 'value-oriented' approaches that ignore the technical questions of implementation. Business eunomics will help organizations identify which ends to pursue, with consideration of both internal structure and external market institutions. As Williamson (1996, p. 11) suggests, eunomics is an exercise for organizations to assess the efficacy of alternative modes (or means), as it is shaped by the changing mechanisms of markets. Barnard (1968, p. 77) referred to this as 'coordination', whereas Fuller termed it as 'organization by common ends' (Fuller, 1955, p. 1316). The theory of business eunomics assesses how we juggle various kinds of industrial organization in relation to the ends we propose to pursue. (Melkevik, 2019, p. 295).

To further explain the main contribution of business eunomics, as Phillips and Margolis (1999, p. 628) observed, the ethical problems faced by individuals and businesses demand a theory grounded in the same context that generates the effects, a theory capable of speaking to those who operate within that social context. The relevant limits that influence the individual and the organization include those of the market place, democracy, values of society, business parameters such as choice of law, risks and so on. Business eunomics will ensure that in trying to balance certain values in society we also balance how much space different institutions occupy in our societies so that we can seek an equilibrium whereby we efficiently realize a set of values, instead of a single value (or end). Melkevik (2019) advocates three theses of business eunomics: first, the inseparability of means and ends; second, the importance of the complementary nature of ends for business ethics where organizations may realize as many objectives at a given time, with relative considerations of the necessary means; third, the suitability of means and ends for a given market scenario therefore we cannot assume away that environment only to make the organization successful. He believes that eunomics should move away from immediate managerial concerns. One should not assume the primacy of a particular end and lose sight of how decisions are implemented with a process that may change the original intended ends. The social responsibility of the firm is to create value in society with its resources. A theory of business eunomics helps us to be concerned with the principles of social order, with an understanding of the internal morality of managerial decisions (Melkevik, 2019 p. 303).

6. Reimagining Higher Education and Value Transformation

Much has been written about 4IR or Industry 4.0. Broom (2019) wrote that predictions are 'futile' in the face of vast complexity and unpredictability of major forces in the world such as the development and adoption of new technologies. The uncertainty of the scale and speed of changes render it somewhat difficult to describe the impending impact of Industry 4.0.

It is acknowledged that 4IR has created the need for new workplace skills and opens up new opportunities for people to create value and invest in lifelong learning. However, new skills that fundamentally assess the values and ethics related to the technological development are needed just as urgently (Philbeck et al., 2018, p. 14). As espoused by Clark (1995, p. 39), social value does not only highlight the social aspects of the economy, it also relates to the theory of valuation. Business and the economy create social relations. Social value is intrinsic in both business and economics. To anticipate the future, educators and decision makers must start by asking 'What values and ethics related skills are needed now for dealing with technologies, will these skills be needed in the future?'

To provide a strong theoretical foundation for an integrated approach for value transformation, it is believed that a set of introductory courses on different value and ethical theories and their application to technical disciplines must be included. This can be learned alongside economic theories and concepts. For example, the topics may include institutional economics, social value, efficiency versus equity, change and regulatory reforms and the environment. These topics set the scene for a broad understanding of society and contexts in which disciplines such as business, engineering and the laws sit. Different ethical theories and applications should then be discussed, including business eunomics, concepts of means and ends and theories and practices of risks and choices.

Dr. Jordan Nguyen (as cited in Eggleton, 2019), who delivered the keynote address at the recent Reimagination 2019 Summit in Melbourne, Australia, acknowledged that technology is currently throwing up numerous ethical issues around the use of big data and surveillance, as well as other 'traumatic issues'. He suggested that one should always put 'humans first'. Dr. Nguyen, an internationally renowned documentary maker, engineer and futurist believes that the future is all about humanity first and technology second. The notion of a human-centered approach by Philbeck et al. (2018) discussed earlier resonates with this.

Whereas some of these topics are already addressed by many educational programs the complexity of converging technologies in fact requires these concepts to be internalized, that is, applied integratively across disciplines such as science, humanities, business and the arts. Indeed, new disciplines may well be developed, as there will be new partnerships and engagement with wider scale of stakeholders and new institutions will emerge. So how are we going to ensure that our higher education institutions can foster value and ethics in light of the changing technological development?

It is also noted that with the diversity of approaches, some countries already see the need to transform future skills from traditional study programs by introducing innovative challenges, experiential learning and industry-led internships. Transformation is developed through a framework of practical (e.g., case based) learning using contemporary scenarios and pedagogies such as debates, challenges and critiques. A humanistic principle is embedded within the educational activities so that a combination of experiential learning and case studies, applying multimedia, can be used.

Apart from the foundational concepts of ethics and social relations, there are changing emphases in addressing future skills for the workplace. An example is *The Future of Jobs*, which identifies the trends in skills changes desired by 2020 (Gray, 2016) as including:

1. ComplexProblemSolving
2. CriticalThinking
3. Creativity
4. PeopleManagement
5. Coordinatingwithothers
6. EmotionalIntelligence
7. JudgementandDecision-Making
8. ServiceOrientation
9. Negotiation
10. CognitiveFlexibility

While 2020 is already upon us, the skills identified to address the complexity of technological development all concern social relations. For example, direct social relationships are embedded within problem solving, people management, coordination, service and negotiation, whereas social relations also influence indirectly the practice of critical thinking, creativity and emotional intelligence. No doubt, other skills, competencies and relations arise in the development of technologies, including the skills to integrate human and artificial intelligence and other robotic technologies.

In an extensive mapping of the global transformation on 21st-century education, Nordin and Norman (2018, pp. 1–7) followed the major areas of impact of the Fourth Industrial Revolution and provided some examples of relevant educational systems. Whereas the discussion was focused on education in general I have included (see Table 4.1) some of the other education efforts that involve ethics and value transformation, in addition to the relevant points made by Nordin and Norman (2018).

Table 4.1 Topics to be considered to embed value and ethics for 4IR

Impact Issues	Nordin and Norman (2018) suggestions on education efforts	Other educational transformation methods/topics
Disruption to jobs and skills	• Gender Parity issues • Women in sustainable environment fields • Educating in early childhood levels on 4IR • Analysis of job market in 4IR • Global trade and digital currencies	• Inclusion of industry engagements and discussions within education programs • Using challenges and debates and inter-institutional exchange to instill critical skills and deeper understanding of values and alternative viewpoints
Innovation and Productivity	• Circular economy • Entrepreneurship and future of enterprise • Innovation and competitiveness • Accessibility of education opportunities • Current technologies such as drones, IoT	• Increase elements of innovative exercises, incubation and other entrepreneurial activities; • Embed ethics and values as core subjects, alongside economics.
Inequality	• Design learning for digital literacies • Understanding digital impact and operationalize for enhancement	• Societal change and policy debates should be included as part of the learning
Agile Governance	• Understanding agile governance—learning to design and apply relevant ecosystems	• Case studies on ethical, cultural and governance issues internationally and nationally

(*Continued*)

Table 4.1 (Continued)

Impact Issues	Nordin and Norman (2018) suggestions on education efforts	Other educational transformation methods/topics
Security and Conflict	• Cyber security as core elements • Security concepts and systems	• Technological, behavioral and psychological aspects of security and conflict are to be introduced
Business Disruption	• Flexible and global learning environment including MOOCs • Designing learning environments for new business models	• Explore different means of learning about business practices • Experiential learning embedded with ethical problems to be explored
Fusing technologies	• Technologies are used in all facets of educational efforts • Educational innovation • Technological advancements blurring physical, digital and biological spheres should be introduced to understand interconnectedness	• Technical workshops on emerging and current technologies with a discussion on social impact
Ethics and Identity	• Ethical issues, identity and privacy to be included • Ethical boundaries and values are cultivated	• Ethics and value discussion with different ethical problems in practice • Research on ethical problems to be included

Higher education, especially in business schools, has employed different efforts to deliver a value-based education program. Reficco, Jaen and Trujillo (2019) carried out a survey with a sample of faculty members and program directors from Latin America. They found that societal demands had influenced the direction of managerial education towards values and social responsibility, changing content and teaching methodologies. Value-based content, such as social responsibility and environmental sustainability, have gained a lot of coverage in the last decade. Case methods are also used extensively. In relation to research in the area, Dierksmeier (2019) reconstructed the change in Michael Jensen's agency theory and has pointed out the transformation of Jensen's outlook in addressing humanistic pedagogy instead of a mechanistic approach in management learning.[7]

The value transformation has begun.

7. Conclusion

The Fourth Industrial Revolution (4IR) or Industry 4.0 has far-reaching impact on society; not does it affect how the economy develops, it also changes business models and human lives and values. This chapter provided an overview of these impacts. The ethics of technology development was examined, with an overview of the importance of a human-centered approach, social relations and business eunomics, an untapped business ethics theory that can be considered for understanding a more holistic than a managerial approach to value transformation. Though it is a more flexible approach to ethical theories, business eunomics untangles the rather rigid presumption of traditional business ethics that is focused on managerial directives and divorces means from ends. A more dynamic method of governance that provides flexibility to tackle the fast-changing technological environment has been advocated.

This chapter supports the importance of humanistic approaches and social relations. This approach facilitates the understanding of values and relationships, locally and globally. I also recommend that value transformation must begin by a strong foundation of an understanding of social value, relations and ethics and applying them to various disciplines that include business and engineering. An integrative method of internalization can be achieved by identifying elements of 4IR skills throughout the education process, highlighting the prevalence of social relations. Finally, I have complemented Nordin and Norman (2018)'s mapping of 21st-century education in relation to 4IR with other topics and educational areas for consideration.

Notes

1. World Economic Forum Data (2018) has a collection of 'big data' that provides some predictions in respect of *Readiness of the Future Production Report 2018* used by Schwab and Davis (2018).
2. Nordin and Norman (2018) provide detailed factors for each of the themes with some recommendations for a range of education topics that are not discussed in detail here.
3. See Figure E3.
4. Daniel Callaghan is the Chief Executive for the *The Human Cloud*, Financial Times.
5. Asevedo (2018) reviews successful factors on human resources management.
6. WISE@NY (2018) is a publication on learning revolutions. It gathered practitioners, thought leaders and creative architects to empower learners for future challenges, foster inclusion, innovating inside and outside the classroom.
7. Dierksmeier (2019) refers to Michael Jensen's shift from using agency theory (1970–1990) in corporate governance and economic policy to employing an 'integrity theory' of management learning.

References

Alvaredo, F., Chancel, L., Piketty, T., Saez, E., & Zucman, G. (2018). *World inequality report*. Retrieved February 21, 2020, from https://wir2018.wid.world/files/download/wir2018-summary-english.pdf

Ardittis, S. (2018). *How Blockchain can benefit migration programmes and migrants*. Retrieved January 12, 2020, from https://migrationdataportal.org/blog/how-blockchain-can-benefit-migration-programmes-and-migrants

Asevedo. T. (2018). *SAP SuccessFactors then and now: Driving a human revolution.* Retrieved February 20, 2020, from https://news.sap.com/2018/10/sap-successfactors-then-now-human-revolution/

Barnard, C. (1968). *The function of the executive.* Cambridge: Harvard University Press.

Benioff, M. R. (2016). Foreword. In K. Schwab (Ed.), *The fourth industrial revolution* (pp. vii–viii). Geneva: World Economic Forum.

Broom, D. (2019). *These 4 scenarios show how we might be working in the future.* Retrieved December 8, 2019, from www.weforum.org/agenda/2019/03/scenarios-for-how-we-might-work-in-future-rsa-uk/

Chiu, M., Manyika, J., Miremadi, M., Henke, N., Chung, R., Nel, P., & Malhotra, S. (2018). *Notes from the AI frontier: Applications and value of deep learning.* Retrieved January 12, 2020, from www.mckinsey.com/featured-insights/artificial-intelligence/notes-from-the-ai-frontier-applications-and-value-of-deep-learning

Clark, C. M. A. (1995). From natural value to social value. In C. M. A. Clark (Ed.), *Institutional economics and the theory of social value: Essays in honour of Marc R Tool* (pp. 29–42). New York, USA: Kluwer Academic Publishers.

Diana, F. (2015). *An interview with Futurist Gerd Leonhard.* Retrieved January 12, 2020, from https://frankdiana.net/2015/01/14/an-interview-with-futurist-gerd-leonhard/

Dierksmeier, C. (2019). From Jensen to Jensen: Mechanistic management education or humanistic management learning? *Journal of Business Ethics.* https://doi.org/10.1007/s10551-019-04120-z

Eggleton, M. (2019). Future mindset, special report, reimagination 2019. *The Australian Financial Review*, S2.

Freeman, R. E. (1984). *Strategic management: A stakeholder approach.* Boston: Pitman.

Friedman, M. (1970). *The social responsibility of business is to increase its profits.* Retrieved January 12, 2020, from http://umich.edu/~thecore/doc/Friedman.pdf

Fuller, L. L. (1954). American legal philosophy at mid-century: A review of Edwin W. Patterson's jurisprudence, men and ideas of the law. *Journal of Legal Education*, 6, 457–485.

Fuller, L. L. (1955). Freedom: A suggested analysis. *Harvard Law Review*, 68, 1305–1325.

Fuller, L. L. (1981). *The principles of social order.* Durham: Duke University Press.

Gray, A. (2016). *The 10 skills you need to thrive in the fourth industrial revolution.* Retrieved February 20, 2020, from www.weforum.org/agenda/2016/01/the-10-skills-you-need-to-thrive-in-the-fourth-industrial-revolution/

Kagermann, H., Lukas, W., & Wahlster, W. (2011). *Industrie 4.0 - Mit dem Internet der Dinge auf dem Weg zur 4. industriellen Revolution.* Retrieved June 26, 2020, from https://www.ingenieur.de/technik/fachbereiche/produktion/industrie-40-mit-internet-dinge-weg-4-industriellen-revolution/

Magruk, A. (2016). Uncertainty in the sphere of the Industry 4.0 – potential areas to research, *Business, Management and Education*, 14(2), 275–291.

Melkevik, A. (2019). A theory of business eunomics: The means-ends relation in business ethics. *Journal of Business Ethics*, 160, 293–305.

Nordin, N., & Norman, H. (2018). Mapping the fourth industrial revolution global transformations on 21st century education on the context of sustainable development. *Journal of Sustainable Development Education and Research*, 2(1), 1–7.

O'Connor, S. (2015). *The human cloud: A new world of work*. Retrieved February 20, 2020, from www.ft.com/content/a4b6e13e-675e-11e5-97d0-1456a776a4f5

Oxford Martin Programme on Technology and Employment. (2013, September). *The future of employment: How susceptible are jobs to computerisation?* (Working Paper). Oxford, UK: Frey, C. B., & Osborne, M.

Philbeck, T., Davis, N., & Larsen, A. M. E. (2018). *Values, ethics and innovation: Rethinking technological development in the fourth industrial revolution* [White Paper]. Retrieved January 12, 2020, from www3.weforum.org/docs/WEF_WP_Values_Ethics_Innovation_2018.pdf

Phillips, R., & Margolis, J. (1999). Toward an ethics of organisations. *Business Ethics Quarterly*, 9, 619–638.

Reficco, E., Jaen, M. H., & Trujillo, C. (2019). Beyond knowledge: A study of Latin American business schools' efforts to deliver a value-based education. *Journal of Business Ethics*, 156, 857–874.

Schneider, P. (2018). Managerial challenges of Industry 4.0: An empirically backed research agenda for a nascent field. *Review of Management Science*, 12, 803–848.

Schwab, K. (2016). *The fourth industrial revolution*. Geneva: World Economic Forum.

Schwab, K., & Davis, N. (2018). *Shaping the fourth industrial revolution*. Geneva: World Economic Forum.

Standing, G. (2011). *The precariat: The new dangerous class*. London, UK: Bloomsbury.

Williamson, O. E. (1996). *The mechanism of governance*. Oxford: Oxford University Press.

WISE@NY (2018). *Learning revolutions: Creating educational environments for empowerment and inclusion*. Retrieved September 22, 2019, from www.wise-qatar.org/new-york-learning-revolutions/

5 Educating the Next Generation of Accountants
How to Promote Ethical Consciousness Through Critical Thinking

Ariela Caglio and Mara Cameran

1. Introduction

Some previous studies have indicated that the ethical orientation of accounting professionals is impacted by *individuals' inborn characteristics*, such as national/societal culture, gender and age. A relation between cultural beliefs and moral reasoning has been documented empirically, as earlier contributors reported ethical differences between auditors raised in different countries. For example, Cohen, Pant and Sharp (1995) analyzed the ethical judgements of 138 auditors from the US, Japan and Latin America through the use of vignettes, finding that the strongest differences exist between Latin American auditors and US auditors. The former belongs to a culture considered as highly collectivist and with high power distance, whereas US auditors belong to a highly individualist and low power distance culture. In particular, Latin American auditors perceived the actions described in the vignettes as significantly less ethical in comparison to the US auditors, thus suggesting the importance of a cultural background/ education landscape in shaping accounting professionals' ethics. Following this line of reasoning, some studies focusing on accounting ethics as a particular facet of business ethics emphasize the role that 'ethics-unfriendly environments' can play (e.g., Coicaud & Warner, 2001). An ethics-unfriendly environment is defined in terms of the widespread perception in a particular society that ethics is not relevant as a social value, given the impunity that often follows fraud, corruption and malpractice observed in the behaviors of managers and public officials, especially when occurring at upper business or government levels. Other works suggest that demographic traits can also influence accounting professionals' behavior. For instance, female auditors show lower intentions to engage in audit quality reduction behaviors (e.g., Sweeney, Arnold & Pierce, 2010) and are less concerned with the commercial side of auditing (e.g., Jonnergård, Stafsudd & Elg, 2010) and generally more ethical (e.g., Bernardi & Arnold, 1997). Age is also associated with variations in auditors' ethical judgements. As an example, Marques and Azevedo-Pereira (2009) find that age is the major determinant of ethical relativism: older accountants reveal themselves to be more relativistic than younger ones. It seems that, as they gain experience, accountants are less willing to follow rules. Sankaran and Bui (2003) additionally note that older students majoring in accounting are significantly less ethical than their younger counterparts.

On the other hand, some previous contributors have underlined the importance of *education* in influencing students' ethical orientations: for example, Marques and Azevedo-Pereira (2009) documented that "students' future ethical behavior can be enhanced through formal courses by increasing their awareness of the consequences of their decisions and actions" (Tormo-Carbó, Seguí-Mas & Oltra, 2016, p. 163). In addition, Swenson-Lepper (2005) reported higher levels of ethical sensitivity among more educated people. The question then becomes whether education can influence the ethical orientations of future accountants beyond inborn, individual factors. The debate is still ongoing about *if* and *how* educators can effectively nurture the ethical orientation of their students.

In our chapter, we seek to answer this question. We will do so by starting with evidence we collected on the perception of accountants' ethical behavior held by students and young workers born between the beginning of the 1980s and the start of the 21st century. They have been labelled as GenMe (i.e., Generation Me) by Jean Twenge, an American professor of psychology. To discuss the effectiveness of education, it is necessary to understand their stance on ethics. Their attitude is also crucial, as, in the near future, the accounting profession and related organizations will have to confront the retirement of millions of older workers and their substitution by young people from the GenMe cohort. As we find, among other things, some signals of a negative association between the level of education and the perception of accountants' ethics, in this chapter, we discuss how universities could better promote ethical consciousness through the accounting courses they offer. We will indicate, as a starting point, a better alignment with the approach proposed by the International Accounting Education Standards Board (IAESB), which emphasizes not only the ability of individuals to perform to the technical standards expected of professional accountants but also an appropriate level of values, ethics and attitudes to achieve that competence. We will specifically examine and evaluate one important standard, i.e., the IES 7 on professional skepticism, which highlights the importance of teaching '*critical thinking*' to students. This latter is related to a hot debate, which is voiced also by the Association to Advance Collegiate Schools of Business (AACSB), according to which the main problem that employers observe among recent graduates is the lack of critical thinking (AACSB, 2019b). Thus, teaching this skill is indeed a global challenge for the future of accounting education.

2. What Is Ethics? Are Accountants Ethical?

Accounting associations (e.g., the International Federation of Accountants [IFAC]) embraced the idea that generational differences matter when dealing with accounting education and professional development (see, for example, IFAC, 2019). Moreover, previous studies have warned about undertaking cross-sectional analyses of the perception prevalent in specific professions, as these may also be impacted by generational differences in values (for a review, refer to Parry & Urwin, 2011). Thus, we decided to map the public's perception(s) concerning the ethics of accountants by specifically concentrating on the opinions of so-called GenMe, i.e., students and young workers born in the 1980s and 1990s.[1] GenMe is the youngest generation in today's workforce and the characteristics of this new cohort of workers will require accounting organizations to adjust their focus and perspective in order to most effectively attract and retain GenMe employees.

Our empirical investigation is based in Italy. This is a suitable setting in which to explore accountants' ethics, as the continental context has always been contrasted with the Anglo-Saxon or Anglo-American one in terms of its relatively weak accounting profession (Di Pietra, McLeay & Riccaboni, 2001): given its characteristics, the integrity and ethical stance of the profession may well be perceived as merely symbolic.

To collect the opinions of GenMe respondents, we used a questionnaire organized in different parts: one aimed at capturing some background information about the respondents, e.g., gender, age and education; one consisting of an open-ended question which asked respondents to specify five characteristics they freely associated in their minds with accountants; one where respondents had to answer to the question, 'Do you think accountants behave ethically?'; and, finally, one core part comprising a list of items, rooted in the previous literature and typically associated with accountants. These items included personal and physical traits (e.g., she/he is shy, she/he dresses in a trendy style, she/he is conscious of her/his duty), professional traits (e.g., she/he has long-term earnings potential, her/his job requires an ability to delegate), as well as some traits included in the definition of ethical behavior provided by extant studies (e.g., she/he is law compliant, she/he is incorruptible). The respondents were asked to express their opinion using a five-point Likert scale (1=strongly disagree; 5=totally agree). The questionnaire was administered to students, prospective certified public accountants (CPAs) and young employees at various auditing firms in order to reach out to GenMe people from different backgrounds (especially in terms of education) and with various degrees of closeness and frequency of contact with accountants, including accountants themselves.

Approximately 2,100 questionnaires were distributed, yielding 1,794 usable responses (response rate=approximately 85 percent). Our final sample was composed of 1,293 university students (773 studying business and economics, with the rest studying other disciplines)[2] and 501 CPA/audit firm employees; 767 students were attending a graduate course. The mean age of the respondents was 22.65 years and there was a slight majority of males (around 52 percent). Concerning CPA/audit firm employees, 232 (46.3 percent) were attending in-house training before starting their professional career, 129 (25.7 percent) had been working for less than one year and the remaining 140 (28 percent) had been working as accountants for more than one year.

We performed various analyses on the data collected by means of our questionnaire.

First of all, we examined the open-question answer indicating five characteristics that were freely associated in the respondents' minds with accountants. We coded as ethical all the responses that used words such as *ethical/ethics* and *honest (honesty), sincere, truthful (true), fair, law-compliant, correct, moral rigidity, respectful, incorruptible, trustworthy, reliable, responsible, dutiful, conscious of her/his duties, rigorous* and *conscientious*. We coded as unethical the opposite of these words/expressions as well as words such as *cheater, swindler, tax dodger* and *involved in bribery and corruption*. Ethical or unethical was indicated in only 13.66 percent of the questionnaires (245 questionnaires out of 1,794) as one of the five characteristics freely associated with 'the accountant'. Among the cases in which ethical was specified, 13 percent mentioned it as the first characteristic, 24 percent as the second, 22 percent as the third, 21 percent as the fourth and 20 percent as the fifth. The 'free' association between accountants and the lack of ethics concerned just around 2 percent of the total sample, whereas around 12 percent of the total sample (i.e., 84.49 percent of those who indicated ethicality/unethicality as one of the five traits freely associated with accountants) considered accountants to be ethical.

Secondly, in order to better understand the opinions on accountants' ethical behavior, we calculated the mean which referred to the specific question where respondents were required to disclose their view of accountants' ethical behavior ('Do you think accountants behave ethically?'). The mean was 3.3 (where 3 represents a neutral opinion): therefore, although the free association does not indicate that ethics is a fundamental concern in the minds of GenMe, overall, respondents have a mildly positive perception of accountants' ethics, which might signal some room for improvement.

Moreover, we tried to understand which characteristics are relevant to GenMe in order to differentiate between ethical accountants and unethical ones by building a correlation matrix between being ethical and the other items included in our questionnaire. We find significant and positive relations between the perception of accountants' behavior as ethical and being 'trustworthy' (0.393), 'incorruptible' (0.405), 'discreet' (0.170) and 'law-compliant' (0.592) and a negative and significant association with being 'easily influenced' (-0.178). We also find high correlation coefficients with items that are not commonly included in the definition of ethics by accounting professional bodies, i.e., with 'sincere' (0.382; $p=0.000$), with 'hard worker' (0.327; $p=0.000$) and with 'collaborative' (0.271; $p=0.000$). These items indicate some characteristics that, in the minds of GenMe, are associated with accountants' ethical behavior in addition to those which are part of the traditional definition proposed by professional bodies or in previous accounting contributions on ethics.

Our analyses thus suggest that, in the minds of GenMe, the perception of accountants' ethical behavior is connected with the idea that accountants need to make decisions based on external codes in order to avoid breaking the law ('law-compliant'), with the importance of professional independence ('being easily influenced') and with individual moral values ('incorruptible' and 'discreet') (Cullen, Parboteeah & Victor, 2003; Martin & Cullen, 2006). The link with the 'trustworthy' element is at the core of accountants' set of practices and suggests a call for transparency and accountability from GenMe as part of the accounting profession's ethical responsibilities and of its role in serving the public interest. Moreover, our results show that there are three additional items, i.e., 'sincere', 'hard worker' and 'collaborative', which are not generally included in the definition of the dimensions of ethics provided by the literature and by professional bodies, but positively associated with the item 'ethical behavior'.

These highlights seem to point to the existence of a more multifaceted perception of accountants' ethics and of the fact that GenMe appears to exhibit a more articulated idea of the dimensions for defining an accountant as an ethical professional. GenMe students and young workers would appear to direct their attention more towards individual characteristics. This indicates that accountants' ethical behavior is also considered to be the product of their personal traits. All in all, the GenMe public demands more than conventional adherence to the law and to the professional standards of ethics: their attention to individual characteristics is in line with the fact that GenMe is a generation in which the importance of the individual supersedes all other concerns (Twenge, 2006). This is additionally consistent with previous literature suggesting that ethicality depends on demographic as well as cultural individual traits.

Further, our evidence suggests that proximity to the profession influences the perception of accountants' ethical behavior. Practitioners have a significantly different (p=0.000) and better (mean=3.64) perception in comparison to students (mean=3.17). However, more experienced professionals have a less positive perception of accountants' ethics than do their less experienced colleagues. It is easy to imagine a young professional at the beginning of her/his career willing to work ethically and being confronted by a deceitful accountancy world, where 'compromises' are an everyday occurrence (Marques & Azevedo-Pereira, 2009). Our findings could be considered good news as the most negative opinion is exhibited by those respondents who are not close to the profession, meaning that this perception is unlikely to be indicative of the actual ethicality of the profession. Yet, it is not such good news from the point of view of the generally mildly positive level of trust in accountants exhibited by GenMe, which leaves room for improvement. In addition, considering the less positive opinion of those respondents with more work experience in accounting and assuming that this group of respondents represents the best-informed view (given that they are more experienced), our evidence raises some concerns about the ethicality of accountants.

In order to understand whether education might play a role, we also investigate the link between the level and type of education of GenMe students and young workers and their perceptions. We find some signals of a negative association between the level of education and the perception on ethics: there is a weakly significant difference (p=0.051) between graduate and undergraduate students, whereas we found no evidence showing that management and business administration students believe that accountants are more or less ethical than other students (p=0.788). Our results do not change when we consider the effect of either having or not having attended an accounting course. Our findings more precisely show that those who attended an accounting course do not have different perceptions of accountants' ethics, compared with those who did not attend any accounting courses (not significant t-test at the 0.473 level).

However, if we consider both whether and when an accounting course was attended, we obtain significant results. Our evidence illustrates (t-test; p=0.001) that a more positive perception was reported by respondents who attended an accounting course at the high-school level (mean=3.5), whereas the others reported a less positive one (3.26, also below the mean of the whole sample, i.e., 3.3). This might be explained by drawing on Hunt, Falgiani and Intrieri (2004), who observed that high-school teachers are focused on the bookkeeping aspect of accounting. A curriculum with such a focus could foster the notion that accountancy is a regular technical activity (Albrecht & Sack, 2000), associated with precision and reliability (Jeacle, 2008) and without much room for subjectivity and a flexible interpretation of rules, which could be understood as potentially unethical behavior.

In sum, the evidence presented here seems to suggest the existence of a multifaceted perception of accountants' ethics by GenMe. Our results also reinforce the need for appropriate actions to enhance the reputation of the profession. Moreover, they cast some doubts on the effectiveness of business and accounting education programs in the case of ethical issues. Indeed, we found no significant difference between the perceptions of management and business administration students and other students. Our results do not change when we consider the effect of either having or not having attended an accounting course. The role of high education and of universities in helping students to develop ethical sensitivity seems to indicate that some progress remains to be made. Finally, our findings are also consistent with the idea that accounting professionals soften their ethical orientation as they become older (Sankaran & Bui, 2003), thus prompting some questions on the effectiveness of professional ethical codes of conduct and the usefulness and contents of continuing education programs in terms of ethical issues. All in all, our evidence is in line with the call from researchers (e.g., Cooper, Leung, Dellaportas, Jackling & Wong, 2008; Sikka, Haslam, Kyriacou & Agrizzi, 2007) and practitioners (e.g., PricewaterhouseCoopers, 2003) for the implementation of more comprehensive accounting education, including ethics, professional skepticism and lifelong learning opportunities with the aim of serving the public interest. Educating accountants "for a global world is a partnership between higher education institutions, professional bodies, employers and regulatory bodies" (Watty, Sugahara, Abayadeera, Perera & McKay, 2014, p. 287).

3. Educating the Next Generation of Accountants

The results of our survey on GenMe in Italy seem to suggest that universities are not systematically exploiting the opportunity to promote ethical consciousness through business and accounting courses for young students. Previous literature has reported a lack of attention among academics given to the importance of incorporating ethical issues in university classroom activities (Gunz & McCutcheon, 1998). According to previous psychological studies, GenMe individuals become stressed when they receive ambiguous signals from the environment: they are perfectionists and apprehensive and show low self-reliance (Twenge, 2006). All these traits make them ill equipped to deal with the dilemmas typically encountered during a career in accountancy. Therefore, it is all the more important that, when they are still students, they are made aware of those potential or actual dilemmas they might face in the course of their future careers (Marques & Azevedo-Pereira, 2009). Explicitly introducing ethical and deontological issues in accounting courses could enhance their understanding that accounting decisions may be complex, due to a "mesh of conflicting obligations that constitutes our lives" (Young & Annisette, 2009, p. 95).

In this regard, universities as well as academics should be aware that they shape a significant part of accounting education. From a broader perspective, this implies the need to question their role in society. We do not believe that there is a unique and easy answer to this, but the first step is the acknowledgement that what happens inside universities might influence what happens in business life. The academic experience should ensure that aspiring accounting professionals are made aware of the complexity entrenched in their future career, which is far from being limited to numerical problems and formula applications. It is definitely worth dedicating part of the teaching time to provide some ethical education to potential future professional accountants in order to ensure they independently think about ethical issues with guidance from their educators. At the end of the day, they will certainly face some ethical dilemmas during their working life and could be completely alone in solving them. Thus, any previous experience and decision-making model seen in class could be a valuable starting point in order to assist them in making the best decisions regarding their personal and the public interest.

A good starting point from which to reflect on how to improve the contribution made by universities in raising awareness among students of the ethical issues they will face could be a better alignment with the approach proposed by the IAESB, which emphasizes not only the ability of individuals to perform in line with the standards expected of professional accountants, but also the importance of an appropriate level of values, ethics and attitudes enacted while achieving that competence. The IAESB is one of the independent standard-setting boards operating under the IFAC umbrella, which focuses on the development and the enhancement of accountants' education. The latter has to be understood in a broad sense, including both pre-qualification education and training of perspective accountants as well as continuing education and development for members of the accountancy profession. The IAESB issues different types of publications, i.e., authoritative and non-authoritative, for IFAC members. The former type includes standards in the area of professional accounting education, namely, International Education Standards (IESs) and International Education Practice Statements (IEPs), whereas the latter type comprises International Education Information Papers (IEIPs) and support materials such as toolkits or interpretation guides.

In a nutshell,

> the IAESB's objective is to serve the public interest by: developing and setting high quality international education standards that enhance the competence of aspiring professional accountants and professional accountants, thereby strengthening the worldwide accountancy profession and contributing to strengthened public trust.
>
> (IAESB, 2017a, p. 3)

In the following pages, centered on aspiring professionals educated through universities, we aim to stimulate instructors as well as academic institutions in order to reflect on what they are doing and what they can do to educate their accounting students so that they can identify and deal with ethical threats.

3.1 Fundamental Principles of Ethics for Professional Accountants

According to the 2018 International Code of Ethics for Professional Accountants (including International Independence Standards) (IESBA, 2018, p. 18), effective as of 15 June 2019, there are five fundamental principles of ethics for professional accountants:

(a) Integrity—to be straightforward and honest in all professional and business relationships.
(b) Objectivity—not to compromise professional or business judgments because of bias, conflict of interest or undue influence of others.

(c) Professional Competence and Due Care—to: (i) Attain and maintain professional knowledge and skill at the level required to ensure that a client or employing organization receives competent professional service, based on current technical and professional standards and relevant legislation; and (ii) Act diligently and in accordance with applicable technical and professional standards.
(d) Confidentiality—to respect the confidentiality of information acquired as a result of professional and business relationships.
(e) Professional Behavior—to comply with relevant laws and regulations and avoid any conduct that the professional accountant knows or should know might discredit the profession.

As the circumstances in which professional accountants operate might create threats in relation to compliance with the fundamental principles, a conceptual framework was developed in order to assist accountants in complying with these fundamental principles and meeting their responsibility to act in the public interest. According to the code, the conceptual framework specifies an approach for a professional accountant to:

(a) Identify threats to compliance with the fundamental principles;
(b) Evaluate the threats identified; and
(c) Address the threats by eliminating or reducing them to an acceptable level.

(IESBA, 2018, p. 24)

In relation to undertaking professional activities, the exercise of professional judgment is required when the professional accountant applies the conceptual framework in order to make informed decisions about the courses of actions available and to determine whether such decisions are appropriate in the circumstances.

(IESBA, 2018, p. 25)

The IAESB has defined professional judgement as "the application of relevant training, knowledge and experience, within the context provided by auditing, accounting and ethical standards, in making informed decisions about the courses of action" (IAESB, 2017a, p. 58).

For the purpose of this chapter, 'IES 4: Initial Professional Development (IPD)—Professional Values, Ethics and Attitudes' is of the utmost importance. IES 4 lists the types and levels of professional values, ethics and attitude that accountants are expected to demonstrate at the end of their initial professional development. Indeed, in the introduction to this principle, it is highlighted that "professional values, ethics and attitudes are the characteristics that identify professional accountants as members of a profession" (IAESB, 2017a, p. 54). In the current version of the principle, which is under revision (it should be effective as of 2021), it is clarified that professional accounting education programs shall provide "a framework of professional values, ethics and attitudes for aspiring professional accountants to (a) exercise professional skepticism and professional judgment and (b) act in an ethical manner that is in the public interest" (IAESB, 2017a, p. 55). Learning outcomes in terms of professional values, ethics and attitudes to be achieved by aspiring professional accountants by the end of IPD are grouped into three areas: (a) professional skepticism and professional judgement; (b) ethical principles; (c) commitment to the public interest. For all these areas, an intermediate level of competence is required.[3] Unfortunately, the compliance to IES 4 seems to be far from being completely reached (Crawford, Helliar, Monk & Veneziani, 2014). The IAESB has recognized that an assessment of the implementation process across the world is critical. Indeed, in its Strategy 2017–2021, both an increase in the awareness of IESs and the development of an implementation support aimed at overcoming application challenges are included as main objectives to be reached (IAESB, 2017b).

In commenting on the new version of the IESs, the European Accounting Association (EAA) clearly stated that

> We do not think it is appropriate to prescribe a level lower than advanced for the following competence areas: "ethical principles" and "commitment to the public interest". At the very root of well-known business scandals that damaged the reputation of the accounting profession worldwide there was the lack of an ethical dimension rather than technical weaknesses. For protecting accountants' reputation and the public trust in the profession, accountants should have and demonstrate advanced levels of ethical standards and commitment to the public interest at all stages of their career.
> (Cameran & Campa, 2016, p. 299)

Indeed, the EAA is an association of academics deeply involved in educational issues and this is clearly a hot topic for educators. University education should provide students with technical skills as well as an indispensable ethical background (Martinov-Bennie & Mladenovic, 2015) in order to make proper accounting judgements. The latter is essential and no less important than technical skills.

Academics and universities are often focused on technical skills.[4] For example, at the introductory level, accounting is generally taught using lectures and solving problems on the board (Williams, 1993), even if, in comparison to a high school education, more and more complex problems are proposed to students. At a certain point during their academic education, students realize there is no unique solution to any problem and that there are circumstances where following the rules might lead to bad outcomes (Correll, Jamal & Robinson, 2007). This is a potentially explosive mix for a generation which, as already discussed, is poor at coping with ambiguity as they are perfectionists and apprehensive as well as show low self-reliance (Twenge, 2006).

However, exams often test students' proficiency in solving problems similar to those presented in textbooks and during lectures (Young & Warren, 2011). The use of standardized measures of student learning outcomes is also incentivized by the aim to make available comparable indicators of institutional effectiveness (Goos & Salomons, 2017). It also makes exam grading faster, reducing also the probability that students will complain about too much subjectivity in grading and the potentially negative impact this will have on course/institution evaluations. This type of assessment reduces the incentives (and the ability) for students to state their own opinions about a problem, encouraging them to enter into the so-called 'right-answer syndrome' (Williams, 1993), which is associated with a passive, non-thinking attitude (Pithers & Soden, 2000).

Correll et al. (2007, p. 134), in describing their experience in Canadian universities with accounting students, wrote that

> students are marks-oriented, if not marks-obsessed. . . . They believe that rules make life easier and they are used to being given a track to run on and rules to follow. These are the students who are happy when GAAP gives them a rule to follow. . . . They are more comfortable dealing with the form than with the substance of a transaction. This is the polar opposite to the exercise of professional judgement. When we are trying to teach them to exercise professional judgement, we want them to see the substance rather than the form.

This is not a new and isolated phenomenon. For example, looking at the UK setting, Brown and McCartney (1995) noted that, since the 1990s, a competence-based education was provided to accounting students. These authors emphasized the need for 'meta-competences' which are a prerequisite for "the development of capacities such as judgement, intuition and acumen upon which competences are based and without which competences cannot flourish" (Brown & McCartney, 1995, p. 43).

Yet, in this respect, academics' constraints cannot be ignored. Indeed, whereas most faculty members sincerely believe that ethics are of the utmost importance for accountants, few of them are trained to teach related competences. Discussing subjects such as ethics most of the time implies dealing with 'controversial/complex' topics, which may hurt the feelings of some students, who could express negative opinions when completing teaching evaluations and performance reviews. Moreover, the emphasis on pedagogy is often not rewarded according to the tenure and promotion criteria (Van der Stede, 2018) of some universities. Efforts spent on this reduces the time spent on other academic obligations, such research, which, instead, weigh more in terms of career progression (Halx & Reybold, 2005).

As an example, let us consider Stephenson's (2017) article, which presents a reflective ethical decision model designed to provide a framework within which students can identify and design their own construct of ethical values. The author suggested that guiding students through the process of developing their own personal code may be more effective than trying to teach ethics to students. This is a very time-consuming process not only in terms of teaching time, but also considering the investment that instructors have to make when preparing lessons, which might conflict with other academic obligations that are more rewarding from the point of view of academic career progression.

All in all, even after having considered all of this, given that future accounting professionals' primary responsibility is to act in the public interest, incorporating ethical principles in students' curricula is critically important. Specifically, the under-revision IES 4 lists, with reference to ethical principles, the related learning outcomes to be achieved by aspiring professional accountants by the end of IPD: (i) explain the nature of ethics; (ii) explain the advantages and disadvantages of rules-based and principles-based approaches to ethics; (iii) identify ethical issues threats and determine when which ethical principles apply; (iv) analyze alternative courses of action to address ethical threats and their related consequences; (v) apply the fundamental ethical principles of integrity, objectivity, professional competence and due care, confidentiality and professional behavior to ethical dilemmas threats and determine an appropriate approach; and (vi) apply ethical principles when accessing, storing, generating, using and sharing data and information (IAESB, 2018, p. 58). The last learning outcome was added during the recent process of standard revision in order to underline the need for professional accountants to apply ethical principles when working with data and information. These outcomes should be pursued before entering the profession and universities should offer courses where teaching time is allocated for this purpose. The challenges remain centered on the 'how'.

3.2 A Proposal About the 'How': Accountants as Critical Thinkers

One possible solution regarding how to help students in accounting to develop their ethical sensitivity could be to introduce, as part of their curriculum, a critical thinking course or some specific sessions on the accounting courses aimed at developing their critical thinking. The already-cited revised IES 4 emphasizes the fact that professional accountants need to apply "a questioning mind when assessing data and information", "critical thinking when identifying and evaluating alternatives to determine an appropriate course of action" (IAESB, 2018, pp. 24–25). In the same vein, the under-revision IES 3 explicitly indicates that accounting professionals need to "apply critical thinking skills to solve problems" and that they must be able to "recommend solutions to unstructured, multifaceted problems" and to demonstrate "intellectual agility" as well as "an awareness of personal and organizational bias" (IAESB, 2018, p. 22). IES 8, in terms of dealing with engagement partners, also explicitly states that they need to "apply a questioning mind to critically assess audit evidence and other relevant information obtained during the course of an audit to reach informed conclusions", "evaluate the potential impact of bias on conclusions", "apply knowledge and experience to challenge management's assertions and representations" and "resolve audit issues using inquiry and critical thinking to consider alternatives and analyze outcomes" (IAESB, 2018, p. 33).

However, the Association to Advance Collegiate Schools of Business (AACSB) expresses unambiguous concerns about the lack of adequate critical thinking among accountants and, in general, among young graduates (AACSB, 2019b). The AACSB provides quality assurance, business education intelligence and professional development services to over 1,600 member organizations and more than 800 accredited business schools worldwide, with the mission to improve the quality of business education on a global scale (AACSB, 2019a).

According to the AACSB website, the main problem that employers observe in recent graduates is the lack of critical thinking. The same organization admits that teaching this ability is indeed a global challenge (AACSB, 2019b). Such statements seem to reinforce the idea that academics and universities need to be more effective in preparing students to enter the real working environment.

As already discussed with reference to ethical orientation, as well as in the case of critical thinking, individual traits play an important role in its development. Indeed, even if there are characterological components that are related to a person's inclination to use critical thinking (Giancarlo & Facione, 2001), these traits should be spotted and nurtured by educators.

According to developmental psychology, developing critical reflection is a process of learning which can be undertaken by adults (Brookfield, 1987, 1991). Practical approaches typically include teaching diaries, role-model profiles, participant-learning portfolios and structured critical conversation (Brookfield, 2017). Watanabe-Crockett (2015) points out that critical thinking is generally overlooked at the primary, secondary and high school levels. This trend may be also exacerbated by cultural traditions and teachers' behaviors. For example, Acharya (2017, p. 31) reported that Nepalese science teachers in high schools "take obedient, compliant, dependent and submissive students as good students and those who are independent and express personal opinions different from teachers are regarded as showing disrespect". Moreover, both students and teachers might find critical thinking discomforting because it requires personal reflection (Halx & Reybold, 2005), whereas, on a basic-level course, the general expectation is that instructors solve problems and students take note of the solution. Furthermore, students cannot learn to think critically by simply watching someone else thinking critically (Gelder, 2005); rather, it requires a willingness to entertain ideas without necessarily accepting them (Halx & Reybold, 2005).

Thinking critically does not always end with the right answer but, more often, results in more questions or contrasting opinions about a topic. This concept could be particularly difficult to convey to GenMe students. Indeed, they are depicted as a generation where the importance of the individual supersedes all other concerns (Twenge, 2006). They are also quite narcissistic, with an expectation that the world owes you something ("I deserve the best", "I need an A because I made efforts") (Twenge, 2009, p. 401).

Critical thinking skills develop slowly in students (Wolcott, Baril, Cunningham, Fordham & Pierre, 2002). Thus, "there must be a coordinated effort among those teaching the introductory courses and the upper-division courses to provide students with multiple opportunities to practice their critical thinking skills and receive feedback on their efforts" (Young & Warren, 2011, p. 862). This would require an active learning style from the very beginning (i.e., on introductory accounting courses). Standardized measures of student learning outcomes are used more and more as they allow to compare the effectiveness of different educational providers. However, the presence of standardized assessments, the limited amount of time during class sessions and large groups incentivize educators to apply a traditional approach during their classes (i.e., the instructor explains and the students take notes). In this framework, it is not surprising that the achieved result is that many students leave the education system without any well-developed critical thinking skills.

Some studies have suggested how to develop critical and creative thoughts in students through innovative ways of teaching. For example, in their study, Samkin and Francis (2008), focusing on an undergraduate accounting class, propose that students' assessment should rely on several components, e.g., classroom assessment techniques and tests aimed at measuring their reflection ability and how they select relevant information (i.e., case studies where students are required to identify problem areas and recognize if and what additional information is needed to solve the problem), with a specific emphasis on students' creativity when dealing with the tasks as reported earlier. A personal journal, where students "monitor their learning goals and progress; interrelate ideas; develop understanding of themselves at work; describe learning plateaux and blocks and how they overcome these and free up the writing process so that it can become a source of freedom, relaxation and fun" (Samkin & Francis, 2008, p. 244), is cited as an assessment tool. Preparing and delivering a course such as the one described in the cited article require a lot of time and dedicated effort.

The importance of critical thinking is of increasing relevance, especially in light of the opportunities brought about by technological advances. In the era of big data, the accounting profession is faced with the challenge of analyzing, evaluating and distilling huge data sets with the objective of extracting value-added insights. Thus, the discussion about how to prepare students for the effective use of these kinds of data is emerging. As noted by McKinney, Yoos and Snead (2017, p. 64), it is crucial that "a decision maker with big judgment skills possesses a healthy and informed skepticism that can assess the factors underpinning the numbers and think critically about the assumptions behind the data". Indeed, the lack of a critical mindset could assume a default position of accepting evidence as reliable without sufficient effort made to express an unbiased opinion about it. The analysis of huge data sets requires integrating critical thinking (Chabrak & Craig, 2013) and data analytic skills (Janvrin, Raschke & Dilla, 2014) into typical accounting topics.

4. Conclusions

The education system, especially at the higher level, needs to prepare professional accountants for entering the real business world and acting in the public interest. Different types of knowledge are required in order to solve complex problems. According to the International Code of Ethics for Professional Accountants, "a distinguishing mark of the accountancy profession is its acceptance of the responsibility to act in the public interest. A professional accountant's responsibility is not exclusively to satisfy the needs of an individual client or employing organization" (IESBA, 2018, p. 16).

Analyzing the perceptions of the GenMe cohort, we find that there is room for improvement regarding accountants' ethics. Well-publicized accounting scandals as well as the financial crisis may have compromised the perception of accountants' integrity and ethics. In addition, in recent years, professional bodies and accounting firms have been concerned with the short supply of talented graduates willing to choose a career in accounting due to the limited appeal of a profession which bears the bean counter's stigma (e.g., McDowall & Jackling, 2010). For this reason, they have extensively sought to promote a less 'conventional' accountant in favor of a more active, sociable and high-status professional. This representation of the 'colorful' accountant might have endangered the idea of professional ethics, thus leading to a discredited image in the public mind (Jeacle, 2008). The results of our survey of GenMe hint at a negative association between the perception of accountants' ethics and the level of education.

This is a wake-up call for faculty members and educational institutions, which underlines their need to reflect on how they can foster the development of students' critical knowledge and appropriate professional values.

This must be done through measures that do not simply include general and vague phrases in universities' mission statements; rather, it requires practical actions such as rewarding academics who dedicate themselves to ethical education and encourage critical thinking. A possible strategy for this purpose is to increase the value ascribed to such encouragement and tailoring the requirements for career progression and tenure evaluation.

Moreover, universities need to think carefully about the balance between teaching hours allocated to academics and practitioners. Indeed, some of them have decided to significantly reduce teaching hours allocated to academics in favor of practitioners, on the assumption that the latter are more equipped than faculty members to teach students how to undertake the practical aspects demanded in the 'real world'. This implies a reduction in the time available for teaching academic theories and business principles or, in general, those meta-competences (Brown & McCartney, 1995) which are a prerequisite for students' ability to think critically.

Overall, accounting educators at the university level do a good job at teaching accounting rules. However, even computers can be programmed to follow such rules reasonably well. Moreover, GenMe students seem to think that they must have all the answers readily available. But this does not make for a good accounting professional. General accounting standards are the minimum and students should be encouraged to investigate how to present financial information better than the minimum. They should not be trained to be extremely good at simply following rules; instead, they should be shown how "to actually think about the rules and to know when the rules are wrong or are leading to bad outcomes" (Correll et al., 2007, p. 134). At the end of the day, an "accountant is paid for his judgment, not for his technical ability" (Zug, 1951, p. 177).

Course instructors may have very different backgrounds, ranging from those with significant professional experience to high-quality researchers with virtual no practical experience in the accountancy field. An effective strategy on the part of universities is to help instructors in investing their time in becoming familiar and keeping up to date with the IAESB's activities and publications. Past literature has stressed that relatively few educators are familiar with the IAESB's activities which seek to achieve the convergence of accounting education standards around the world (McPeak, Pincus & Sundem, 2012; Sugahara & Wilson, 2013). Moreover, as a result of "different traditions, steeped in history and culture, the current accounting education life cycle operates differently across the globe" (Helliar, 2013, p. 514). This is true both at the entrance level and for the continuing professional development (De Lange, Jackling & Basioudis, 2013) of accounting professionals. Differences in regulatory environments also play a highly significant role in differentiating forms of accounting education found in the world (Karrenanen & Needles, 2013). All this implies that, other than the already-cited familiarity with IAESB activities, it is also necessary to adapt the IES content to the specific educational setting and the characteristics of educators and students sitting in specific classes.

Notes

1. The complete results of this research are reported in Caglio and Cameran (2017). Is it shameful to be an accountant? GenMe perception(s) of accountants' ethics. *Abacus*, Vol. 53, No. 1, March: 1–27.
2. These include law (17.2 percent), architecture (15 percent), engineering (11.8 percent), classics and literature (8.5 percent), political science (8.3 percent) and mathematics and statistics (5.9 percent).
3. The IAESB describes the 'intermediate' level in terms of its learning outcomes as follows: "independently applying, comparing, and analyzing underlying principles and theories from relevant areas of technical competence to complete work assignments and make decisions; combining technical competence and professional skills to complete work assignments; applying professional values, ethics, and attitudes to work assignments; and presenting information and explaining ideas in a clear manner, using oral and written communications, to accounting and non-accounting stakeholders. Learning outcomes at the intermediate level relate to work situations that are characterized by moderate levels of ambiguity, complexity, and uncertainty" (IAESB, 2017a, pp. 16–17).
4. Some of the comments related to accounting education are built on Cameran and Campa. Critical thinking in today's accounting education. A reflection note following the International Ethics Standards Board for Accountants Consultation Paper 'Professional Skepticism—Meeting Public Expectations'. *Accounting Finance and Governance Review*, forthcoming.

References

AACSB. (2019a). *Who we are*. Retrieved October 1, 2019, from www.aacsb.edu/about

AACSB. (2019b). *Critical thinking*. Retrieved October 1, 2019, from www.aacsb.edu/events/seminars/curriculum-development-series/critical-thinking

Acharya, K. P. (2017). Exploring critical thinking for secondary level students in chemistry: From insight to practice. *Journal of Advanced College of Engineering and Management*, 3, 31–39.

Albrecht, W. S., & Sack, R. J. (2000). *Accounting education: Charting the course through a perilous future* (Vol. 16). Sarasota, FL: American Accounting Association.

Bernardi, R. A., & Arnold Sr, D. F. (1997). An examination of moral development within public accounting by gender, staff level, and firm. *Contemporary Accounting Research*, 14(4), 653–668.

Brookfield, S. D. (1987). *Developing critical thinkers*. Milton Keynes: Open University Press.

Brookfield, S. D. (1991). The development of critical reflection in adulthood. *New Education*, 13(1), 39–48.

Brookfield, S. D. (2017). *Becoming a critically reflective teacher*. San Francisco, CA: John Wiley & Sons.

Brown, R. B., & McCartney, S. (1995). Competence is not enough: Meta-competence and accounting education. *Accounting Education*, 4(1), 43–53.

Caglio, A., & Cameran, M. (2017). Is it shameful to be an accountant? GenMe perception(s) of accountants' ethics. *Abacus, 53*(1), 1–27.

Cameran, M., & Campa, D. (2016). Comments by the European Accounting Association on the International Accounting Education Standards Board Consultation Paper 'Meeting future expectations of professional competence: A consultation on the IAESB's future strategy and priorities'. *Accounting in Europe, 13*(2), 295–303.

Chabrak, N., & Craig, R. (2013). Student imaginings, cognitive dissonance and critical thinking. *Critical Perspectives on Accounting, 24*(2), 91–104.

Cohen, J. R., Pant, L. W., & Sharp, D. J. (1995). An exploratory examination of international differences in auditors' ethical perceptions. *Behavioral Research in Accounting, 7*(1), 37–64.

Coicaud, J. M., & Warner, D. (Eds.). (2001). *Ethics and international affairs: Extent and limits*. New York: United Nations University Press.

Cooper, B. J., Leung, P., Dellaportas, S., Jackling, B., & Wong, G. (2008). Ethics education for accounting students: A toolkit approach. *Accounting Education: An International Journal, 17*(4), 405–430.

Correll, R., Jamal, K., & Robinson, L. A. (2007). Teaching professional judgement in accounting. *Accounting Perspectives, 6*(2), 123–140.

Crawford, L., Helliar, C., Monk, E., & Veneziani, M. (2014). International accounting education standards board: Organisational legitimacy within the field of professional accountancy education. *Accounting Forum, 38*(1), 67–89.

Cullen, J. B., Parboteeah, K. P., & Victor, B. (2003). The effects of ethical climates on organizational commitment: A two-study analysis. *Journal of Business Ethics, 46*(2), 127–141.

De Lange, P., Jackling, B., & Basioudis, I. G. (2013). A framework of best practice of continuing professional development for the accounting profession. *Accounting Education, 22*(5), 494–497.

Di Pietra, R., McLeay, S., & Riccaboni, A. (2001). Regulating accounting within the political and legal system. In S. McLeay & A. Riccaboni (Eds.), *Contemporary issues in accounting regulation* (pp. 59–78). Boston, MA: Springer.

Gelder, T. V. (2005). Teaching critical thinking: Some lessons from cognitive science. *College Teaching, 53*(1), 41–48.

Giancarlo, C. A., & Facione, P. A. (2001). A look across four years at the disposition toward critical thinking among undergraduate students. *The Journal of General Education, 50*(1), 29–55.

Goos, M., & Salomons, A. (2017). Measuring teaching quality in higher education: Assessing selection bias in course evaluations. *Research in Higher Education, 58*(4), 341–364.

Gunz, S., & McCutcheon, J. (1998). Are academics committed to accounting ethics education? *Journal of Business Ethics, 17*(11), 1145–1154.

Halx, M. D., & Reybold, L. E. (2005). A pedagogy of force: Faculty perspectives of critical thinking capacity in undergraduate students. *The Journal of General Education, 54*(4), 293–315.

Helliar, C. (2013). The global challenge for accounting education. *Accounting Education, 22*(6), 510–521.

Hunt, S. C., Falgiani, A. A., & Intrieri, R. C. (2004). The nature and origins of students' perceptions of accountants. *Journal of Education for Business, 79*(3), 142–148.

IAESB. (2017a). *Handbook of international education pronouncements*. Retrieved October 1, 2019, from www.ifac.org/system/files/publications/files/2017-Handbook-of-International-Education-Pronouncements.PDF

IAESB. (2017b). *Strategy 2017–2021 and work plan 2017–2018.* Retrieved October 1, 2019, from www.ifac.org/system/files/publications/files/IAESB-Strategy-and-Work-Plan.pdf

IAESB. (2018). *Proposed revisions to IESs 2, 3, 4, and 8: Information and communications technologies and professional skepticism.* Retrieved October 1, 2019, from www.ifac.org/system/files/publications/files/IAESB-Exposure-Draft-Proposed-Revisions-IES-2-3-4-8.pdf

IESBA. (2018). *International code of ethics for professional accountants.* Retrieved October 1, 2019, from www.ethicsboard.org/iesba-code

IFAC. (2019). *Professional accountants: The future.* Retrieved October 1, 2019, from www.accaglobal.com/gb/en/professional-insights/pro-accountants-the-future.html

Janvrin, D. J., Raschke, R. L., & Dilla, W. N. (2014). Making sense of complex data using interactive data visualization. *Journal of Accounting Education, 32*(4), 31–48.

Jeacle, I. (2008). Beyond the boring grey: The construction of the colourful accountant. *Critical Perspectives on Accounting, 19*(8), 1296–1320.

Jonnergård, K., Stafsudd, A., & Elg, U. (2010). Performance evaluations as gender barriers in professional organizations: A study of auditing firms. *Gender, Work & Organization, 17*(6), 721–747.

Karrenanen, J. K., & Needles, B. E. (2013). *Global accountancy education recognition study 2012.* Retrieved October, 1, 2019, from https://nasba.org/app/uploads/2013/08/GAER_2012_Study_Final.pdf

Marques, P. A., & Azevedo-Pereira, J. (2009). Ethical ideology and ethical judgments in the Portuguese accounting profession. *Journal of Business Ethics, 86*(2), 227–242.

Martin, K. D., & Cullen, J. B. (2006). Continuities and extensions of ethical climate theory: A meta-analytic review. *Journal of Business Ethics, 69*(2), 175–194.

Martinov-Bennie, N., & Mladenovic, R. (2015). Investigation of the impact of an ethical framework and an integrated ethics education on accounting students' ethical sensitivity and judgment. *Journal of Business Ethics, 127*(1), 189–203.

McDowall, T., & Jackling, B. (2010). Attitudes towards the accounting profession: An Australian perspective. *Asian Review of Accounting, 18*(1), 30–49.

McKinney Jr., E., Yoos II, C. J., & Snead, K. (2017). The need for 'skeptical' accountants in the era of Big Data. *Journal of Accounting Education, 38*(March), 63–80.

McPeak, D., Pincus, K. V., & Sundem, G. L. (2012). The international accounting education standards board: Influencing global accounting education. *Issues in Accounting Education, 27*(3), 743–750.

Parry, E., & Urwin, P. (2011). Generational differences in work values: A review of theory and evidence. *International Journal of Management Reviews, 13*(1), 79–96.

Pithers, R. T., & Soden, R. (2000). Critical thinking in education: A review. *Educational research, 42*(3), 237–249.

Pricewaterhousecoopers. (2003). *Educating for the public trust: The PricewaterhouseCoopers position on accounting education.* Retrieved October 1, 2019, from www.pwc.com/us/en/faculty-resource/assets/educatingfortrust.pdf

Samkin, G., & Francis, G. (2008). Introducing a learning portfolio in an undergraduate financial accounting course. *Accounting Education: An International Journal, 17*(3), 233–271.

Sankaran, S., & Bui, T. (2003). Ethical attitudes among accounting majors: An empirical study. *Journal of American Academy of Business, Cambridge*, 3(1–2), 71–77.
Sikka, P., Haslam, C., Kyriacou, O., & Agrizzi, D. (2007). Professionalizing claims and the state of UK professional accounting education: Some evidence. *Accounting Education: An International Journal*, 16(1), 3–21.
Stephenson, S. S. (2017). Reflective ethical decision: A model for ethics in accounting education. *The Accounting Educators' Journal*, 26, 11–37.
Sugahara, S., & Wilson, R. (2013). Discourse surrounding the international education standards for professional accountants (IES): A content analysis approach. *Accounting Education*, 22(3), 213–232.
Sweeney, B., Arnold, D., & Pierce, B. (2010). The impact of perceived ethical culture of the firm and demographic variables on auditors' ethical evaluation and intention to act decisions. *Journal of Business Ethics*, 93(4), 531–551.
Swenson-Lepper, T. (2005). Ethical sensitivity for organizational communication issues: Examining individual and organizational differences. *Journal of Business Ethics*, 59(3), 205–231.
Tormo-Carbó, G., Seguí-Mas, E., & Oltra, V. (2016). Accounting ethics in unfriendly environments: The educational challenge. *Journal of Business Ethics*, 135(1), 161–175.
Twenge, J. M. (2006). *Generation me: Why today's young Americans are more confident, assertive, entitled- and more miserable than ever before*. New York: Free Press.
Twenge, J. M. (2009). Generational changes and their impact in the classroom: Teaching generation me. *Medical Education*, 43(5), 398–405.
Van der Stede, W. A. (2018). Multitasking academics. *Issues in Accounting Education*, 33(3), 85–94.
Watanabe-Crockett, L. (2015). The importance of teaching critical thinking. *Critical Thinking*. Retrieved October, 1, 2019, from https://globaldigitalcitizen.org/the-importance-of-teaching-critical-thinking
Watty, K., Sugahara, S., Abayadeera, N., Perera, L., & McKay, J. (2014). Towards a global model of accounting education. *Accounting Research Journal*, 27(3), 286–300.
Williams, D. Z. (1993). Reforming accounting education. *Journal of Accountancy*, 176(2), 76.
Wolcott, S. K., Baril, C. P., Cunningham, B. M., Fordham, D. R., & Pierre, K. S. (2002). Critical thought on critical thinking research. *Journal of Accounting Education*, 20(2), 85–103.
Young, J. J., & Annisette, M. (2009). Cultivating imagination: Ethics, education and literature. *Critical Perspectives on Accounting*, 20(1), 93–109.
Young, M., & Warren, D. L. (2011). Encouraging the development of critical thinking skills in the introductory accounting courses using the challenge problem approach. *Issues in Accounting Education*, 26(4), 859–881.
Zug, H. C. (1951). Courses of study leading to CPA certificates should not be narrow, nor fixed by law. *Journal of Accountancy*, 92(2), 175–179.

6 Ethical Virtues, Norms and Values in Accounting Education

Domènec Melé

1. Introduction

The first attempts at introducing ethics into accounting education, which go back to the beginning of the 20th century (Loeb, 1988), were mainly based on ethical standards associated with the accounting profession, and later on rationalist ethical principles (e.g., Loeb & Bedingfield, 1972; Loeb, 1978; Langenderfer & Rockness, 1989; Cottell & Perlin, 1990; Armstrong, 1993; Maurice, 1996; Gowthorpe & Blake, 1998; Duska & Duska, 2003). The dominant idea was that ethics was rules or principles and ethics in accounting, as in other matters, is an "application of ethics or morality . . . to practical issues" (Cottell & Perlin, 1990, p. x).

Later, with the eruption of virtue ethics in different fields of applied ethics, this approach arrived in accounting ethics too. The lack of importance assigned to virtues probably stems from the fact that the tradition of virtues—entered on the agent—has been overshadowed for centuries. This privileges approaches based on norms or principles and oriented to specific ethical issues and to solve dilemmas.

According to Armstrong, Ketz and Owsen (2003), who explored ethics education literature in accounting at the beginning of the current century, there was a prevalence of action-centered ethics, based on rules, as opposed to agent-centered ethics focused on moral character of the agent. Two important exceptions were Francis (1990) and Mintz (1995, 1996), who focused on virtue ethics. However, in the last two decades, the number of scholars working on an agent-centered ethics in accounting has increasing significantly. Among them, there are McMillan (2004), Melé (2005), Mintz (2006), Cheffers and Pakaluk (2007) and West (2018). In professional education, the value of appropriate training in the virtue of practical wisdom has been emphasized by Schwartz (2011) and Harrison and Khatoon (2017).

In this chapter, I argue that ethical accounting education should pay attention to virtues, in particular practical wisdom, rooted in human goods (intrinsic values), as well as to principles or rules. To a great extent, this chapter is an updated version of a previous paper (Melé, 2005), expanded in some parts. It is structured as follows. Firstly, we discuss why rule and principled-based approaches are insufficient. Then we present some objections to agent-based virtues proposals disconnected from human goods and principles. In the following section, we explain why practical wisdom and other person-rooted virtues are so important. Then, we debate the connection between virtues and principles and their dependence on human goods. Finally, we connect this approach to the psychological elements of ethical behavior and discuss implications of the previous arguments for ethical education in accounting.

2. Insufficiency of Codes and Principles-Based Approaches

Accountants can carry out their work in many different areas, including auditing, managerial accounting, tax accounting, financial planning, consulting and, of course, simply preparing accounts. In each of these spheres, ethical issues appear (Armstrong, 2002) and accountants perceive that opportunities exist in their work to engage in unethical behavior.[1]

For accountants, as with any other profession, codes of conduct give guidelines for proper behavior in the job. Codes are the most concrete cultural form in which professions acknowledge their societal obligations (Abbott, 1983). Codes, and possibly some procedures for reinforcing them, are a public commitment of the profession and a basic element in achieving social recognition of, and public trust in it.

Codes of conduct contain a set of principles and rules that specify what society expects to be considered in decision making. According to Bowie and Duska (1985), from a practical perspective, codes of conduct are useful in several ways: 1) They motivate through the use of peer pressure; 2) provide a stable and permanent guide to right or wrong rather than leaving the question to continual *ad hoc* decisions; 3) give guidance, especially in ambiguous situations, orienting the behavior of the employees and controlling the autocratic power of employers over employees; 4) help to specify the social responsibility of business; and 5) contribute to the interest of business itself, for if businesses do not police themselves ethically, others will do it for them.

In spite of these benefits, codes of conduct have not been immune to criticism. One is the 'mechanistic' application of such codes. Although some ethical values or principles can easily be recognized in most codes of conduct for accountants, in practice, the rules are often applied in a mechanical way, without presenting their ethical foundation. A second criticism is that using exclusively codes for ethical education in accounting, students might confuse ethics with a set of rules, legal standards or other regulations, whereas ethics is much more than rules. In addition, as Adams, Malone and James (1995) suggested, in today's legalistic society, the question of 'what is the right thing to do?' is often confused with 'what is legal?' Whereas they refer to accountants in the United States of America, this statement could be applied to other countries.

A third criticism regards the lack of effectiveness of codes. Lere (2003) suggests that it is rare to have a situation where codes of ethics impact decision-making. He believes that whereas enforcement provisions can increase the likelihood that an individual will select (forego) the action that a code of ethics indicates to be ethical (unethical), there are limits as to how effective enforcement provisions can be.

A fourth important criticism is the existence of particular situations in which rigid rules falls short. In such cases, there can be a question of whether the best ethical behavior is always to follow the established rules. Adams et al. (1995) studied several cases regarding auditing client confidentiality in which disclosure could be the best ethical behavior, in spite of the applicable rules, which state that a Certified Public Accountant (CPA) member, acting in public practice, shall not disclose any confidential information without the specific consent of the client. A survey among CPAs showed that a substantial percentage (between 30 and 47 percent) thought that the best ethical behavior would be not to follow the rules of the code for these specific cases.

Finally, and from a different perspective, Velayutham (2003) points out that the focus of codes of ethics has been to progressively replace the 'true and fair view' requirement by 'compliance with accounting standards'. Thus, codes have moved from focusing on moral responsibility to a public good to that of a technical specification for a product or service. In this way, technique has supplanted character.

The limitations of codes of conduct are accepted even by some of those who include rules and codes in accounting ethics textbooks. Thus, Loeb and Rockness (1992), two experts in ethical education in accounting, recognized: "our collective experience indicates that both college students and practicing accounting professionals are interested in accounting ethics education that moves beyond the rules of a code ethics and the code's corresponding official interpretation" (Loeb & Rockness, 1992, p. 488).

In some fields of professional activity, there is a tendency to emphasize basic principles from which particular norms derive. Thus, in 1957, the American Medical Association replaced its Code of Ethics, which stated the duties that American physicians owed to their patients, their society and to one another, with a statement of moral principles, supplemented by opinions and commentaries on specific cases and questions (Roth, 1994, p. 695). Currently, this tendency is also observed in accounting codes, which entail a few generic principles as framework for rules. The American Institute of Certified Public Accountants (AICPA) Code of Professional Conduct consists of principles and rules as well as interpretations and other guidance for accountants. The principles mentioned refer to responsibility as professionals (exercise sensitive professional and moral judgments in all their activities): public interest, integrity, objectivity, independence and due care (AICPA, 2014). The International Code of Ethics for Professional Accountants published by the International Ethics

Standards Board of Accountants (IESBA) of the International Federation of Accountants, which highlights a set of crucial principles as the main reference for the entire code: integrity, objectivity, professional competence and due care, confidentiality and professional behavior (IESBA, 2019).

Considering the general principles that serve as a rule's basis provides a broader perspective for ethical behavior in accounting. With this approach, it may well be easier to avoid a legalistic vision of ethics in accounting or a mechanistic application of rules in decision-making.

Frequently, principles adopted come from rationalistic theories that propose diverse methods of moral reasoning to apply them properly to solve dilemmas or to justify certain actions. Ethical education in accounting usually includes teaching several normative theories, such as Kantianism, Utilitarianism and other rationalistic ethical theories. These theories are presented as useful to identify moral dilemmas and provide a pathway for moral reasoning.

There is no doubt that "identifying moral conflicts, thinking them through, discussing them with colleagues and others and utilizing the tools of ethical analysis are useful, in fact, indispensable activities" (Cottell & Perlin, 1990, pp. ix–x). To this end, some teachers explain different ethical theories and encourage students to use them as a tool for ethical reasoning. Thus, they may present the Kantian theory, with its categorical imperatives or the Utilitarian principle of 'the greatest happiness for the greatest number' or any other ethical theory based on aprioristic principles of morality.

A number of objections can be presented to this approach. Firstly, and depending on the aprioristic principle accepted, the action may be seen only as a set of *duties* (Kantian and Neo-Kantian theories) or only as a set of *consequences* (Utilitarianism, if they are evaluated in terms of satisfaction, or consequentialism if they are evaluated in terms of other chosen values). Authors in favor of understanding ethics only as duties criticize others that think only consequences are relevant and vice versa. In contrast with these approaches, common moral sense might consider both the action itself and also the action's foreseeable and avoidable consequences relevant.

Secondly, principle-based ethics are questioned for different reasons, including the well-known criticism of Anscombe (1958) of the lack of attention in principle-based ethics to the psychological aspect of moral behavior, and others (e.g., Duska, 1993) regarding the understanding of ethics and the foundations of modern moral theories.

Third, teaching rationalist theories can develop students' skills in solving ethical dilemmas, applying such theories and determining what is right according to a set of duties or systematically analyzing the consequences, but this does not motivate students to act well. Ethics cannot become a sort of 'technology' for solving moral dilemmas. In this regard, in teaching business ethics—and the same can be said for accounting ethics—Cooley (2004) observed that students memorize enough of the moral theories to pass their tests, but never understand the motivating spirit underlying the theories. He concludes students know how to apply the moral principles to various situations but produce the wrong results due to their illicit biases and rationalizations. Fulfilling your (self-evident) duties (Kantianism) or calculating the consequences in terms of satisfaction (Utilitarianism) does not seem enough for ethical behavior, because human behavior is far more complex than accepting aprioristic principles and knowing how to apply them. As will be discussed, motivation and habits are also very important for correct behavior. Similarly, Shaub (1994) pointed out several potential weaknesses in implementing accounting ethics education in the classroom and criticized the current overreliance on ethical dilemmas.

The fourth shortcoming has to do with the lack of consideration of the decision-maker's character in moral reasoning (e.g., Anscombe, 1958; Veatch, 1968; MacIntyre, 1984). In particular, Pincoffs (1986) criticized the problems with theories used to solve ethical dilemmas. He stated deontological or utilitarian ethical theories are reductive, because they eliminate what is morally relevant (character) and they legislate the form of moral reflection (duties and consequences). In addition, rationalist theories exclude the contribution (or not) of every free action to human flourishing.

Principle-based theories are a heritage of the enlightenment and of modern moral philosophy, which emphasizes duties and norms without examining the personal disposition of the person making the moral judgment in a specific situation (except maybe the good will for acting well), and without considering the habits acquired by deciding and acting in a certain way. In addition, and similarly to what has said regarding codes of conduct, there are particular situations that are extremely difficult to solve exclusively by universal principles.

In contrast to modern moral philosophy, the Aristotelian view argues that moral judgment "is not merely an intellectual exercise of subsuming a particular under rules, norms, or hyper-norms. Judgment is an activity of perceiving while simultaneously perfecting the capacity to judge actions and choices and to perceive being" (Koehn, 2000, p. 17). This vision contrasts with Kantian theory and Utilitarianism, which, as has been pointed out, take this capacity for granted and consider it irrelevant in making moral judgments.

3. Are Values and Virtues Sufficient?

Teaching values could counter a concept of ethical training reduced to a mere application of rules or the shortcomings of the rationalistic theories mentioned before. Values can also go as far as to provide a motivation to act well. "Value in general may best be glossed as that which is worth having, getting, or doing. . . . Value, thus understood, is essentially *relational*, that is, it is value for some person(s) or living being(s)" (Bond,

2001, p. 1745). Values, in the context of business, are generally understood as motives for acting correctly. Codes present the grounding moral values as principles. However, teaching values is not enough. Accountants, like every professional, have to make practical judgments about specific situations and, above all, have to behave correctly. Both conditions require not only bearing values in mind but also having good character, as we will explain later.

In addition, having values does not entail having virtues—the strength of character for moral behavior. From Aristotle a diversity of virtues has been presented rooted in the human nature. However, defenders of principle-based ethics often argue that the only relevant virtue, at least implicitly stressed, is the disposition to fulfill the obligations prescribed by code or by normative ethical theories. This latter misses the richness of virtue ethics theory.

As noted earlier, several scholars have strongly criticized those approaches that reduce ethical education to presenting ethical theories to solve ethical dilemmas rather than considering personal virtues. In contrast, Francis (1990) emphasized the role of the agent's moral character beyond rules and the possibility of accounting to be a virtuous practice. As an alternative to teaching ethical theories, Pincoffs (1986, p. 150) presented the primary objective of moral education as encouraging the development of the person. This means encouraging the development of virtues, that is to say, permanent dispositions that favor ethical behavior.

Introducing virtues in ethical education makes sense, because, according to Rest (1984) moral behavior depends on four factors: moral sensibility, moral judgment, motivation and character, and virtues shape moral character.

In line with Pincoffs (1986) other scholars have presented significant insights into the role of virtue in accounting, both in practice and education. Thus, Mintz (1995, 1996) presented significant pedagogical insights in the teaching of virtue to accounting students. He mentioned several virtues that enable accountants to withstand environmental pressures and to act in accordance with the moral point of view: 1) benevolence and altruism, 2) honesty and integrity, 3) impartiality and open-mindedness, 4) reliability and dependability and 5) faithfulness and trustworthiness. Why these virtues and not others? The question that arises is on what are virtues founded, and which virtues are relevant?

Introducing virtues in accounting education sounds good. However, not all proposals regarding virtue ethics seem equally acceptable. Some approaches only judge as virtues that which fosters outcomes, for instance, industriousness for a productive life, justice for achieving good relations, loyalty that maintains adhesion, truthfulness to increase the reputation of being a reliable person. According to some authors, virtues are virtues only if they are accepted in a particular context. Thus, Solomon

(1992, p. 107) defines virtue as "a pervasive trail of character that allows one to 'fit into' a particular society and excel in it". In spite of Solomon's valuable contribution in introducing virtues in business ethics, his definition of virtue is more than questionable. Some traits of character can be considered 'virtues' in a particular society, but not in other. What is more, some 'virtues' can dubious examples of human excellence. In professional life, some 'virtues' can be applauded, whereas they are contrary to common decency. As Ewin (1995, p. 833) says,

> given Solomon's account of what virtues are, the obvious virtues in business might well seem to be those traits that make somebody (say) a good salesperson, traits which might include excellence at persuading people to accept falsehoods as much as they might include honesty.

Another problem is found in certain approaches in which virtues are proposed without any reference to norms or principles, which according to some authors is a failure to supply the means to resolve moral dilemmas (e.g., Messerly, 1994).

Both problems arise from considering virtues apart from rules and values or principles instead of simultaneously considering rules, values and virtues. At this regard a valuable contribution is that by Mintz (1995, 1996), who, as noted, emphasized the role of virtues in accounting education, seems to have been aware of the necessity to integrate virtues with rules (standards), duties and values. He states: "Ethics refers to standards of conduct that indicate how one ought to behave based on values and moral duties and virtues arising from principles about right and wrong" (Mintz, 1995, p. 251). However, he did not go further by integrating these three elements. In fact, it would be very difficult to do so, because he considers universalistic perspectives ('principles about right and wrong') and subjective perception of values: "values are basic and fundamental beliefs that guide or motivate attitudes or actions" (Mintz, 1995, p. 251) which are one of the sources for standards of conduct (standards of conduct, based on values and moral duties).

Our proposal, as we explain next, is based on the centrality of practical wisdom and other fundamental virtues, which can be used to group others. These virtues foster human good and subsequently human flourishing.

4. Practical Wisdom in Making Moral Judgments and Influence of the Other Virtues

Regarding practical judgments, Armstrong (2002, p. 145) affirms that "accounting is an art, not a science. It requires significant judgments and assumptions and ten accountants, given complex circumstances, will probably arrive at several different net income or taxable income figures". Accountants must determine the significance of each situation whereas acting with objectivity, independence, professional competence, due care, confidentiality, professional behavior, confidentiality, integrity and so on. Rules cannot determine what to do in every situation. Universal principles can give guidelines, but each situation is unique. Accountants have to judge each situation and, among others, judge what objectivity and integrity mean in a given context; and then act in accordance with the judgment made.

It has been rightly said that a "practical judgment is, at the very least, crucially dependent upon perception" (Koehn, 2000, p. 4) and the ethical perception depends on certain human capacities, related with moral character, which is different from others capacities, such as logic or aesthetics. The capacity to perceive the ethical dimension of reality and to discern good from bad is 'practical wisdom'. This is an intellectual virtue, called *phronesis* in Greek and defined by Aristotle as "the virtue which enables a person to identify the right end to pursue and to select the best means to attain it" (Aristotle, 1941, pp. 6, 5). Practical wisdom may be expressed, for instance, in being sincerely objective, truly unbiased and independent and in following the 'spirit of the law' rather than its letter.

In the Aristotelian tradition, the character of a person is made up of habits (good habits—or virtues, or bad habits—or vices). According to Aristotle, the virtue of man is also "the state of character which makes a man good and which makes him do his own work well" (Aristotle, 1941, pp. 2, 6). In other words, virtuous individuals habitually perform moral actions in contribution to the human good, that is, what contributes to human flourishing. Thus, courage drives us to do what is good and justice to give to each what is his or hers by right.

Habits are acquired by the repetition of acts. Aristotle described the process by which virtues—and similarly skills—are acquired as following:

> virtues we get by first exercising them, as also happens in the case of the arts as well. For the things we have to learn before we can do them, we learn by doing them, for example, man become builders by building and lyreplayers by playing the lyre; so too we become just by doing just acts, temperate by doing temperate acts, brave by doing brave acts . . . by doing the acts that we do in our transaction with other men we become just or unjust, and by doing the acts that we do in the presence of danger, and being habituated to feel fear or confident, we become brave or cowardly.
> (Aristotle, 1941, pp. 2, 1)

Because human virtues are acquired through habit, they provide promptness or readiness to do good, ease or facility in performing a good action and joy or satisfaction in doing so. Human virtues, or virtues proper to human beings as such, are traditionally grouped in four major categories called 'cardinal virtues': practical wisdom (or prudence); justice, which includes all 'transitive virtues' or virtues related with dealing with others; and two self-mastery virtues: fortitude (sometimes known as courage) and temperance (or moderation) (Pieper, 1965; Houser, 2004), which many consider genuine human virtues (Geach, 1977). These virtues are not arbitrary but respond to human tendencies that are moderated by virtues: the tendency of possession (related by justice and other transitive virtues), the tendency to fight to get valuable good (fortitude) and the tendency to pursue pleasure (temperance or moderation).

Practical wisdom plays an important role in the Aristotelian theory of virtues, because each virtue is in the right means between two vices, one relating to deficiency and the other to excess. Thus, courage is between cowardice and temerity. Practical wisdom determines what the precise content of each virtue is in each circumstance (for example, what being courageous means in a particular situation). Focusing on the basic virtues, practical wisdom indicates the right means in each situation regarding transitive and self-mastering virtues. In turn, practicing these latter virtues is a sure way to develop practical wisdom, because this wisdom is practiced in determining the right means. Finally, transitive and self-mastering virtues have reciprocal influences (for example, fairness requires courage and being fair is fostered by the development of courage needed to act fairly). Thus, there is unity and interdependence among virtues (Simon, 1986). Aristotle, summarizing the unity of virtues, said: "it is not possible to be good in the strict sense without practical wisdom, nor practically wise without moral virtue" (Aristotle, 1941, pp. 6, 13).

5. Virtues and Rest's Four Elements of Good Behavior

Virtues, which shape moral character, are necessary for good behavior, but they are not the only element. As noted earlier, according to Rest (1984) moral behavior depends on four factors: moral sensibility, moral judgment, motivation and character. This obviously also applies to the moral behavior of a person in accounting. These factors are related with practical wisdom, transitive virtues and self-mastering virtues, as we will see next.

- *Moral sensitivity* could be described as how the subject comprehends the ethical dimension of a situation. Human beings have a certain capacity to feel other peoples' needs. In the face of certain situations, we experience feelings of compassion, solidarity, sympathy for a noble cause and other moral sentiments. In any professional practice, including accounting, one might feel that a certain practice would adversely affect people, or sense the right thing to do in a given situation. But there are also sentiments of greed, self-sufficiency or even fear that can be stronger than those related to good behavior. Sentiments can also lead to attitudes of sentimentalism, the morality of which could be questioned. Therefore, moral sentiments do not seem sufficient for authentic moral sensibility;[2] practical wisdom is also required. Practical wisdom helps one to grasp the moral good in each particular action. External influences, including the perceptions of peers, education and ethical knowledge can cultivate (or discourage) moral sentiment.

- *Moral judgment*, or capacity to judge which alternatives are ethically acceptable and which are not and to determine the uprightness of the intention. Good behavior requires deliberation and a decision to carry out an action. Making sound moral judgments is previous to making a good decision. Practical wisdom plays a crucial role in this deliberation. It fosters upright moral reasoning by taking into account universal principles and the pertinent circumstances of each situation. Furthermore, some other relevant virtues in accounting—such as objectivity, open-mindedness, insight and perspicacity—can be considered as integrated within practical wisdom.

  Ethical knowledge, including a right understanding of rules, principles and values, which could be seen as accumulation of wisdom throughout time can also help to make sound ethical judgments. This is especially valuable for those without experience and without a great deal of practical wisdom. However, rules, principles and values have to be considered as only an aid, and not as a substitute for practical wisdom.

- *Moral motivation*, understood as willingness to take the moral course of action, valuing moral values (human goods) over other values and taking personal responsibility for moral outcomes. Frequently, moral motivation is the driving force for making good moral judgments and plays a crucial role in selecting the right action and in executing it. Practical wisdom and moral transitive virtues (indirectly also self-mastering virtues) foster moral motivation, because they give a permanent motivation to act well. External motivation, such as moral role-modeling, ethical leadership, culture and education, can also play a significant role in motivating people towards moral behavior.

- *Moral virtues* or permanent attitudes and interior strength for moral behavior. Some virtues include in transitive virtues are especially relevant in accounting. Among them, justice, fairness, integrity, truthfulness, honesty, loyalty, faithfulness, trustworthiness, service to the common good, gratitude and benevolence. Courage perseverance, competence, diligence, professional will, humility and other self-mastering virtues can help to defeat inner resistance to act in a proper way.

6. Goods, Principles and Virtues in Accounting Ethical Education

Considering these four elements, the goal of ethical education is to achieve good behaviors, trying to develop moral sensibility, increasing capacity to make sound moral judgments, stimulating moral motivation and encouraging the students to acquire moral virtues. Understanding ethical education as being only about developing moral reasoning in students is a narrow view. What does it matter is students know how to reason well in ethics in accordance with a certain theory if they are not motivated to act ethically.

The key question is how to develop moral sensibility, promote good judgment, motivate and fostering virtues. Can virtues be taught? (Hartman, 2006). The acquisition of virtues depends on each student's will, but this can be motivated via exemplarity and in the classroom, for instance, present stimulating narratives. In this sense, Crossan, Mazutis and Seijts (2017, p. 676), citing several sources, affirm: "Personal life stories are used to help students reflect on who they are and why they have become the person they are today". A complementary way is using case studies and helping students identify virtues—or lack of virtues—in people who are protagonists of these cases (Hartman, 2006). For his part, Malloch (2017) suggests that ethical training in companies can motivate employees to acquiring virtues.

Whereas virtues can only be shown rules and human goods can be taught and these are connected with virtues. It may be illustrative to discuss briefly the connection between human goods, rules (principles) and virtues by following Aristotle and Thomas Aquinas—a celebrated commentator on Aristotle—along with some insights taken from MacIntyre (1992).

Human goods are 'intrinsic moral values', rooted in human nature. They can be defined as those which, when one lives in accordance with them, contribute to 'the good of the person', that is to say, to the perfection or flourishing of individuals as a human being. Following Aquinas (1981, I-II, q. 94, a. 2), moral goods can be known by human reason from the spontaneous inclinations of human nature, such as the good of life from the inclination to conserve life, the good of true knowledge from the inclination to know and the good of a harmonic and peaceful social life from the inclination to live in society. Truthfulness, justice and loyalty, which are crucial values in accounting, are human goods—intrinsic ethical values, if you like—tied to the goods of true knowledge and sound social life. Without these values, social life deteriorates and trust—a cement of social life—is destroyed.

Humans are responsible for their own acts and, therefore, for their human development, which at the same time produces a good society. Human development requires following rules associated with moral goods. Some rules need extensive study due the complexity of their application in each profession or environment. But there are some elemental moral rules that are relatively easy to learn. Thus, practically everyone can discover the 'golden rule' (treat others in the same way you would like to be treated), the rule of respecting human dignity, 'giving people their rights', honoring promises and fulfilling contracts and some others.

Likewise, abusing power by exploiting human need, manipulating people and considering persons as mere instruments for the sake of one's own interests, are ethical rules regarding what must be avoided.[3]

By acting in accordance with these rules and consequently with moral goods, the individual acquires virtues. These virtues acquired by acting according to moral goods and the corresponding rules can be called 'human virtues'. Understanding rules, goods (values) and virtues in this way entails that they are interrelated.

Moral values (goods) entail rules and acting in accordance with these develops human virtues, which make it easier to grasp moral values. Practical wisdom has a crucial role in this endeavor, because this virtue provides the capacity to perceive human good in every action—practical reason is "right reason about things to be done", says Thomas Aquinas (1981, I-II, q. 65, a. 1).

Rules, goods and virtues, understood in this way, are indeed interconnected. Furthermore, "virtues, rules and goods . . . have to be understood in their relationship or not at all" (MacIntyre, 1992, p. 11); and "rules, conceived apart from virtues and goods, are not the same as rules conceived in dependence upon virtues and goods; and so it is also with virtues apart from rules and good and good apart from rules and virtues" (MacIntyre, 1992, p. 12).

One problem, as we have discussed, is that generally, rules, principles, values and virtues in current ethical education are presented in a fragmented fashion in accounting. But, if moral values, rules and virtues are so closely intertwined, ethical education ought to present all of the elements in their interrelation. The main emphasis although should be on virtues (character) because these are critical for moral behavior, as explained in the preceding section.

Teaching rules, starting with prohibitions, makes sense and should be promoted. Thus, the knowledge of rules contained in codes of conduct is still necessary, but they have to be critically examined and understood in their relation with human values.

Thus, human values and general principles related to them should occupy a central role in ethical education as well. Rather than presenting enlightened ethical theories to students, it appears better to challenge them to reflect on what is really good. This question is not so common because some might view the answer as a mere personal choice. Certainly, each person has to discover what is good for him or her. But such a choice entails great responsibility.

> According to MacIntyre (1992), the starting point of moral reasoning for ordinary and plain people—those who have not received any philosophical influence—is the question "What is my good?". When an ordinary person asks "What is my good?" he or she is asking about what he or she values, but he or she could be wrong and might

re-think the real value for him or her. This leads to "the further, already philosophical question: 'What in general is the good, for my kind of history in this kind of situation?' And that in turn will lead to a fundamental philosophical question 'What is the good as such for human being as such?'"

(MacIntyre, 1992, pp. 3–4)

An accountant is involved in a professional practice which demands reputation and a contribution to the public interest or the common good, but he or she is, above all, a person who asks him or herself, 'what is my good here and now?'. From a relatively early age we follow rules given by parents, teachers, clergy or other people who elicit our confidence. Afterwards, we may realize that some of these were social conventions or organizational rules and came from reasons of efficacy or utility, but others we discover to have a moral sense (e.g., fairness, truthfulness, loyalty). Through this process of trial and error one discovers moral values and the difference between them and their opposites.

Wisdom accumulated over centuries recognizes some ethical values rooted in human nature, which ordinary persons have a certain capacity to adhere to, for instance, the value of human life, contributing to the well-being of others or living together in a peaceful and amiable way. The latter includes a set of moral values that most people can understand as such. Ethical education should be aware of this and present questions and comments regarding human values and how rules correspond to them.

Ethical education is different from rules and values regarding virtues, because the acquisition of virtues is not a question of knowledge but a result of personally deliberated and free actions. As Aristotle realized it takes place by repetition of good actions. Here arises the age-old question, coming from the times of Socrates and Plato over whether virtues can be taught. If virtues are acquired through deliberated and free actions, it is clear that ethical education cannot by itself produce virtues, but virtues can be highlighted as examples. Furthermore, the importance of virtues can be emphasized to motivate students towards moral behavior, which generates virtues. Several authors have given suggestions in this respect. For Mintz (1995) educators should inform students about the importance of virtues and facilitate the learning of virtue through case analysis, cooperative and collaborative learning techniques and role-playing. Dobson and Armstrong (1995) stressed the essential role played by moral exemplars or role models, or 'white-hat' accountants. Stewart (1997) urges the use of narrative to enhance moral motivation. At the same time, he points out how the accounting faculty must be role models to students in the execution of their professional responsibilities. All of these proposals can contribute to foster ethical behavior, if they are applied together with rules and human goods in an integrated manner.

7. Conclusion

This chapter has attempted to present some shortcomings to approaches of ethical education in accounting that consider separately rules (and principles), values and virtues, or in a fragmentary manner. It also holds that the main goal for ethical education in accounting—and of course, in any other professional field—should be to impact the ethical behavior of those receiving the education, and not only to provide a set of theories tools to solve ethical dilemmas. Ethical behavior primarily has to do with character, although ethical knowledge and external motivation must also be an influence. Consequently, ethical education has to be oriented towards motivating moral behavior and acquiring virtues, as some scholars have pointed out in recent years.[4] However, virtues are not a matter of knowledge but of personal moral development. What ethical education can do is to show virtues, exhort and motivate the student to acquire them and explain how to do so. This includes the presentation and discussion of rules, generally from codes, and principles and values that are necessary for acquiring virtues.

From a practical perspective, this proposal requires, first of all, changing the *status quo* of teaching that exclusively presents rules and enlightened ethical theories. Teaching material should also seek a different focus than what is common in many places, which is presenting dilemmas based on cases and providing little or no information about the people involved. What we have proposed is a comprehensive ethical approach interrelating rules, values and virtues. Cases studies should include not only dilemmas but also descriptions of specific people involved in a particular situation, significant facts of their life, traits of their character, as well as other relevant information about factors with an influence on moral behavior, such as how people are motivated by their organization (incentives, moral role modeling, leadership, organizational culture and so on) and by the socio-cultural environment.

Notes

1. Finn, Chonko and Hunt (1988), surveying the responses of 332 members of the AICPA, found that the most frequent ethical issues in the accounting profession (CPAs) were client proposals of tax alteration and tax fraud (47 percent), conflict of interest and independence (16 percent), client proposal of alteration of financial statements (10 percent) and other issues (15 percent).
2. In Aquinas words, virtue overcomes inordinate passion; it produces ordinate passion" (Aquinas, 1981, I-II, q. 60, a.2). Note: passion in Aquinas has the current sense of emotion or sentiment.
3. According to Aquinas (1981, I-II, q. 100, a.1), the Ten Commandments, apart from being a set of fundamental moral rules for both Jews and Christians, contain the whole of natural law. These rules contribute to the

good of the person who fulfills them and one can easily realize that the Commandments are indispensable rules of all social life.
4. See a similar goal for ethical education, although from a different perspective, in Armstrong et al. .2003.

References

Abbott, A. (1983). Professional ethics. *American Journal of Sociology, 88,* 856–885.
Adams, B. L., Malone, F. L., & James, W. (1995). Confidentiality decisions: The reasoning process of CPAs in resolving ethical dilemmas. *Journal of Business Ethics, 14*(12), 1015–1020.
AICPA. (2014). *Code of professional conduct.* Retrieved March 20, 2020, from www.aicpa.org/content/dam/aicpa/research/standards/codeofconduct/downloadabledocuments/2014december15contentasof2016august31codeofconduct.pdf
Anscombe, G. E. M. (1958). Modern moral philosophy. *Philosophy, 33*(124), 1–19.
Aquinas, T. (1981). *Summa theologica: Translated by fathers of the English Dominican province.* New York: Benziger Brothers.
Aristotle. (1941). *Nichomachean ethics.* In R. McKeon (Ed.), *The basic works of Aristotle* (pp. 935–1126). New York: Randon House.
Armstrong, M. B. (1993). *Ethics and professionalism for CPAs.* Cincinnati: South-Western.
Armstrong, M. B. (2002). Ethical issues in accounting. In N. E. Bowie (Ed.), *The Blackwell guide to business ethics* (pp. 145–164). Oxford: Blackwell.
Armstrong, M. B., Ketz, J. E., & Owsen, D. (2003). Ethics education in accounting: Moving toward ethical motivation and ethical behavior. *Journal of Accounting Education, 21*(1), 1–16.
Bond, E. J. (2001). The concept of value. In L. C. Becker & C. B. Becker (Eds.), *Encyclopedia of ethics* (pp. 1745–1750). New York: Routledge.
Bowie, N. & Duska, R. (1985). *Business ethics.* New Jersey: Prentice Hall.
Cheffers, M., & Pakaluk, M. (2007). *Understanding accounting ethics* (2nd ed.). Sutton, MA: Allen David Press.
Cooley, D. R. (2004). The moral paradigm test. *Journal of Business Ethics, 50*(3), 289–294.
Cottell Jr., P. G., & Perlin, T. M. (1990). *Accounting ethics: A practical guide for professionals.* New York: Quorum Books.
Crossan, M., Mazutis, D., & Seijts, G. (2017). Developing character in business schools. In A. J. Sison, G. R. Beabout & I. Ferrero (Eds.), *Handbook of virtue ethics in business and management* (pp. 671–680). Dordrecht: Springer.
Dobson, J., & Armstrong, M. B. (1995). Application of virtue ethics theory: A lesson from architecture. *Research in Accounting Ethics, 1,* 315–330.
Duska, R. F. (1993). Aristotle: A pre-modern post-modern? Implications for business ethics. *Business Ethics Quarterly, 3*(3), 227–249.
Duska, R. F., & Duska, B. S. (2003). *Accounting ethics.* Oxford: Blackwell.
Ewin, R. E. (1995). The virtues appropriate to business. *Business Ethics Quarterly, 5*(4), 823–832.
Finn, D. W., Chonko, L. B., & Hunt, S. D. (1988). Ethical problems in public accounting: The view from the top. *Journal of Business Ethics, 7*(8), 605–615.

Francis, J. R. (1990). After virtue? Accounting as a moral and discursive practice. *Accounting, Auditing and Accountability Journal*, 3(3), 5–17.
Harrison, T., & Khatoon, B. (2017). *Virtue, practical wisdom and professional education*. Birmingham: University of Birmingham.
Hartman, E. M. (2006). Can we teach character? An Aristotelian answer. *Academy of Management Learning & Education*, 5(1), 68–81.
Geach, P. T. (1977). *The virtues*. Cambridge: Cambridge University Press.
Gowthorpe, C., & Blake, J. (Eds.). (1998). *Ethical issues in accounting*. New York: Routledge.
Houser, R. E. (Ed.). (2004). *The cardinal virtues. Aquinas, Albert and Philip the chancellor*. Toronto, Canada: Pontifical Institute of Mediaeval Studies.
IESBA. (2019). *International code of ethics for professional accountants*. Retrieved March 19, 2020, from www.ifac.org/system/files/publications/files/IESBA-Handbook-Code-of-Ethics-2018.pdf
Koehn, D. (2000). What is practical judgment. *Professional Ethics Journal*, 8(3/4), 3–18.
Langenderfer, H. Q., & Rockness, J. W. (1989). Ethics into accounting curriculum: Issues, problems and solutions. *Issues in Accounting Education*, 4, 58–69.
Lere, J. C. (2003). The impact of codes of ethics on decision making: Some insights from information economics. *Journal of Business Ethics*, 48(4), 365–379.
Loeb, S. E. (Ed.). (1978). *Ethics in the accounting profession*. New York: Wiley.
Loeb, S. E. (1988). Teaching students accounting ethics: Some crucial issues. *Issues in Accounting Education*, 3(2), 316–329.
Loeb, S. E., & Bedingfield, J. P. (1972). Teaching accounting ethics. *The Accounting Review, October*, 811–813.
Loeb, S. E., & Rockness, J. (1992). Accounting ethics and education: A response. *Journal of Business Ethics*, 11(7), 485–490.
MacIntyre, A. (1984). *After virtue: A study in moral theory* (2nd ed.). Notre Dame, IN: Notre Dame University Press.
MacIntyre, A. (1992). Plain persons and moral philosophy: Rules, virtues and goods. *American Catholic Philosophical Quarterly*, 66(1), 3–19.
Malloch, T. R. (2017). Teaching virtues to business professionals. In A. J. G. Sison, G. R. Beabout & I. Ferrero (Eds.), *Handbook of virtue ethics in business and management* (pp. 681–690). Dordrecht: Springer.
Maurice, J. (1996). *Accounting ethics*. London: Pitman.
McMillan, K. P. (2004). Trust and the virtues: A solution to the accounting scandals? *Critical Perspectives on Accounting*, 15(6–7), 943–953.
Melé, D. (2005). Ethical education in accounting: Integrating rules, values and virtues. *Journal of Business Ethics*, 57(1), 97–109.
Messerly, J. G. (1994). *An introduction to ethical theories*. Lanham: University Press of America.
Mintz, S. M. (1995). Virtue ethics and accounting education. *Issues in Accounting Education*, 10(2), 247–267.
Mintz, S. M. (1996). The role of the virtue in accounting education. *Accounting Education: A Journal of Theory, Practice and Research*, 1, 67–91.
Mintz, S. M. (2006). Accounting ethics education: Integrating reflective learning and virtue ethics. *Journal of Accounting Education*, 24(2/3), 97–117.
Pieper, J. (1965). *Four cardinal virtues*. Notre Dame, IN: Notre Dame University Press.

Pincoffs, E. L. (1986). *Quandaries and virtues*. Lawrence: University Press of Kansas.
Rest, J. R. (1984). The major components of morality. In W. M. Kurtines & J. L. Gerwitz (Eds.), *Morality, moral behavior, and moral development* (pp. 24–38). New York: Wiley.
Roth, J. K. (1994). *Ethics*. Pasadena, CA: Salem Press.
Schwartz, B. (2011). Practical wisdom and organizations? *Research in Organizational Behavior, 31*, 3–23.
Shaub, M. K. (1994). Limits to the effectiveness of accounting ethics education. *Business & Professional Ethics Journal, 13*(1/2), 129–145.
Simon, Y. (1986). The definition of moral virtue. In V. Kuic (Ed.), *The definition of moral virtue* (pp. 91–124). New York: Fordham University Press.
Solomon, C. R. (1992). *Ethics and excellence: Cooperation and integrity in business*. New York: Oxford University Press.
Stewart, I. (1997). Teaching accounting ethics: The power of narrative. *Accounting Education: A Journal of Theory, Practice and Research, 2*, 173–184.
Veatch, H. (1968). *For an ontology of moral*. Evanston, IL: Northwestern University Press.
Velayutham, S. (2003). The accounting professions code of ethics: Is it a code of ethics or a code of quality assurance? *Critical Perspectives on Accounting, 14*(4), 483–503.
West, A. (2018). After virtue and accounting ethics. *Journal of Business Ethics, 148*(1), 21–36.

7 Building Moral Courage Through a Wisdom-Focused Accounting Ethics Course

Michael K. Shaub

1. Introduction

Accounting ethics course requirements in the United States have allowed ethics educators to gain insight into accounting students' moral reasoning and, to a lesser extent, moral sensitivity. However, the evidence is limited to show that these courses actually affect ethical behavior in the workplace. In the end, the public judges accountants and auditors not based on their recognition skills or judgment, but on their actions.

In Rest's (1986) four-component framework of ethical decision-making, moral sensitivity precedes moral judgment; you must be able to recognize an ethical issue in order to reach a judgment. An accounting ethics course necessarily sensitizes students to certain issues and then the instructor has the chance to incorporate moral decision-making models to help students reach judgments. The third component of Rest's framework is moral intention, which is the behavior that the subject intends to carry out based on the judgment reached in stage two. Stage four, then, is the actual behavior.

> Moral Sensitivity → Moral Judgment → Moral Intention → Moral Behavior

A primary limitation on enacting moral behavior is the subject's unwillingness to act on moral intention because of a number of constraints: pressure from superiors or peers, personal cost to the subject, fear of rejection or job loss and unwillingness to get involved. Many people who have been aware of scandals sat idly by while they unfolded because they lacked the moral courage to step in when necessary. This lack of moral courage has become newsworthy recently in the United States because of the 'Me Too' movement surrounding sexual harassment and because of the revelations regarding the United States Olympic Gymnastics team's doctor, Larry Nassar. But accountants and auditors have had knowledge of information that would have exposed most of the major financial scandals and they are often accused, in retrospect, of not stepping forward with what they knew. Often their unwillingness is seen as collusion with a corrupt management, when in fact it may simply have been a lack of moral courage.

Sekerka and Bagozzi (2007, p. 135) define moral courage as "the ability to use inner principles to do what is good for others, regardless of threat to self, as a matter of practice". Kidder (2003) sees moral courage as something that is learned and its development happens in three stages: discourse and discussion, modeling and mentoring and practice and persistence. For accounting students, the accounting ethics course provides the opportunity for discourse and discussion and classroom speakers may provide a model of moral courage as well. Persistent moral courage comes only through a principled commitment to the concept, practiced consistently, and the support of mentors in the workplace.

Moral courage aligns with the concept of professional skepticism. The auditor's job is to provide an objective viewpoint and to push back against management assertions that are not credible, or those that could have a material impact on the financial statements. Pushing back against a powerful management is difficult, especially when there is a significant level of power difference, as there is early in an auditor's career. Exercising professional skepticism requires that the auditor not just exercise judgment about a transaction or a circumstance in the audit. The auditor must have the moral courage to act on that judgment through testing, questioning and sometimes even confronting the client. In addition, on occasion the auditor must have the moral courage to challenge those above them within the audit firm about the necessity of pursuing an issue with a client.

Students can be taught to recognize the supportability of client assertions in an auditing classroom and they can be taught to understand the moral judgments underlying their audit judgments in an accounting ethics classroom. However, nowhere in an accounting curriculum are they taught the necessary moral courage to follow through on their judgments to act morally in a situation. The accounting ethics classroom is potentially the perfect environment to wrestle with the issues involving moral courage, including understanding what enables and inhibits it. Building a culture in an organization that enables moral courage can short circuit major moral failures before they are allowed to come to fruition.

This chapter describes an accounting ethics course designed to build wisdom into accounting students, particularly those who have already been exposed to the profession through an accounting internship. The development of wisdom is facilitated by the course's focus on the development of dialogical and dialectical reasoning, with a view to minimizing students' susceptibility to the five fallacies of thinking: egocentrism, omnipotence, omniscience, invulnerability and unrealistic optimism (Jordan & Sternberg, 2007). Whereas these fallacies enable unethical behavior, they also enable moral cowardice (or suppress moral courage) in those who observe the unethical behavior, primarily because these fallacies reflect a purely self-interested view of the world. Dialogical reasoning develops through a series of interactions that require the ability to alternately listen to others' viewpoints and communicate one's own in ways that others can understand. Dialectical reasoning tests one's thesis against another's opposing viewpoint, or antithesis, with a view to creating from the tension an adequate synthesis of the ideas. Both dialogical and dialectical reasoning contribute to a more balanced view of others' interests rather than a complete focus on self.

Robinson (1990) characterized Plato's threefold concept of wisdom:

> as (a) *sophia*, which is found in a contemplative life in search of truth; (b) *phronesis*, which is the kind of practical wisdom shown by statesmen and legislators; and (c) *episteme*, which is found in those who understand things from a scientific point of view.
>
> (Sternberg, 2003, p. 394)

As described in Shaub (2017), those in the accounting profession should be interested in all three concepts. The accounting ethics course is by nature contemplative, but it also can potentially include practical examples of wisdom introduced by outside speakers and by studying cases of moral failure and moral courage. In addition, the college classroom is an ideal place to begin to wrestle with the scientific findings from the literature describing morality, through either syllabus assignments or students' outside research.

Seeking to develop wisdom in the accounting ethics classroom opens the door to the development of moral courage. Dialogue in accounting ethics often arises from the tension between duty and consequences that is present in many moral dilemmas and sometimes from the tension between conflicting duties. The need for moral courage arises directly out of these tensions and students are able to confront their need to have ordered values and priorities that will guide them through these decisions. But, even more, they need to understand how hard it will sometimes be to do what they genuinely believe that they *should* do.

In those difficult situations, following through takes moral courage. And, for accountants, there is no better place to learn how to develop it than in an accounting ethics classroom. This chapter will describe what that classroom looks like and how the course can be developed and implemented.

The remainder of the chapter is organized as follows. The next two sections describe the inhibitors and enablers of moral courage in the workplace, followed by a discussion of moral courage in public accounting firms and what the academic research says about moral courage. The next three sections describe the accounting ethics course itself, how wisdom is incorporated in the course and, using the Sekerka and Bagozzi (2007) model, how the course impacts the development of moral courage in accounting students. Conclusions follow.

2. What Inhibits Moral Courage?

What inhibits moral courage? The threat of real harm to the person, or the loss of significant benefits, is the most obvious reason for people failing to do what they believe they should do morally. When standing up for the truth can cost a job or potentially result in indictment, fines or the loss of a license, it is difficult to act with moral courage. This is particularly true when the person choosing the action has been involved for a period of time in sanctionable behavior and becomes interested in making it right.

Others are unwilling to take courageous steps because of the sense that it will do no good. Either the problem is so pervasive, or those responsible for the situation are so powerful that they can squelch any attempt to do the right thing, or the problem does not cause concern to outside authorities, so acting on it seems like a waste of time.

Many are unwilling to step forward because of conflicting duties, including a duty of loyalty to a supervisor or the company. Sometimes a duty to family and the fear of losing a job inhibit speaking up about something that happens at work. This reinforces the threat of consequences. Often there is a conflict between the person's duty to the organization and the duty to tell the truth or, for an accounting professional, the duty to protect the public interest.

Sometimes acting with moral courage is impeded because a profession focuses on rule-based behavior. For example, most codes of conduct governing accountants require that they maintain client confidentiality, with few exceptions. In addition, the exceptions are generally initiated from outside the organization, such as the receipt of a subpoena to testify in court, or they are the result of an accountant or auditor's judgment that is invisible to the public, such as a violation of generally accepted accounting principles or auditing standards. But if the information is unknown outside the organization, such as the type of information that would lead to an SEC investigation or a subpoena, then waiting to exercise moral courage until the investigation is triggered is hardly a protection for those who might be harmed. And it is arguably not moral courage at all at that point.

There is no way to gauge the percentage of accounting misstatements and audit failures that go undetected simply because an accountant or auditor does not have the moral courage to correct the situation. But it is likely significant, in light of the resistance that is detailed in the stories of those who have acted in the best interests of others, at personal cost to themselves. Cynthia Cooper made the cover of *Time* magazine as one of its Persons of the Year in 2002, when she was the whistleblower at WorldCom. But she did so at significant personal cost, as outlined in her book, *Extraordinary Circumstances* (Cooper, 2008). Halliburton whistleblower Tony Menendez invested nine years in the whistleblowing process and its aftermath (Eisinger, 2015). Whistleblowing is not for the faint of heart.

3. What Enables Moral Courage?

Academic research demonstrates that the involvement of a whistleblower in corporate financial misrepresentation events is associated with more significant civil and criminal penalties for those involved in the misrepresentation and higher financial penalties for the company involved (Call, Martin, Sharp & Wilde, 2018). In other words, whistleblowing, at some level, works. But it does not appear to work because people generally feel a duty incumbent upon them to maximize the truth in the marketplace. Despite the presence of a modest number of whistleblowers acting in the public interest, most must be enticed into telling what they know.

Not all whistleblowers are exercising moral courage and moral courage is demonstrated in other ways than whistleblowing. For example, sometimes whistleblowers are compelled to blow the whistle because of charges against them. However, understanding why whistleblowing takes place is informative in understanding more broadly how ethical judgments and ethical intentions can be translated into ethical behaviors, whether through influencing consequences or making duties more salient to the decision maker.

Recent legislation (including the Dodd-Frank Act) and regulations have provided a variety of incentives for whistleblowers to come forward, because awards from the IRS and SEC can range from 10–30 percent of the total recovery. Congress and the executive branch of the federal government have recognized how difficult it is for a sense of duty to overcome the potential negative consequences to the employee's career of speaking up in a situation. The requirements of the laws and regulations generally require a process that involves some level of reporting internally to the organization first, as well as extensive fact gathering by the employee on behalf of the regulatory authority. This data gathering creates an additional moral conflict in the individual who can no longer be seen as loyal to the organization and appears to be operating as a 'mole,' gathering evidence.

Moral courage is at a premium even in the classroom. My business school's classrooms ban food and drink, except for water. In trying to demonstrate professional skepticism in an Auditing classroom recently, I confronted an academically excellent student who was sitting in the front row drinking a cup of coffee. He was largely unaffected and unapologetic about the incident as I described the situation to the class. Then I asked the class how many of them had confronted him about his behavior, because every one of them knew that he was violating an explicit rule of the organization. The answer, of course, was none. One student stated that she might need coffee to get through another class, so confronting him would eliminate that possibility. (I ignored the implications for the quality of my class.)

As I explained to my students, although the coffee was a minor violation, it was an explicit violation fully known to everyone in the room. Yet no one felt any pressure to say anything; in fact, it would have been deeply embarrassing (and was slightly so for me, despite my authoritative role) for them to say anything at all. The social pressure is immense with respect to calling out anyone for modestly disrespectful behavior.

Generally, moral courage is enabled when someone becomes convinced that a commitment to truth or duty trumps consequences. Sometimes this is prompted by perceived injustice in circumstances, or by the violation of others' rights. In the accounting ethics classroom, most cases that are discussed involve someone's choice to step into a situation or to avoid it when the circumstances were perceived as ethically problematic.

What I am trying to provide my students is what a recent PwC-sponsored report (Ramanna, 2019) called 'air cover' to challenge others' thinking. I am trying to give my students explicit permission to call out behavior and ask about the motivations behind it. Whereas it was less natural to do it in my Auditing classroom than in my Accounting Ethics classroom, auditing is supposed to be a profession that maximizes truth telling in the marketplace. So it should be a safe place to have open and honest conversations. But, in the thirty years that I have taught Auditing, I have found those open and honest conversations to be rare and, for many students, awkward at first.

In the workplace, two of the primary enablers of moral courage are exemplars and express permission provided by influential people, both of which are versions of the mentoring seen as key by Kidder (2003). Exemplars came to the forefront as the Olympic gymnastics scandal unfolded. Once one or two people stepped out and identified morally repugnant behavior, the floodgates of moral courage opened. This resulted in an open confrontation of Larry Nassar in the courtroom by a series of the women he had harmed, despite any feelings of personal shame. This happens in the business world when whistleblowers like Cynthia Cooper at WorldCom reveal what is going on in a corporation to mislead financial statement users, despite consequences.

The second empowering force for moral courage, leaders providing express permission to speak out against moral wrongs, is rare. When leaders grant this permission, it is likely to be the result of an unfolding scandal and its granting can be seen as an attempt at reputation management. Even when a leader is not engaged in bad behavior and does not condone it, the uncertainty of the consequences can make it difficult for the leader to empower others to reveal the extent of the problem. In addition, if the moral wrong has been kept secret for a long time, those consequences can be devastating to both the reputation and the finances of an organization. Michigan State University's involvement in the gymnastics scandal resulted in a $500 million settlement (Smith & Hartocollis, 2018). It is this potential for damage to the organization, and not just the consequences to an individual, that can make a leader hesitate, or a whistleblower reluctant to speak.

Many leaders do not find professional skepticism difficult when it comes to questioning subordinates' performance. A wise leader takes the same approach with moral issues rather than simply accepting assertions at face value when there is contradictory evidence. This allows the leader to gauge more effectively the organization's potential exposure to everything from a harassment suit to bribery allegations. This approach is similar to the effect achieved by letting the air slowly out of a balloon rather than having to pop it later. A wise leader minimizes the need for significant moral courage in the organization by proactively searching out potentially dysfunctional behavior.

No leader can accomplish this task alone and so it falls to the wise leader to grant express permission throughout the organization to engage in uncomfortable conversations in hopes of short circuiting major moral failures. Granting this permission to speak and calling out those who are engaged in bullying subordinates to adopt misplaced duties to the team or the organization, is how a leader becomes a moral exemplar. This type of leader empowers the moral courage that turns moral judgment into moral action.

Because, in the end, moral courage is an individual decision made by the professional and it is rare. Wise leaders do well to minimize the situations within the organization in which it is necessary. They do better when they act intentionally to enable moral courage when it is required.

4. Moral Courage in Public Accounting Firms

As I interact with accounting firms, I note professionals' reticence to criticize even egregious behavior by competitors. There is an undercurrent of fear, or perhaps a personal awareness, that those behaviors could happen in their own firms. Just like the young woman in my classroom who refused to challenge her classmate for bringing coffee into the classroom, criticizing a behavior seems like casting stones when one's own firm could fall victim to the same behavior by its members.

Because I direct a large accounting program, I must confront sexual harassment events involving my students. These circumstances often arise while students are on their internships at large accounting firms and, surprisingly, the harassment often takes places at unofficial or sanctioned firm events with a large number of people present. Of course, alcohol is regularly involved, but many people are standing by in the situations described to me who could step in to prevent them, whether as peers or superiors in the firm. By the time the situation arrives on my desk, the woman often stands alone, with her word against the accused assailant. Public accounting firms are uniquely problematic in that the supervisory structure means that people two or three years older than their subordinates regularly make decisions about work schedules and assignments that have significant impact on those under them, often with little recourse for the junior employees. Complaining about these things is seen as a form of rebellion and an unwillingness to work hard for the good of the whole. Loyalty to the team is the paramount value, and this is helpful to the successful completion of an audit or a consulting project on a timely basis.

However, this loyalty also undermines the firm's ability to change harmful parts of the firm culture. In addition, this preeminent value of loyalty, combined with the calculations of potential harm from pushing back against it in a whistleblowing sense, embeds in the employee the reluctance to confront the behavior. Bystander reactions to these situations cannot simply be described as 'blaming the victim' in the situations that I have observed, because those who are reluctant to come forward are aware that the victim did not precipitate the situation. In fact, those colleagues who witness the harassment may well be a source of comfort or protection to the victim afterwards. However, that does not make the employee willing to undermine the value of loyalty to the firm to bring about justice for the victim. Few volunteer to testify on behalf of the victim without somehow being compelled. I have even observed a situation where another intern (from a different university), who was allegedly harassed by the same accounting firm employee, was unwilling to come forward to support my student, despite the fact that she was turning down her offer from the firm whose employee harassed her.

I always fully disclose these situations through our campus Title IX office as a matter of legal policy, so I am not handling these situations in a vacuum. Nevertheless, it is important to understand how difficult moral courage is in the accounting profession even in egregious situations. It takes great wisdom to balance people's interests while seeking to bring about justice and create the kind of culture that maximizes truth telling in the marketplace. It should not be surprising that it is difficult for accounting firms to create the kind of environment that will require truth telling by clients, an atmosphere where professional skepticism is woven into the firm culture. Teaching both Auditing and Accounting Ethics provides me with multiple reinforcement points for challenging students' thinking about their responsibility to question and confront assertions made by others in ways that lead to a constructive resolution of disagreement.

Near and Miceli (1995, p. 679) note that whistleblowing "is not an unqualified good; its benefits are gained only when the complaint is valid and is effectively handled, resulting in positive change". They suggest that it is wrong to expect it to happen when the whistleblower will be personally harmed and change from the whistleblowing action cannot reasonably be expected. My students seem to sense that this describes their situation when they are harassed. In addition, as in any situation that reveals unknown information, the motives of whistleblowers can be either egoistic or altruistic (Brief & Motowidlo, 1986; Near & Miceli, 1995). The perceived motives of the whistleblower potentially impact the credibility of the claims being made.

Recent whistleblowing revelations regarding sexual harassment in Big Four public accounting firms (Marriage, 2019) in the United Kingdom indicate the need for moral courage to come forward with allegations. The stories of twenty whistleblowers from all of the Big Four public accounting firms provide insight into the challenges in changing egregious behavior by powerful partners and managers and into the firms' use of non-disclosure agreements and protracted litigation to discourage outside reporting.

Moral courage in public accounting firms, or the lack thereof, is particularly relevant to my Accounting Ethics classroom, as most of my students have just returned from an audit internship at a Big Four public accounting firm. These ten-week internships during busy season allow the students a realistic glimpse into life in the Big Four at a pressurized time of the year, where there is potentially the greatest need for moral courage and for wisdom.

How can young professionals develop the moral courage that would stand in the face of forces that cause most people to simply mind their own business and do their jobs? The evidence seems to be that most do not even attempt to do so and choose to simply leave their positions if situations become uncomfortable enough. But if accounting is to be a moral profession, it cannot simply ignore the challenges that go with that, whether it is challenging dishonest audit or tax clients, refusing consulting engagements that are morally questionable, or insuring fair treatment of accounting firm employees.

These young people have the potential to become the moral exemplars discussed earlier, but they need the support of wise leaders in the firms who provide express permission to speak out against moral wrongs. This permission is more effectively used to change culture when it is not simply the result of a scandal, but represents the vision of a leader or a group of leaders. To encourage literally means to 'give courage' to others; what the Big Four needs is a broad and deep set of encouraging leaders who are not afraid to hear the truth and deal with the problems that arise from knowing. The accounting profession needs leaders with moral courage to model that quality for those entering the profession. This moral courage enables real accountability internally within the firm and can provide an impetus for holding clients accountable as well.

5. What the Research Says About Moral Courage

Sekerka and Bagozzi (2007, p. 132) describe true moral courage as everyday behavior, seeing it as "what can be achieved by most people", and not just something that exists in a crisis. Sekerka, Bagozzi and Charnigo (2009) focus on five themes that describe what they refer to as 'professional moral courage': moral agency, multiple values, endurance of threats, going beyond compliance and moral goals.

First, those with moral courage see themselves as moral agents and assume that they should engage with moral issues; they are quick to assume responsibility. They are moral responders, principled moral reasoners who embody a set of organizational, professional and personal values. They are able to prioritize the order of competing values. They also serve as models for others in the workplace.

Morally courageous individuals are not fearless, but they know how to endure threats such as loss of their jobs, self-esteem or respect. In fact, their moral adherence to duty can actually be a complicating factor that can undermine their moral courage, particularly when they feel a duty to those in authority over them. Sekerka et al. (2009) indicate that this is particularly true in hierarchical organizations like the military, which was the population from which their sample was selected. Many accounting graduates begin their careers in public accounting firms that possess hierarchical characteristics similar to the military, with each rank carrying significant authority over the ranks below them.

Whereas morally courageous people normally comply with rules and restrictions, they do not limit themselves to compliance, instead adopting a more proactive approach to ethics in the work environment. They see ethics aspirationally, as the pursuit of "what is right, just and appropriate" (Sekerka et al., 2009, p. 570), and not as simply an exercise of following rules.

Finally, those with moral courage have explicit moral goals to their behavior, exercising 'prudence, honesty and justice' in the pursuit of a virtuous outcome. They "show respect and consideration for others and the larger whole, which transcends self-interest" (Sekerka et al., 2009, p. 570).

Thorne (1998) describes the ethical intention stage of Rest's (1986) four-component framework of ethical decision-making as the place where ethical motivation is derived from moral virtue. To Thorne (1998, p. 298),

> *moral virtue* is the positive attribute of character which describes an individual's direct concern for the interests of others despite personal risks (Pincoffs, 1986) and *ethical motivation* describes an individual's willingness to place the interests of others ahead of his or her own.
> (Rest, 1994)

The intention stage is the stage at which the auditor assumes the moral duty to protect the public interest and the place where the decision maker needs the moral courage to take the next step into ethical action.

6. The Accounting Ethics Course

The goal of the accounting ethics course described here is for students to develop in wisdom by increasing their commitment to dialectical and dialogical reasoning and by minimizing their susceptibility to the five fallacies of thinking as described by Jordan and Sternberg (2007). Although Shaub (2017) more fully describes the course, the following section summarizes the course content and its potential impact on the development of wisdom.

The course normally meets for six weeks, four days a week, with most of the students having just completed a ten-week audit internship at one of the Big Four public accounting firms. As a result, many of the students approach ethical issues with an auditor's mindset, which can see ethics as a combination of duty and compliance.

A primary deliverable of the course is the formation of ten or fewer self-chosen principles to guide the students' professional lives. They develop these principles in the context of ethics accountability groups with whom they regularly discuss the issues that arise in the course.

All students select their outside reading to guide their search for principles. I have historically given great latitude in the students' choice of reading, as long as the reading has ethical content, and there is a minimum hourly weekly reading requirement. The students prepare a 350-word 'weekly ethics reading summary' that they circulate in their ethics accountability group to be annotated with comments by its members. The group discusses similarities and differences in issues raised by and perspectives taken by their respective authors. This allows students to practice dialogical reasoning and some of the contrasting perspectives arising from students' readings allow them to engage in the tension of dialectical engagement as well. Each group then prepares one question out of its discussion to challenge the thinking of the rest of the class. We spend the next portion of the class addressing these questions as an entire class. I grade the annotated memos for each person.

Each student also keeps a weekly ethics journal in a Google Doc for my review. This journal may include issues from the student's reading, comments on ethical issues in the news, or discussion of perspectives provided by in-class speakers. I invite a wide variety of speakers to address topics, including some who have been involved in or who have investigated accounting fraud. Students provide a three-sentence summary the class day after each speaker's presentation, forcing the student to provide the speaker's basic message, the reasons why the speaker's arguments were or were not persuasive and the ethical viewpoint the speaker appealed to most.

The first week of the course provides the basic language necessary to enable students to speak about ethical issues. This includes coverage of the basic ethical viewpoints from a philosophical perspective and a decision-making model built around Rest's (1986) cognitive moral developmental model, specifically as applied by Hunt and Vitell (1986). Once this language is learned, the students are better able to listen for the concepts of duty, virtue, consequences and rights in people's arguments.

Because the course is in accounting ethics, the accountant or auditor's duty is fundamental to the course's discussions. The Hunt and Vitell (1986) model provides a good picture of the tension between duties and consequences in the moral decision-making process described by Rest, particularly in the second stage of moral judgment. Hunt and Vitell model the potential consequences as having a direct impact on intentions independent of the moral judgment reached. For example, people may decide they need to speak up about an issue, but the circumstances make it difficult to follow up on their intentions.

We also typically study a major fraud in depth using a case study developed by an expert in the case and we bring that expert in to lead the case discussion, particularly focusing on the auditors' behavior. Sometimes we bring in one of the key figures actually involved in that fraud to provide management's perspective about what was happening at the time. I grade the case solutions prepared by each ethics accountability group that they hand in on the day of the discussion.

7. Wisdom in the Accounting Ethics Course

A number of the students taking Accounting Ethics have developed ethical mindsets that are purely, or largely, calculation-focused and primarily centered on self-interest. To some, the idea of moral duties is a relatively unfamiliar concept, even if they informally adopt some in their personal relationships. For these students, early discussions in the course center around the question, 'What will happen to me if I do that?'. Although this is an important question to ask, it is not the only question and it is often not the most important question.

Calculations are not just incomplete and self-interested, but they are often inaccurate in both the moral intensity of the effect (Jones, 1991) and the breadth of parties affected. This is one reason that rules are put into place to constrain purely self-interested moral behavior. It is also a good motivation for considering what duties a person has in a situation, apart from the consequences.

The accounting ethics course also allows the consideration of others' rights in situations, particularly in tandem with considering how to do what is just. The focus on rights in a search for justice makes students aware of others' interests, even when they believe that self-interest is the rational focus of all decision-making, a view that is readily reinforced in most business school courses (Ghoshal, 2005).

Ethical complexity can be humbling for young decision makers and make them more willing to search for wisdom instead of settling for easy rules. It is not always apparent how one should respond, even when values are clear.

Stories of leaders' fall from grace undermine the presumption of invulnerability. Students who have not experienced the consequences of ethical failures may overestimate their ability to control circumstances or to anticipate obstacles to accomplishing their goals. The stories they encounter, particularly from speakers in the classroom, but reinforced by other forms of storytelling, broaden their perspective about how they could be vulnerable to moral temptation.

All three of Plato's concepts of wisdom are activated in the Accounting Ethics classroom described here: the search for truth by reading and contemplation, the practical wisdom that comes from considering the impact of moral actions on a broader set of people and the development of respect for the research around ethical decision-making. The syllabus readings, students' self-chosen outside readings, the reflective journals and the ethics speaker memos contribute to the search for truth. Ethics accountability group discussions and classroom interactions involving the entire class help students understand the broader impact of ethical decisions, as do certain speakers and videos. Understanding the ethical decision-making research is a significant focus in the front end of the course and helps provide a common language for discussion. All of these approaches are reflected in the group presentations that complete the course.

8. How a Wisdom-Focused Accounting Ethics Course Impacts Moral Courage

An accounting ethics course ought to be designed not just to teach moral reasoning, but also to maximize moral behavior, because people are judged by their behaviors, not their reasoning. Consistent moral behavior in challenging situations is only possible if processes are put in place to enable moral courage in the presence of duty. The course is meant to prepare people for a profession, not just a job, and a duty to others (or to the public) to prevent harm is implicit in the designation of any field as a profession. This duty requires both competence and integrity.

Every code of professional conduct implies duties in uncomfortable situations and conflicts of interest, and accountants are no exception. Other professions are roundly condemned when they are moral cowards in the face of duty. Hospitals and nursing homes that cover up mistreatment of patients and hierarchies that shield clergy from prosecution for sexual abuse, are just two examples of professions where censure accompanies revelation of moral cowardice by those who knew of the abuse. Others' interests must be taken into account by any profession.

Seeking to develop wisdom in the accounting ethics classroom opens the door to the development of moral courage and the undermining of moral cowardice. The need for wisdom and for moral courage both arise out of the complexity often involved in moral decision-making in accounting, balancing competing interests and duties. Clearly ordered values and priorities are helpful to students in guiding them through moral decisions and the classroom provides an ideal opportunity to clearly think through those values and priorities.

In addition to the development of wisdom, an explicit goal of the course as it is currently being taught is to impact the third stage of Rest's (1986) four-component framework of ethical decision-making, the intention stage. Wisdom can potentially influence both of the first two stages, in that it sensitizes an accountant or auditor, based on experiences and knowledge, to the types of situations that may prove to be ethical in nature. Shaub, Finn and Munter (1993) found auditors less sensitive to certain moral situations and this was impacted by their moral orientation. Wisdom should have its most direct impact on the moral judgment stage, influencing both the understanding of duties and consequences and the potential for justice to be undermined through a moral failing. Moral courage has its most direct impact on the third stage, development of the moral intention that follows a moral judgment.

Moral courage results from a person's willingness to consider the interests of others despite personal costs incurred. According to Sekerka and Bagozzi (2007, p. 135), moral courage "is a practice, consistently doing what one knows one ought to do". A morally courageous person "consistently makes decisions in the light of what is good for others, despite personal risk" (Sekerka & Bagozzi, 2007, p. 135). These moral habits are consistent with the Aristotelian view of virtue.

Sekerka and Bagozzi (2007) (see Figure 7.1) propose factors that influence movement to and from the desire and decision to act morally. The decision-making process begins at the left of Figure 7.1 with an ethical challenge that has been recognized by the decision maker (Shaub et al., 1993). This recognition results in a variety of responses labeled A-D in Figure 7.1, which in turn impact the person's first-order desire to act ethically. Of these responses, the Accounting Ethics course described here seeks to influence variables B through D.

First, the course is aspirational and thus encourages a sense of self-efficacy (variable B) and choice in the student to make ethically consistent decisions. It also encourages the student that, although not all outcomes can be controlled, they are not merely victims of their circumstances and their choices can actually affect outcome expectancies (variable B), especially when they act consistently over a long period. As noted earlier, this consistency is actually the definition of moral courage.

Second, the course is designed to modify generally accepted subjective and group norms (variable C). Most accounting students taking Accounting Ethics have considered little beyond ethical compliance, which is covered in their Auditing course and perhaps in accounting firm training on their internships. Our university, for example, does not require a general ethics or business ethics course. The class discussions and speakers are designed to make the students think beyond 'mere compliance' to consider what they *ought* to do in a situation, setting a potentially higher bar for behavior than simple compliance with rules or group norms. The goal is to develop accountants and auditors who engage in the pursuit of "what is right, just and appropriate" (Sekerka et al., 2009, p. 570).

Third, the course is meant to increase students' affect toward the means of attaining an ethical goal (variable D). These "sentiments toward morally courageous actions" (Sekerka & Bagozzi, 2007, p. 133) are not automatically positive, particularly if group conformity is important to the individual. The instinctive consideration of self-interest first may also have a negative affective influence on the person faced with an ethical challenge. The dialectical reasoning that comes from consideration of long-term effects of moral decisions is important in activating affect in students, whether it comes from the courage demonstrated by an exemplar's willingness to stand for the truth, or from stories of harm prevented and wrongs corrected by the willingness to take a stand.

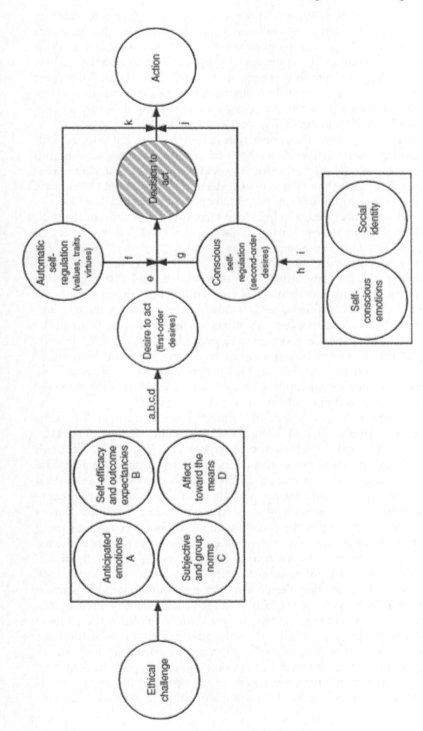

Figure 7.1 Factors That Influence Movement to and from the Desire and Decision to Act

Source: From Sekerka and Bagozzi 2007, p. 134

In the upper right of Figure 7.1, the course explicitly seeks to shore up automatic self-regulation by encouraging students to identify, document and embrace self-chosen principles to guide their professional lives. Self-regulation is a particularly important component of an effective professional life: "So important is this function (self-regulation) that Baumeister and Exline (1999) proposed that self-regulation might be the master virtue, inasmuch as virtues entail overcoming selfish impulses for the sake of the collective" (Sekerka & Bagozzi, 2007, p. 140).

As students develop these principles through their self-selected outside reading, they test the ideas with others in their ethics accountability groups through discussing their weekly ethics reading summaries. Employing dialogical and dialectical reasoning helps students hone these values into something that can potentially provide guidance for life.

The course is also meant to influence second-order desires, or the individual's conscious self-regulation as pictured in the lower right section of Figure 7.1. This is accomplished primarily by trying to redefine the students' social identity as professionals and not just employees of an accounting firm or corporation. This restructuring emphasizes personal responsibility consistent with ethical codes of conduct rather than being content with simply following orders. Students in an early stage relationship with their accounting firm are subjected by accounting firms to the type of recruiting activities designed to engender unquestioning loyalty. They tend to see themselves as employees of their particular firm rather than as members of a profession. This is particularly true because these students have not yet taken the CPA exam or gone through the licensing procedures involved in certification.

Second-order desires as seen in Figure 7.1 are also affected by self-conscious emotions such as "empathy, pride, guilt, shame, embarrassment, envy and jealousy" (Sekerka & Bagozzi, 2007, p. 142). Although the readings and speakers in the course are not meant to manipulate these desires, almost all accounting ethics stories appeal to some subset of these emotions. Guilt, shame and embarrassment often accompany ethical failure and these are reinforced by the reporting that accompanies the incident, as well as by the professional punishment resulting in a loss of prestige or the ending of a career. Some of these emotions are activated by the circumstances or by the firm as well and they may actually undermine conscious self-regulation. For example, a person's self-esteem may be driven by the pride they derive from being identified with the firm.

The combination of a potentially redefined social identity and the activating of self-conscious emotions can powerfully impact self-conscious regulation. If self-regulation is indeed the 'master virtue', it is helpful not to have to rely solely on automatic self-regulation from an individual's values. If being identified with a profession and taking pride in that identity is an effective reinforcement to personal values, it has the potential to influence the accountant's or auditor's decision to act in response to an ethical challenge. And if that person's first-order desire to act morally was strong to begin with (path e in Figure 7.1), the influence of the ethics course (or of effective mentoring) may help to provide the moral courage necessary to take moral action.

9. Conclusion

A student once walked into my office and told me about accepting an offer with the Big Four firm with whom the student did an internship. This would not be remarkable for a student in our accounting program, except that I had kicked that student out of our five-year accounting program for a cheating incident, and I told the student of the need to be transparent with the firm about what had happened. The student was certainly fearful of the response in having to tell several key individuals in the firm, one of whom replied that it was "like a punch in the gut". It took a significant level of moral courage for that student to have those conversations after a moral failure. But our conversation reaffirmed what I sensed when I wrote the dismissal letter nine months earlier—that if the student were willing to be transparent as a habit, life would be more fulfilling. The student did not have to circle back to tell me about receiving an offer; in fact, the purpose was to thank me for the impact that truth-telling session had on that student's life. And the student was humble enough to ask whether it would be permissible to recruit on our campus, rather than simply presuming, after the cheating incident, that it was permissible.

Even when a person knows the right thing to do, the moral courage to act is not automatic. Engaging in conversations and activities that promote wisdom by making students dialogue and test their ideas with one another, as well as broadening the interests they consider in moral decision-making, has the potential to influence the development of the moral courage necessary to be a true professional. The accounting ethics classroom can be uniquely designed as an environment to promote the wisdom that leads to moral courage.

References

Baumeister, R. F., & Exline, J. J. (1999). Virtue, personality and social relations: Self-control as the moral muscle. *Journal of Personality*, 67(6), 1165–1194.

Brief, A., & Motowidlo, S. (1986). Prosocial organizational behaviors. *Academy of Management Review*, 11(4), 710–725.

Call, A., Martin, S., Sharp, N., & Wilde, J. (2018). Whistleblowers and outcomes of financial misrepresentation enforcement actions. *Journal of Accounting Research*, 56(1), 123–171.

Cooper, C. (2008). *Extraordinary Circumstances*. Hoboken, NJ: John Wiley & Sons.

Eisinger, J. (2015). *The Whistleblower's Tale: How an accountant took on Halliburton*. Retrieved December 3, 2019, from www.propublica.org/article/the-whistleblowers-tale-how-an-accountant-took-on-halliburton

Ghoshal, S. (2005). Bad management theories are destroying good management practices. *Academy of Management Learning & Education*, 4(1), 75–91.

Hunt, S. D., & Vitell, S. (1986). A general theory of marketing ethics. *Journal of Macromarketing*, 6, 5–16.

Jones, T. M. (1991). Ethical decision making by individuals in organizations: An Issue-Contingent Model. *Academy of Management Review*, 16, 366–395.

Jordan, J., & Sternberg, R. (2007). Wisdom in organizations: A balance theory analysis. In E. Kessler & J. Bailey (Eds.), *Handbook of organizational and managerial wisdom* (pp. 3–20). Thousand Oaks, CA: Sage Publications, Inc.

Kidder, R. (2003). *Moral courage*. New York: William Morrow.

Marriage, M. (2019). *Betrayed by the Big Four: Whistleblowers speak out*. Retrieved November 20, 2019, from www.ft.com/content/78f46a4e-0a5c-11ea-bb52-34c8d9dc6d84.

Near, J. P., & Miceli, M. P. (1995). Effective whistle-blowing. *Academy of Management Review*, 20(3), 679–709.

Pincoffs, E. (1986). *Quandaries and virtues*. Lawrence, KS: University Press of Kansas.

Ramanna, K. (2019). *Building a culture of challenge in audit firms*. PwC UK. Retrieved December 18, 2019, from www.pwc.co.uk/who-we-are/future-of-audit/building-a-culture-of-challenge-in-audit-firms.pdf

Rest, J. R. (1986). *Moral development: Advances in research and theory*. New York: Praeger.

Rest, J. R. (1994). Background: Theory and research. In J. Rest & D. Narvaez (Eds.), *Moral development in the professions* (pp. 1–26). Hillsdale, NJ: Lawrence Erlbaum Associates.

Robinson, D. N. (1990). Wisdom through the ages. In R. J. Sternberg (Ed.), *Wisdom: Its nature, origins, and development* (pp. 13–24). New York: Cambridge University Press.

Sekerka, L. E., & Bagozzi, R. P. (2007). Moral courage in the workplace: Moving to and from the desire and decision to act. *Business Ethics: A European Review*, 16, 132–149.

Sekerka, L. E., Bagozzi, R. P., & Charnigo, R. (2009). Facing ethical challenges in the workplace: Conceptualizing and measuring professional moral courage. *Journal of Business Ethics*, 89, 565–579.

Shaub, M. K. (2017). A wisdom-based accounting ethics course. *Advances in Accounting Education: Teaching and Curriculum Innovations*, 20, 181–216.

Shaub, M. K., Finn, D. W., & Munter, P. (1993). The effects of auditors' ethical orientation on commitment and ethical sensitivity. *Behavioral Research in Accounting*, 5, 145–169.

Smith, M., & Hartocollis, A. (2018). *Michigan State's $500 million for Nassar victims dwarfs other settlements*. Retrieved December 17, 2019, from www.nytimes.com/2018/05/16/us/larry-nassar-michigan-state-settlement.html.

Sternberg, R. (2003). WICS: A model for leadership in organizations. *Academy of Management Learning and Education*, 2, 386–401.

Thorne, L. (1998). The role of virtue in auditors' ethical decision-making: An integration of cognitive-developmental and virtue-ethics perspectives. *Research on Accounting Ethics*, 4, 291–308.

8 Moral Competence
What It Means and How Accountant Education Could Foster It

Georg Lind

1. Accountants as Moral Agents

The title of this section might sound strange in the ears of those who follow the media news: "A major accounting firm has been sued for almost $5.5 million after the Federal Court ruled it attempted to conceal an error that is costing a business client $660.000 annually" (Zuchetti, 2018, para. 1). The CEO of Audi, a major Germany carmaker, has been arrested and is now in custody (Spiegel Online, 2018). Reports like this are only the tip of an iceberg (Costa, 2016; Beasley, Carcello, Hermanson & Committee of Sponsoring Organizations of the Treadway Commission, 1999). Accountants were mostly involved. "A corporate scandal involves alleged or actual unethical behavior by people acting within or on behalf of a corporation. Many recent corporate collapses and scandals have involved false or inappropriate accounting of some sort" (Wikipedia-eng, 2019).

Yet we must not forget that the profession of an accountant is highly demanding, not only intellectually but also morally. Those who are never tempted to transgress the law will hardly ever do so. But dealing daily with business matters is a real moral challenge. Accountants and their superiors often have to try out new ways of business making and take risks in order to make their firm survive and prosper. This is not only an intellectual challenge but also a moral one.

Traditionally accountants' education addresses only the intellectual tasks of accountants. But in response to many business scandals, accountants' education is offering now also business ethics. The aims and methods of business ethics focus on enforcing old legal and new ethical rules for accounting by promoting respective "values, ethics and attitudes" (IFAC, 2019). However, there are hardly any programs for fostering moral competence in its graduates. Can wrongdoing be prevented only by conveying values, ethics and attitudes, or by adding more rules to the ethical code of accountants? How can the skills and competence be fostered that are needed for applying these rules in everyday decision-making and for solving the problems and conflicts that these rules may cause? For example, firms want its accountants to maximize their profits but also to respect the legal constraints. They want to utilize all tricks for saving revenues but also want to be considered honest. Besides, accountants are confronted with their own dilemmas. They want to make a sufficient income that supports them and their families and protects them against future poverty, but also to stay out of trouble. They need to be loyal to their employers and do a good job, but also to report errors and rule breaking of their firm.

Obviously the increase of legal and ethical rules has also increased the number of possible conflicts as a simple calculation shows: if there are two rules, such as (1) maximizing the firms profit and (2) staying honest, only these two rules can come into conflict with each other and the accountants have to learn only how to handle this type of conflict. This can be hard enough. Of course, this is not the actual number of instances in which this single type of conflict occurs. But once an accountant has learned how to handle this type of conflict, he or she can handle it regardless how often it happens.

Now imagine that there is a third rule added—for example, (3) to report any error of accounting to the compliance officer. Then there can be already three types of conflicts: namely between rules 1 and 2, between rules 2 and 3 and between rules 1 and 3. In general, if 'N' designates the number of existing rules, there are $[(N-1) * N] / 2$ types of conflicts possible. When we apply this formula to our case, the result confirms our calculation: $[(3-1) * 3] / 2 = 3$ types of conflicts. You can see that the number of possible conflicts (and troubles!) increases dramatically (not only linearly) with the number of rules with which an accountant must comply. To give an example: if there are ten rules which need to be observed, the number of potential conflicts raises to $[(10-1) * 10] / 2 = 45$! In other words, if we teach accountants ten legal or ethical standards, they must be prepared to solve 45 different types of moral conflicts in their professional work.

This simple calculation explains why merely increasing the number of rules and enforcing them is a self-defeating strategy. New rules may help to solve certain conflicts, but at the same time they also increase the probability of conflicts. This may also explain why schools that teach business ethics find it hard to increase the moral competence of their students (see later). It may also explain why strict enforcement of compliance rules in firms often hamper the aims and operations of their firms, as Schütz and Beckmann (2019) have observed. When employees fear repercussions by the compliance officer they avoid risky decisions that their company would need in order to succeed.

Therefore, accountants' education must undergo a paradigm shift. Instead of adding more rules and trying to enforce them, it must equip accountants with the level of moral competence that they need to solve their moral dilemmas. Plato stated that "Good people do not need laws to tell them to act responsibly, while bad people will find a way around the laws" (as cited in Costa, 2016, p. 97). Hence, if they are sufficiently trained to act responsibly, they do not need to find ways around the law. Generally, accountants bring high moral ideals to their profession; yet many lack the ability to solve moral dilemmas in an adequate way. When they feel pressure on the job, they may feel the need to find a way around the rules. Does present accountant education promote moral competence or 'does economics and business ethics wash [it] away?' (Hummel, Pfaff & Rost, 2016). Before we can address this question, we need to clarify what moral competence means and how it can be made visible through scientific methods.

2. The Meaning of Moral Competence

Moral competence must not be confused with ethical competence as "is common in ethical decision-making literature" (Pohling, Brdok, Eigenstetter, Stumpf & Strobel, 2017, p. 450). Moral competence deals with our real behavior, whereas ethical competence means the ability to reflect on moral behavior. As the famous moral philosopher Max Scheler has allegedly responded to an accusation of immoral conduct: Like a street sign, a philosopher does not necessarily go the way that he shows. This may be the reason why business schools with the strongest ethical code often are perceived by their students as having the least ethical culture (Desplaces, Melchar, Beauvais & Bosco, 2007). Moral competence is different from moral orientations, values or motivation and should be clearly distinguished from them although there is a link to be made. However, people hardly differ with regard to central moral orientations like freedom, justice, cooperation and truth. Already the Greek philosopher Socrates, who lived two and half thousand years ago, made this observation: "But if this be affirmed, then the desire of the good is common to all and one man is no better than another in that respect?" (Plato: dialogue with Meno, online Gutenberg project).[1] Surveys have confirmed his observation in modern time (Lind, 2019). Thus, moral orientations do not need to be educated and hence do not concern us here as much as the education of moral competence does.

We define *moral competence* as *the ability to solve problems and conflicts on the grounds of moral principles through thinking and discussion, instead of using force and deceit, or submitting to an authority*. Our definition is not only a rewording of Kohlberg's (1964, p. 425) definition of *moral judgment competence* as "the capacity to make decisions and judgments which are moral (i.e., based on internal principles) and to act in accordance with such judgments". It is an extension as it also includes the dimension of communication. Humans are social beings who depend not only on their own capacity to reason but also on the ability to obtain advice from and discuss problems, with others. Thus, moral reason does not mean only individual reflection but also "the eradication of those relationships of violence which are inconspicuously embedded in the communication structures and which prevent conscious conflict resolution and consensual conflict regulation through intrapsychic as well as personal barriers to communication" (Habermas, 1976, p. 34; see also Habermas, 1990).

Solving conflicts and problems through deliberation and discourse, in turn, requires the ability *to judge arguments with regard to their shared moral principles instead merely with regard to their opinion agreement.* If participants in a debate have low moral competence, they use any argument, regardless of its moral quality, just to support their stance on a controversial issue and reject all good arguments of their opponents. Yet, if a controversy cannot be settled through the exchange of arguments, they might culminate into a fight in which each side will use deception and violence to subdue the other side. A peaceful agreement can be reached only by participants who have the ability to understand and appreciate the moral quality of their opponent's arguments and support their own cause only with morally good arguments.

3. How to Make Moral Competence Visible

If we want to study the impact of accounting education on its graduates' moral competence, we need to find a way to make this competence visible. In the past, this was only possible with so-called 'qualitative' methods like clinical interviews. But because such methods are very time-consuming and costly and because they lend themselves to subjective biases (Lind, 1989), we have developed a new kind of test, the *Moral Competence Test* (MCT), which is fully objective. It is available in forty languages and used in many research and evaluation projects (Lind, 1978; 1982, 2019).[2]

For making moral competence visible, the MCT is designed as an Experimental Questionnaire (Lind, 1982). It looks like an ordinary questionnaire but actually it is a multivariate behavioral experiment, applied to individual participants (also called a N=1 experiment), with three design- factors: (1) dilemma context, (2) supporting versus rejecting arguments and (3) six types of moral orientation.

The MCT consists of two dilemma stories representing two different dilemma contexts, followed by several questions. One story deals with a case of mercy killing ('doctor's dilemma'), the other one with a case of eavesdropping of workers by their management ('workers' dilemma'). After reading each story, the participants are asked to rate the protagonist's decision on a scale from -3 to 3 (from 'very wrong' to 'very right'). This sets the stage for the *moral task* that the participants have to cope with: they have to rate arguments supporting the protagonist's decision and arguments rejecting it, six on both sides. We know from experience as well as from systematic studies, that it takes moral competence to rate the arguments with regard to their moral quality. People with low moral competence can evaluate arguments only with regard to their opinion agreement or other non-moral criteria (Lind, 2019). In order to make this visible, all arguments are of different moral quality. All were carefully crafted to represent one of the six types of moral orientation, which, according to Kohlberg's theory, are typical for each stage of moral development (Kohlberg, 1984). The moral quality of the altogether 24 arguments has been checked by several experts.

Because of its special design, the MCT works like an X-ray device. Like X-rays, it is a very valuable instrument for measuring moral competence and the efficacy of educational programs but will also have undesirable side effects if used improperly. It produces valid data only if it used anonymously and without time pressure.

We can literally see a person's competence after sorting the responses by type of moral orientation their arguments have rated. It manifests itself in his or her pattern of ratings. Figure 8.1 shows the response pattern of two fictitious persons, which illustrates this. The response pattern of person 'A' exhibits a very low moral competence. That person rejects all arguments disagreeing with her stance on the issue, even the good ones and accepts all argument supporting her decision, even the bad ones. In contrast, the response pattern of person 'B' exhibits a very high moral competence. That person rates the arguments clearly with regard to their moral quality without paying much attention to their opinion agreement. That is, she rejects bad arguments even though they support her stance on the issue, but accepts arguments even though they are at odds with her decision. We can imagine that people like 'B' are more likely to find a solution for a conflict between opposing courses of action or a conflict with opponents on a controversial issue than people like 'A' who cannot understand the moral quality of the arguments.

Figure 8.1 also teaches us some methodological lessons. It shows that we cannot infer moral competence, or any other trait, from a *single* test item, but that we must always look at the pattern of responses to several test items and that these test items should not merely be in repetitions ('parallel') but should be systematically varied according to the nature of the trait which we want to measure. For example, if the responses of the two persons to the Type-6 argument in favor of the protagonist's decision (encircled) are identical, they mean something different for them. Person 'A' rates this argument very high ('4'), obviously because it supports her stance, but not because it is better than the other arguments. In contrast, person 'B' rates this argument as '4', obviously because she understands and appreciates the different moral qualities of the arguments.

The second lesson that we can learn from Figure 8.1, is that *consistency* is not a trait of the measurement instrument ('reliability') but oft the participants. Moreover, it teaches us that we have to be specific what we mean by 'consistency'. The two persons in Figure 8.1 respond consistently but in completely different ways. Person 'A' consistently defends her stance on the particular issue, whereas person 'B' consistently evaluates arguments with regard to their moral quality. Without saying which kind of consistency we refer to, this term remains meaningless.

160 Georg Lind

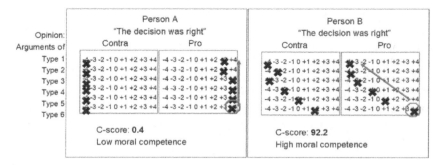

Figure 8.1 Making the Moral Competence of Two Persons Visible

Note: Different levels of moral competence are manifested in different *pattern* of judgments: "A" judges the arguments consistently with regard to their opinion-agreement. "B" judges the arguments consistently with regards to their moral quality.

Finally, Figure 8.1 proves that we can make moral competence visible through using ideas originating in experimental psychology. Donders (1868) proved through an ingenious experiment that people do not always react mechanically, as behaviorist psychologists used to think, but pause to think when they face a dilemma. His experiment laid the grounds for the methods of modern brain research. The concept of Experimental Questionnaires has been inspired by Brunswik's (1955) diacritical method. Like many psychologists, Brunswik was aware of the fact that human behavior is usually determined by more than one trait, as most test makers assume. He was the first one who had an idea how we could disentangle the traits involved in producing a certain behavior. He called it 'diacritical method', which is the same as the method of multivariate experimental design. The *Moral Competence Test* is the first application of his idea in psychological research (Lind, 1982).

The fact that a single response typically has more than meaning has important implications for the selection of methods for assessing moral competence and human traits in general. It excludes the use of all methods that are based on the idea that single items (or a sample of similar items) contain all that we need to know about a trait and therefore can be the basis of analysis. This excludes methods like item analysis ('reliability') and correlation and regression analysis because they are based on the assumption that a single response of a person has a single meaning and, therefore, we can put all people on the same item-based scale. However, our examples show also that we can compare them with respect to their pattern of responses. We only need to construct a proper index for this.

4. The Index for Moral Competence: C-Score

For analyzing the nature, relevance and education of moral competence, we can translate the visual impressions depicted in the Figure 8.1 into adequate numbers. We do this with the help of multivariate analysis of variance (MANOVA). With this method, we can express in a number how much each design factor determines a person's responses. This number is called 'C-score', whereas 'C' stands for competence. The C-score tells us what proportion of the person's judgments is influenced by the moral quality of the arguments. It reaches from 0 (no moral competence) to 100 (maximum moral competence). As we can see in Figure 8.1, this score corresponds well with what we see. 'A', who evaluates argument only with regard to their opinion agreement, get a very low score, whereas 'B', who rates arguments with regard to their moral quality, gets a very high C- score.

The C-score is a pure measure of moral competence. It is not conflated with moral orientations like Kohlberg's Stage score. Yet the MCT provides also independent measures of the six moral orientations that are built in the test. This makes it possible to test the Piagetian hypothesis of cognitive-affective parallelism, which predicts that both aspects of moral judgment, moral competence and moral orientations, correlate highly. Indeed, they correlate almost perfectly (Lind, 2002). However, this correlation can break down when the participants have reasons to believe that the MCT is used as a high-stakes test.

The MCT is theoretically and empirically valid. It is theoretically valid because its construction has been guided by an elaborate theory and is grounded in several decades of moral psychological research. This has been possible because this research has produced resilient knowledge about the nature of moral competence, which we can use as criteria for checking the MCT's empirical validity. The MCT is also empirically valid. Like no other test, the MCT and most of its translations, have been submitted to very rigorous empirical validity tests, which use four criteria that root in moral competence theory (Lind, 2019): (1) Experimental studies show that participants cannot simulate the C-score upward (Lind, 2002). If they could, as is the case with most other tests, it would measure only a moral orientation, value or attitude. As Pohling et al. (2017, p. 466) states: "since the MCT is the only measure with an inbuilt task to assess pro- and counter- arguments and thus simulates a moral discourse, we agree . . . that the MCT . . . measures a cognitive competence aspect of moral judgment". (2) By and large, all participants prefer the six Types of moral orientations represented by the arguments in the same order as moral philosophers do. (3) These types correlate as Kohlberg predicted: the correlations between 'neighboring' types are the highest and between more 'distant' types are the lowest. (4) Finally, the MCT data conform almost perfectly Piaget's (1976) hypothesis of affective-cognitive parallelism.

Although the *a priori* probability of confirming these four criteria by chance is extremely small, much smaller than the conventional p-value of 0.05, the MCT meets all these criteria nearly perfectly (Lind, 2002, 2019). Data from validated and certified MCT versions are fully equivalent and, therefore, can be compared with one another. New tests or translations of the MCT must meet the last three of these criteria in order to become certified as valid. Non-certified MCT versions should me mistrusted.

Some researchers think that the content (story) of the MCT should be adapted to the purpose of the study. We do not recommend this because it would make comparison of different studies almost impossible. Note that the participants' stance on the story plays no role in calculating the C- score.

However, certain dilemma stories can depress the C-score in certain participants, namely when they make them think that their answers will be judged for 'correctness' by an authority. Then, it seems, they hold back their own thinking about the dilemma. This results in low C-scores. For example, accounting students tend to get lower C-scores on an accountant dilemma than they get on the standard MCT (Kodwani & Schillinger, 2009a, 2009b; Costa, 2016, p. 125). Obviously, they feel that they are not free to say what they think but try to please the institution that has commissioned the survey. Similarly, people with dogmatic religiosity refrain from thinking about it when their religion considers it to be a sin (Bataglia & Schillinger, 2013) and soldiers refrain from thinking when they have to discuss a military dilemma story (Senger, 2010). This phenomenon of *moral segmentation* would deserve further studies. Conventionally we speak of moral segmentation when the C-scores of the two dilemma-stories differ 8 points or more.

5. The Relevance of Moral Competence for Behavior[3]

Moral competence has a strong impact on a variety of behaviors that are of high relevance for accounting professionals. This has been shown by many carefully planned experiments and correlation studies, which have used Kohlberg's qualitative *Moral Judgment Interview* or objective tests like the MCT by Lind (2019) and the DIT by Rest (1979). Most effects are not only statistically significant (which does not mean much when large samples are involved) but are mostly very strong as can be seen in the original reports. There appears to be no other human trait that has shown to be as powerful as moral competence.

The following discussion looks at characteristics of moral competence and their application in experiments.

Criminal behavior: already four decades ago, Blasi (1980) has shown in his review article, that criminal behavior is strongly associated with low moral judgment competence. Wischka (1982) reports that the inmate of a German prison who have been convicted of white collar crime, had an average C-score of only 22.2, whereas a parallel sample of non-prisons had a C-score of 39.7. Similarly, Hemmerling (2014), who has done an intervention study in a large detention center in Germany, found that its inmates had a much lower moral competence than comparable persons without a criminal record. These findings suggest that high moral competence immunizes people against criminal behavior.

Honesty: in fact, three experiments show that when participants take a test and are not supervised, those with higher moral competence rarely take advantage of this in order to cheat, whereas those with low moral competence mostly do (see summary report by Kohlberg, 1984, p. 549). This could mean that only accountants with low moral competence actually need to be supervised by compliance forces and that these forces would be superfluous if accountants would get an opportunity to develop this ability.

Keeping a contract: with a rather simple experiment, Krebs and Rosenwald (1977) demonstrated how important moral competence is for keeping contracts. They assessed their participants' moral development and then asked them to fill out and return a questionnaire afterwards by mail, purportedly for time reasons. The participants were given an envelope with return address and stamps. They explicitly agreed. But only in the group of the higher morally competent, nearly all kept the contract. In low moral competence group, the return rate was very low.

Withholding retaliation: Jacobs (1975) ran several rounds of a prisoner dilemma game with the same pairs of participants, in which one was her confidante who she instructed to frustrate the other one. While in the first rounds, all subjects punished their partners for their apparent misbehavior, those with higher moral competence corrected themselves later during the game series. One can easily see how this finding applies to accountants who feel frustrated by the peers or their superiors. Like in the game, communication is often blocked so that the actors have to rely on their judgment how to react.

Assessing *the moral competence of others*: the success of communication in a conflict situation depends much on the perception of the other person. Is this person approachable or not? Does he understand my arguments? Wasel (1994) tested the hypothesis that people with high moral competence are better able to assess the moral competence of other people. He first assessed all participants' moral competence using the MCT. Then they asked them to fill out the MCT a second time as if they thought that a colleague would fill it out, a person whom they knew through their collaboration. Indeed, participants with higher C-scores were better in simulating the responses of their colleagues to the MCT than those with lower moral competence were. Again, one can imagine many occasions when accountants' ability to rate other people's moral competence can play a role, for example, when evaluating customers, when choosing a job or when blowing the whistle.

Whistle blowing: moral competence is indeed important for moral culture in an organization. As two experiments show, people with higher moral competence are more likely to blow the whistle when they discover the breaking of a rule (Brabeck, 1984; Roberts & Koeplin, 2002).

Resisting immoral orders: moral competence seems to be even more important when accountants are asked to follow illegal orders of their superiors. As Milgram (1974) showed in his famous experiments on obedience, many people submit to disparaging orders if they come from an authority. They obey even when they do not have to fear any consequences for not obeying. However, in his experiments not all participants obeyed. In a follow-up experiment Kohlberg (1984) showed that of the participant with high moral competence almost all stopped following these orders in the middle of the experiment, whereas those with lower moral competence all continued to obey the very end.

More positive traits: in their study of undergraduates, Pohling et al. (2017, p. 458) found more evidence that moral competence correlates positively with a number of traits, at least when these traits are self-assessed: positive traits in their study in which the correlated the moral competence: perspective tasking (0.17), emphatic concern (0.20), fantasy (0.16), openness to experience (0.18), agreeableness (0.30), straightforwardness (0.33) and tender-mindedness (0.31).

Moral competence beats motivation: in a series of experiments Mansbart (2001) demonstrated that participants with higher moral competence make difficult decisions more swiftly than those with lower moral competence. The effect of size was rather large. In contrast, various indicators of motivation showed hardly any influence on the time they needed to reach a decision.

Helping people in distress: the ability to make moral decisions appears to play a role in helping behavior, as the experiment by McNamee (1977) demonstrates. She created an emergency situation and observed how participants reacted to it. Participants with higher moral development scores showed a quick readiness to help. However, of those with a lower moral competence, only a few helped immediately. When interviewed before, nearly all participants said that they would help in such a situation, also those who did not. When asked about their actual behavior they mostly said that they were paralyzed by conflicting thoughts. Obviously, the more morally competent participants could resolve these inner conflicts swiftly.

Avoiding drugs: not being able to resolve urging conflicts over a longer time-period can become painful for others and for oneself. This can result in lack of concentration and sleep, which can in turn hamper learning and work performance. People handle such situations quite differently. Some look up a friend or a therapist. Others, for whom such aid is not available, try to solve this problem with the help of cigarettes, alcohol, hashish or other drugs. In her study of ninth-graders, Lenz (2006) found that adolescents with higher moral competence avoided such 'solutions'.

Uncomforting moral competence: given all these positive effects of high moral competence, one should expect that companies would welcome employees who exhibit it. However, in her experimental Assessment Center exercise Eigenstetter (2008, p. 205) found that personnel officers give applicants with higher moral competence worse aptitude ratings. The global ratings which applicants received correlated highly negative ($r = 0.46$) with their C-score. Ironically, the same personnel recruiters attested these applicants a higher quality of work (p. 170).

These and other experimental studies on the importance of moral competence for professional life and beyond, suggest that it does not take a real high moral competence to impact behavior (Lind, 2019). Already a C-score of 20.0 seems to make a big difference. People that develop their moral competence though learning experiences can improve their moral behavior. Of course, a score of C = 20.0 is not a cut-off point. Moral behavior improves even more when moral competence increases beyond this point and we should not hesitate to offer moral learning opportunities also to those who have already higher scores. But if we had to choose between the promotion of a moral elite and the education of the moral competence of everyone above 20.0, we would be well advised to do the latter.

6. The Impact of Accountants' Education on Moral Competence Development

Given the great importance of moral competence for performing well as an accountant, one should hope (1) that this profession would attract applicants with higher moral competence and (2) that accountants' education fosters moral competence of those who lack it.

As we will see, studies have produced mixed results with regard to the first hope and clearly negative results with regard to the hope that the endeavors to promote moral competence are not in vein. How morally competent are accountants? The moral competence scores of accounting students in different countries vary greatly, most likely because of the great variation of the quality of their secondary education, but apparently less because of specific selection processes. However, the data are spotty and should not be generalized unless more representative studies become available.

In several countries, the average moral competence of students is below the critical value of 20.0. Some do have a higher moral competence but a majority lacks the amount of moral competence needed to act morally. Again, we should remember that these are all statistical numbers that apply to many but not all people. Brazilian business students showed a C-score of 15.0 (Schillinger, 2006, p. 99), in Portugal certified accountants were reported to have an average C-score of 13.9 (Costa, 2016), Mexican management students showed a mean C-score between 15.0 and 16.0 (Robles, 2015), business school students in the US are reported to have an average of C = 18.0 (Desplaces et al., 2007).

The situation looks somewhat better in Swiss and German samples. In Switzerland students of economics and business education have a moral competence score of 23.0 (Hummel et al., 2016). In Germany, such students have got C-score of and C = 29.0 (Schillinger, 2006) and 28.1 (Pohling et al., 2017). Because these are average scores, in these samples there are many people whose moral competence is lower than 20.0.

These studies do not provide a sufficient basis for judging the moral competence of accounting students in these countries, nor do they tell us

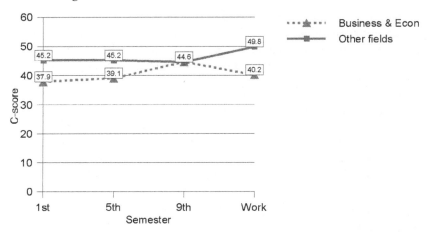

Figure 8.2 The Development of Moral Competence of Business and Economic Students, Germany 1977–85. N = 746, Core Sample

anything about the situation in the rest of the world. However, they give us some signs that there is a need of fostering this key competence for the accounting profession.

Does business and accountant education promote moral competence? The longitudinal study of our FORM Project in the 1970s and 1980s (Bargel, Markiewicz & Peisert, 1982), business and economic students showed a slight increase of their moral competence from first semester to the first year of their employment (see Figure 8.2). Interestingly, their initial moral competence was much higher (C = 37.9) than the findings reported earlier. This may suggest that the moral competence of university students has diminished in the past three to four decade. This could mean that secondary schools have become less effective in promoting moral competence. Other studies point in a similar direction but we do not have enough evidence for such a conclusion. There is too little research done in this area.

7. What Can Promote Moral Competence?

Force seems to be the least effective method to promote moral competence. The more that students feel pressure from family, peers and faculty to excel academically, the lower is their moral competence (Desplaces et al., p. 82).

Can special ethics programs promote moral competence? The *Association of Chartered Certified Accountants* (ACCA), located in the United Kingdom, commissioned a cross-sectional study to find out. ACCA had recently introduced a *Professional Ethics Module* (PEM) in their accountants' education program. The study was designed to assess students' moral competence at four levels of education. Their scores showed no increase of moral competence, but a slight decrease (Kodwani &

Schillinger, 2009a, 2009b). Moreover, this study also showed that the moderate level of moral competence declined after they entered the labor market. Because the data do not come from a longitudinal study, we cannot know whether accountants' moral competence regresses or whether accountants with higher moral competence leave this profession because, as we have seen, their moral competence is not welcome at their workplace (Eigenstetter, 2007).

Other studies showed that if ethics is integrated into the course it has a slightly positive impact on students' moral competence. The absolute effect size is about three C-points increase (Desplaces et al., 2007; Bosco, Melchar, Beauvais & Desplaces, 2010).

Better ways in which accountants' education could foster moral competence are suggested by a cross-sectional and cross-national study of the development of moral competence of students of psychology, medicine and business (Schillinger, 2006). The findings show that moral competence of those students increased during study time whose learning environment was favorable in the sense that it provided them with sufficient opportunities to practice and develop their moral competence. The moral competence of students whose learning environment was 'unfavorable' decreased dramatically. The absolute effect size is 13.5 points [= (27–25.3)—(23.6–11.8)] (see Figure 8.3).

Both approaches seem to work quite well. But both afford a rather large input of time. The effects were produced through four years of study. We

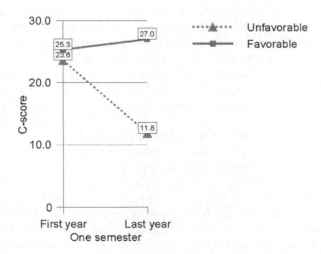

Figure 8.3 Change of Moral Competence of University Students (Business, Psychology, Medicine) Over Four Years as a Function of Their Learning Environment; Absolute Effect Size = 13.5 C-points [(27.0–25.3)–(11.8–23.6)]

Source: Schillinger, 2006, Table 5.1, p. 90

8. A Method for Fostering Moral Competence Efficiently: The KMDD

As we have seen, teaching legal and ethical rules to accountants is very important but it is does not improve students' moral competence. All studies have shown that moral competence does not increase when students are taking business ethics courses. Some studies show that the moral competence of students who took ethics courses or attended course in which ethics was taught, was slightly higher than the moral competence of the other students. However, this difference may have been the effect of self-selection: students who feel more comfortable dealing with ethical standards are more likely to choose courses that expose themselves to these standards. Therefore, business ethics courses would probably attract more students and produce better results if students would be prepared for them through a training of their moral competence.

Teaching only legal and ethical rules without moral competence is unlikely to prevent wrongdoing Knowing rules does not guarantee that people behave accordingly. When they feel overburdened by them or do not know how to solve the conflicts that come up when they try to follow them, they will try to find ways around them.

Many decades of moral psychological research and educational practice have taught us that people's moral competence develops best when they can apply it (Kohlberg, 1984; Lind, 2019). As in sports, we can train people's moral competence best when we provide a challenging and supporting learning environment, that is, opportunities for responsibility-taking and for guided reflection (Schillinger, 2006).

Such training can be effectively done with the *Konstanz Method of Dilemma Discussion* (KMDD).® The KMDD is in use in many institutions of education in many countries for more than twenty years (Lind, 2002; Hemmerling, 2014; Reinicke, 2017). The rationale behind the KMDD and how it works is described in Lind (2019).[4]

Like a theater play, a KMDD session is set up in nine acts: (I) The teacher opens the session with presenting a story of a protagonist (P) who has to make a difficult decision. His (or her) decision is not intellectually difficult but morally; (II) The participants are asked whether they can see P's moral dilemma and which thoughts might crossed P's mind before he or she made the decision. They get time to think this over individually; (III) Then the teacher asks them to talk about this in the whole group: did the protagonist really have a dilemma? What makes it a dilemma? What thoughts might cross his or her mind? (IV) The teacher lets the participants vote on P's decision: was it right or wrong? (V) On the basis of their votes they are divided into two groups; before they discuss they get time to prepare for the discussion in small groups; (VI) The teacher instructs them to convince their opponents that their vote was wrong. The participants must obey only two rules: (1) they are free to anything can be said, but must not qualify any people; (2) The right to speak will be granted by the opponent who spoke last. The teacher only supervises these two rules; (VII) After the discussion they are asked to recall the arguments of their opponents and nominate their best argument for a fictitious prize; (VIII) They are asked to judge the protagonist's decision a second time. (IX) Finally, the teacher asks the participants to evaluate the KMDD session: was it fun? Did they learn something from it?

Several experimentally designed intervention studies have shown that the KMDD is not only highly effective but also very efficient. A single KMDD session of ninety minutes can produce an increase of moral competence between five and ten C-points. Moreover, teachers report that after a KMDD session, students engage more actively in their courses and learn better in all subject areas. It seems that students with a higher moral competence, who can better free their minds from the burden of moral problems and conflicts, have more capacity for learning the academic matter and the ethical rules of their profession. It could also be that students who have a moral cause can appreciate more the value of learning.

Triggered by the teachers' reports I integrated the KMDD into most of my teaching, not only into my moral competence courses during my active time as a university teacher. In most courses, I offered one KMDD session at the beginning of the semester. Aside from this, in my lectures, I adhered to the traditional format. However, I changed the didactics of my seminars from the traditional paper-presentation format to a KMDD-style workshop format. I evaluated the efficacy of this reform of my teaching over the period of eight years, involving more than 3,000 students (Lind, 2015). I tested all students' moral competence before and after each lecture and seminar.

The findings show that this didactical innovation was very effective. Within only a semester, the mean moral competence of the participants of my KMDD-enriched courses increased much more than it would in many years of good education. Remember that bad education does not foster moral competence at all or makes it even regress. The gross effect size was 13.1 C-points. KMDD-style teaching is even more effective than *favorable learning environments*, although their effect size looks similar (13.5; see Figure 8.3). However, it takes four years to produce a similar effect. In other words, the KMDD is four times as *efficient* as the provision of a favorable learning environment.

The KMDD produces high effects with little costs of time and money. But these effects do not come for free because they require a thorough training and certification of the KMDD Teachers. Studies show that untrained teachers do not produce any gains of moral competence in their students even when they offer several KMDD sessions in a row (Lind, 2019). Therefore, we would need centers for moral competence education that offer KMDD Teacher training and certification.

9. Conclusion

This chapter presents evidence that moral competence is real: it manifests itself in the pattern of people's responses to carefully designed measurement instruments. It has also been shown that moral competence has a real impact on many kinds of human behavior that are essential for the accounting profession and, therefore, should be considered a key competence. In spite of this fact, accountants' education seems to undertake no efforts to foster moral competence. Teaching conveying legal and ethical rules has no impact on students' moral competence. The studies reviewed in this chapter clearly show: students in this field suffer from a lack of moral competence when they enter university and show the same lack when they leave.

On the base of this finding, it is strongly recommended that accountant education is supplemented with teaching modules that foster moral competence. This can be done without any changes of the curriculum because modules like the KMDD use up only ninety minutes. These modules could be offered at the beginning of each semester. However, one should not offer them too often. Students could get weary of them. Moreover, they will have diminishing returns.

Presently, any efforts in this direction are constrained by the lack of trained and certified KMDD teachers. The improvement of accountants' education would require centers of moral competence education that educates KMDD Teachers and promote research in this field.

Firms could also foster their accountants' moral competence. They could make their learning environment more favorable:

> If business organizations offer their employees possibilities and requirements for participatory, democratic, decision-making then, because such participation has an educative influence, the workers experience political efficacy. In the long run, they will transfer their readiness to bear responsibility and to act democratically to the larger society in which they demonstrate political engagement as active citizens.
> (Weber & Unterrainer, 2013, p. 249; see also Weber, Thoma, Ostendorf & Chisholm, 2012)

Firms could also amplify the efficacy of these measures by offering KMDD sessions, directed by trained KMDD teachers, once or twice a year.

Notes

1. Retrieved March 9th, 2020, from www.gutenberg.org/files/1643/1643-h/1643-h.htm
2. The old name of the MCT is *Moral Judgment Test* (MJT), which we have renamed in order to avoid confusion with tests that focus on ethical judgment competence.

3. In the following review of empirical findings, I report only numbers of relative effect size (correlations r) and numbers of absolute effect size (mean C-scores). I leave it to the reader to look up the results of statistical significance tests. Note that statistical significance does not tell us whether the findings are meaningful, but only whether the researcher has drawn a large enough sample to get an effect, as tiny as it may be: "There is no good excuse for saying that a statistically significant result is significant because this language erroneously suggests to many readers that the result is automatically large, important, and substantial" (Carver, 1993, p. 288; see also Meehl, 1978).
4. More publications can be found in the list of references and in the internet (www.uni-konstanz.de/ag- moral/home-e.htm).

References

Bargel, T., Markiewicz, W., & Peisert, H. (1982). University graduates: Study experience and social role. Empirical findings of a comparative study in five European countries (FORM-Project). In M. Niessen & J. Peschar (Eds.), *Comparative research on education* (pp. 55–78). Oxford: Pergamon.

Bataglia, P., & Schillinger, M. (2013). Moral segmentation in studies with the Moral Judgment Test in Brazil. In E. Nowak, D. Schrader & B. Zizek. (Eds.), *Educating competencies for democracy* (pp. 71–82). Frankfurt am Main: Peter Lang.

Beasley, M. S., Carcello, J. V., Hermanson, D. R., & Committee of Sponsoring Organizations of the Treadway Commission. (1999). *Fraudulent financial reporting: 1987–1997: An analysis of U.S. public companies.* Retrieved December 15, 2019, from https://egrove.olemiss.edu/cgi/ viewcontent.cgi?article= 1330&context=aicpa_assoc

Blasi, A. (1980). Bridging moral cognition and moral action. *Psychological Bulletin, 88,* 1–45.

Bosco, S. M., Melchar, D. E., Beauvais, L. L., & Desplaces, D. E. (2010). Teaching business ethics: The effectiveness of common pedagogical practices in developing students' moral judgment competence. *Ethics and Education, 5*(3), 263–280.

Brabeck, M. (1984). Ethical characteristics of whistle blowers. *Journal of Research in Personality, 18*(1), 41–53.

Brunswik, E. (1955). Representative design and probabilistic theory in a functional psychology. *Psychological Review, 62*(3), 193–217.

Carver, R. P. (1993). The case against statistical significance testing, revisited. *Journal of Experimental Education, 61*(4), 287–292.

Costa, A. J. (2016). *A competência moral dos contabilistas certificados portugueses* (Dissertation). Retrieved December 2, 2019, from https://ria.ua.pt/handle/10773/18656

Desplaces, D., Melchar, D. E., Beauvais, L. L., & Bosco, S. M. (2007). The impact of business education on moral judgment competence: An empirical study. *Journal of Business Ethics, 74,* 73–87.

Donders, F. C. (1868). Die Schnelligkeit psychischer Prozesse. *Reichert's und du Bois-Reymon's Archiv.* Retrieved December, 1, 2019, from http://psydok.psycharchives.de/jspui/bitstream/20.500.11780/1038/1/F_C_Donders_1868.htm

Eigenstetter, M. (2007). *Verantwortung in Organisationen: Entwicklung und Validierung simulationsorientierter Instrumente zur Diagnostik verantwortungsvollen Entscheidens und Handelns im Arbeits-, Gesundheits- und Umweltschutz* (Dissertation). University of Jena.

Habermas, J. (1976). Was heißt Universalpragmatik? [What does universal pragmatics mean?]. In K. O. Apel (Ed.), *Sprachpragmatik und Philosophie* (pp. 174–272). Frankfurt: Suhrkamp.

Habermas, J. (1990). *Moral consciousness and communicative action.* Cambridge: MIT Press.

Hemmerling, K. (2014). *Morality behind bars: An intervention study on fostering moral competence of prisoners as a new approach to social rehabilitation.* Frankfurt: Peter Lang.

Hummel, K., Pfaff, D., & Rost, K. (2016). Does economics and business ethics wash away moral judgment competence? *Journal of Business Ethics.* Retrieved December 10, 2019, from https://static.nzz.ch/files/0/9/9/Ökonomen_1.1874 4099.pdf_1.18744099.pdf

IFAC. (2019). *Handbook of international education pronouncements.* Retrieved December 2, 2019, from www.iaesb.org/publications/2017-handbook-international-education-pronouncements

Jacobs, M. K. (1975). *Women's moral reasoning and behavior in a contractual form of prisoner's dilemma* (Dissertation). University of Toledo, Ohio.

Kodwani, D., & Schillinger, M. (2009a). *Teaching ethics to accountants: Study of accountant's dilemma as part of ACCA professional ethics module.* Report submitted to *Association of Chartered Certified Accountants*, Glasgow. Retrieved December 1, 2019, from www.uni-konstanz.de/ag-moral/mut/mjt-references.htm#kodwani_2009

Kodwani, D., & Schillinger, M. (2009b). *Ethics to accountants: Challenges of a global qualification.* Paper presented at the 3rd International Symposium 'Can morality be taught? Is it a competence?', Konstanz, Germany.

Kohlberg, L. (1964). Development of moral character and moral ideology. In M. L. Hoffman & L. W. Hoffman (Eds.), *Review of child development research*, Vol. 1 (pp. 381–431). New York: Russel Sage Foundation.

Kohlberg, L. (1984). *The psychology of moral development: The nature and validity of moral stages.* San Francisco: Harper & Row.

Krebs, D. L., & Rosenwald, A. (1977). Moral reasoning and moral behavior in conventional adults. *Merrill Palmer Quarterly, 23*, 77–87.

Lenz, B. (2006). *Moralische Urteilsfähigkeit als eine Determinante für Drogenkonsum bei Jugendlichen* (Unpublished masters thesis). University of Konstanz, Konstanz.

Lind, G. (1978). Wie misst man moralisches Urteil? Probleme und alternative Möglichkeiten der Messung eines komplexen Konstrukts. In G. Portele (Ed.), *Sozialisation und Moral* (pp. 171–201). Weinheim: Beltz.

Lind, G. (1982). Experimental questionnaires: A new approach to personality research. In A. Kossakowski & K. Obuchowski (Eds.), *Progress in psychology of personality* (pp. 132–144). Amsterdam, NL: North-Holland.

Lind, G. (1989). Measuring moral judgment: A review of 'The measurement of moral judgment' by Anne Colby and Lawrence Kohlber. *Human Development, 32*, 388–397.

Lind, G. (2002). *Ist Moral lehrbar? Ergebnisse der modernen moral-psychologischen Forschung* (2nd ed.). Berlin: Logos-Verlag.

Lind, G. (2015). Favorable learning environments for moral competence development: A multiple intervention study with nearly 3.000 students in a higher education context. *International Journal of University Teaching and Faculty*

Development, 4. Retrieved December 11, 2019, from www.novapublishers.com/catalog/product_info.php?products_id=53411

Lind, G. (2019). *How to teach moral competence: New: Discussion theater.* Berlin: Logos.

Mansbart, F.-J. (2001). *Motivationale Einflüsse der moralischen Urteilsfähigkeit auf die Bildung von Vorsätzen* (Unpublished masters' thesis). University of Konstanz, Konstanz.

McNamee, S. (1977). Moral behavior, moral development and motivation. *Journal of Moral Education, 7*(1), 27–31.

Meehl, P. E. (1978). Theoretical risks and tabular asterisks: Sir Karl, Sir Ronald, and the slow progress of soft Psychology. *Journal of Consulting and Clinical Psychology, 46,* 806–834.

Milgram, S. (1974). *Obedience to authority: An experimental view.* New York: Tavistock.

Piaget, J. (1976). The affective unconscious and the cognitive unconscious. In B. Inhelder & H. H. Chipman (Eds.), *Piaget and his school* (pp. 63–71). New York: Springer.

Pohling, R., Brdok, D., Eigenstetter, M., Stumpf, S., & Strobel, A. (2017). What is ethical competence? The role of empathy, personal values, and the five-factor model of personality in ethical decision-making. *Journal of Business Ethics, 137*(3), 449–474.

Reinicke, M. (2017). *Moral competence reloaded.* Chemnitz, self-published. Order from martina.reinicke@outlook.de.

Rest, J. (1979). *Development in judging moral issues.* Minneapolis: University of Minnesota Press.

Roberts, D. H., & Koeplin, J. P. (2002). Impact of cognitive moral judgment ability on knowledge of red flags. *Research on Accounting Ethics, 8,* 125–143.

Robles, V. (2015). Moral judgment competence between systems and administration students. *Ethics in Progress, 6*(2), 26–37.

Schillinger, M. (2006). *Learning environments and moral development: How university education fosters moral judgment competence in Brazil and two German-speaking countries.* Aachen: Shaker-Verlag.

Schütz, M., & Beckmann, R. (2019). *Jenseits der Regeln. Fast jedes Unternehmen bekennt sich zur 'Compliance'—doch mehr Kontrolle birgt Probleme. Es gibt Grauzonen.* Retrieved December 13, 2019, from www.sueddeutsche.de/wirtschaft/forum-jenseits-der-regeln-1.4432729

Senger, R. (2010). Segmentation of soldiers' moral judgment. In G. Lind, H. A. Hartmann & R. Wakenhut (Eds.), *Moral judgments and social education* (pp. 221–242). New Brunswik, NJ: Transaction Publisher.

Spiegel online. (2018). *Audi-Chef Rupert Stadler vorläufig verhaftet.* Retrieved December 2, 2019, from www.spiegel.de/wirtschaft/unternehmen/audi-chef-rupert-stadler-festgenommen-a-1213533.html

Wasel, W. (1994). *Simulation moralischer Urteilsfähigkeit* (Unpublished master's thesis). University of Konstanz, Germany.

Weber, W. G., Thoma, M., Ostendorf, A., & Chisholm, L. (Eds.). (2012). *Democratic competences and social practices in organizations.* Wiesbaden: Springer.

Weber, W. G., & Unterrainer, C. (2013). Democratic education potentials in business organizations. In E. Nowak, D. Schrader & B. Zizek (Eds.), *Educating competencies for democracy* (pp. 249–263). Frankfurt am Main: Peter Lang Verlag.

Wikipedia-eng. (2019). *List of corporate collapses and scandals.* Retrieved December 2, 2019, from https://en.wikipedia.org/wiki/List_of_corporate_collapses_and_scandals

Wischka, B. (1982). *Moralisches Bewusstsein und Empathie bei Strafgefangenen* (Unpublished master's thesis). University of Marburg, Germany.

Zuchetti, A. (2018). *Accountant sued for $5m for counseling error.* Retrieved December 8, 2019, from www.mybusiness.com.au/management/5313-accountant-sued-5-5m-for-concealing-error

Index

Note: Page numbers in **bold** indicate a table on the corresponding page.

3D printing 83, 90

abaco schools 4–7, 9–10
accountancy profession 107, 114
accountants xvi–xvii, 33, 38, 44, 47, 53, 55, 58–62, 64, 66, 68, 116n1, 121–122, 125–127, 132, 137, 139–140, 149–150, 163, 168; aspiring/future/prospective 53, 55, 59, 64, 68, 101; codes of conduct for 121; as critical thinkers 111–114; educating the next generation of 100–116; education and moral competence 165–167, 170; education of 107, 155–156, 165–167, 170; ethics of 60, 101–105, 114, 116n1; moral competence of 163, 165, 167, 170; as moral agents 155–157; perception of 101, 103–105, 114, 116n1; professional 101, 106–109, 111, 114; 'white hat' 132; *see also* Certified Public Accountant (CPA)
accounting: bodies 59; codes 122; curricula xvi, 44–46, 51, 53–57, 56, 59–60, 64–66, 138; faculty 45, 59, 64–65, 67, 132; firms 36, 53, 59, 114, 139, 143–146, 150, 152, 155; historians 6; internship 138; journals 51; managerial 121; organizations 102; profession xviii, xix, 53, 58–59, 66, 101–102, 109, 114, 120, 133n1, 139, 144–145, 166, 170; professionals xvi, xviii, 58, 60, 62–63, 100, 103, 105–106, 111–112, 115, 122, 140, 162; programs 59, 64, 143, 153;

researchers 45; rules 115; scandals 114; standards 115, 122; students xvii, xix, 46–47, 54–55, 59–60, 62–65, 107, 110, 121, 125, 137–139, 150, 162, 165; tax 121
accounting curriculum xvi, 44–46, 51, 54–57, 56, 59–60, 138; ethics in 64–66; issues in 66–67; stand-alone courses vs. integration 65–66
accounting ethics xvi, 31, 33, 37–41, 45, 47, 51–52, 62, 65–67, 69, 100, 120, 123, 139, 152; vs. business ethics 69; courses xvii–xviii, 65, 137–139, 142, 144–153; history of 31–41; research 41; textbooks 122; *see also* accounting ethics education research
accounting ethics education xvi–xvii, xix, 44–47, 51–64, 56, 66–69, 122, 124; *see also* accounting ethics education research
accounting ethics education research xvii, 44–69; themes 46, 55–67, 56
Accounting Review, The 50, 51
advocacy culture 38
Africa 3
agency theory 36, 96, 97n7
Albania 54
altruism 40, 125, 144
Amazon 86
American Institute of Certified Public Accountants (AICPA) 122, 133n1; Code of Professional Conduct 62, 122
apprenticeship 5–6, 9, 26
Aquinas, Thomas 130–131, 133n2, 133–134n3

Index

Aristotle 16, 125, 127–128, 130, 132; Aristotelian view 124, 127–128, 150
Arthur Andersen (accounting firm) 53
artificial intelligence 83, 85, 89–90, 95
Association of Chartered Certified Accountants (ACCA) 166
Association to Advance Collegiate Schools of Business (AACSB) 101, 112
Audi 155
auditing xvii, 26, 40, 51, 58, 100, 102, 108, 121–122, 138, 140–142, 144, 150
auditors xvi–xvii, 100, 137, 148–150
Augustine, St 18
Australia 44, 52–53, 60, 83, 94
Austria 12

bankers 4–5, 8, 11, 52
Bankers Trust 52
banking 3, 8, 11, 13, 23, 25; see also merchant banking
banks 4, 8–9, 11, 23
Barlow Clowes 52
barter 11, 15
behavior xvii, xix, 12, 33, 36–37, 39–40, 55, 60–64, 67, **96**, 100, 103, 112, 121, 124, 137, 141–146, 148–150, 157–158, 160, 162, 164–165, 170; autonomous 90; bad 36, 142; correct 35, 124; criminal 162; helping 164; mis- 39, 163; organizational 90; professional 108, 111, 123–127; prosocial 37; righteous 35, 39; rule-based 140; sanctionable 140; selfish 40; see also behavioral attitudes; ethical behavior; moral behavior
behavioral attitudes xvii
Bellandi, Simone 5
benevolence 125, 129
BHS xvi
big data 94, 97n1, 114
Big Four public accounting firms 144–146, 153
blockchain 83, 86
Bond Corporation 52
book closure process 27n3
bookkeepers 3, 5–9, 11, 19–20; merchant- 24–26
bookkeeping 3, 5–11, 20, 22, 26, 105; single entry 4; see also double entry bookkeeping
Brazil 165

breakthrough technologies 90
business ethics 26, 44, 46–47, 54, 66–67, 69, 90–93, 97, 100, 123, 126, 155–157; courses 54, 66, 150, 168
business eunomics 84, 92–94, 97

capitalism 31, 35–36, 38, 92
cardinal virtues 128
Carillion xvi
Casanova, Alvise 8
case studies xvi, 34, 55, 57–58, 68, 94, **95**, 113, 130, 147
Catholic Church 11–13, 16
Certified Public Accountant (CPA) 60, 102, 122, 133n1, 152; see also CPA examination
character xviii, 16, 62, 120, 122, 124–129, 131, 133, 146
China 53–54, 60, 86; guanxi 60
Christopher Quintex 52
Code of Justinian 16
codes of conduct xvi–xvii, 44, 62, 105, 121–122, 124, 131, 140, 152
cognitive-affective parallelism hypothesis 161
common good 12, 88, 129, 132; see also public good; public interest
compliance 20, 62, 89, 108–109, 122, 145–146, 150, 156, 163; see also compliance officer
compliance officer 156
confidentiality 108, 111, 122–123, 127, 140
conflicts of interest 107, 133n1, 149
Constantinople 3
consulting 121, 143, 145
Cooper, Cynthia 140, 142
corporate governance 36, 66, 90, 97n7
Corporate Law Economic Reform Program (CLERP) 9 Act 44
cost/benefit analysis 31
Cotrugli, Benedetto 6, 9–11, 13–19, 25–26; *Book of the Art of Trade* 9–10, 13
CPA examination 60, 152
credit 3–4, 8–9, 11, 14, 16–17, 20, 22–25
critical thinking xvi, 57, 95, 101, 115, 116n4; teaching of 111–114
cultural beliefs: and moral reasoning 100
cyber security 86, **96**

Index 177

data analytics xvii
Datini, Francesco di Marco 5, 7–9
debt 3–5, 8–9, 11, 14, 20, 23–25
democracy 38, 89, 92
dependability 125
De Raphaeli, Marino 9–11, 13
diacritical method 160
dialectical reasoning 138–139, 146–147, 150, 152
dialogical reasoning 138–139, 146–147, 152
DIT 162
Dodd-Frank Act 141
double entry bookkeeping xvi, 3–4, 7, 9–10, 20, 26
due care xvii, 108, 111, 122–123, 127
duties xviii, 37, 61, 89, 102–103, 122–124, 126, 139–143, 146–149; *see also* moral duties

economics 33, 40, 90, 93, 95, 102, 157, 165
egocentrism 138
e-learning 56–57
empowerment 84–86
England 12; London 3; *see also* United Kingdom
enlightenment, the 124
Enron xvi, 53, 58
ESM Government Securities 52
ethical action xviii, 35, 38, 41, 62, 146
ethical behavior xvi, xviii, 40–41, 53, 59, 61–62, 66–67, 101–104, 121–125, 132–133, 137; un- 61, 105, 121, 138, 155
ethical challenge 150, 153
ethical codes 34, 37, 62, 105, 152, 155, 157
ethical competence 157
ethical consciousness 54, 100–101, 106
ethical decision-making 53, 56, 60–63, 67–68, 137, 146, 148–149, 157
ethical decision-making models xvii, 66, 90
ethical dilemmas xvi, 57, 67, 106, 111, 123–125, 133
ethical intent/intentions xviii, 61, 141, 146
ethical motivation 146
ethical orientation xvii, 33, 62, 100–101, 105, 112
ethical principles 109, 111, 120

ethical relativism 100; and age 100–101; and education 101
ethical research 35, 37–38, 40–41, 88
ethical rules 131, 155–156, 168–170
ethical sensitivity xvii, 33, 54, 61, 65, 68, 101, 105, 111
ethical standards 108–109, 120, 156, 168
ethical theories xviii, 57, 66, 93–94, 97, 123–125, 131, 133
ethical values 13, 19, 111, 121, 130, 132
ethical virtues 120–133
ethics: accountability groups 147–148, 152; action-centered 120; agent-centered 120; Buddhist 54; courses 53, 62–63, 65, 88, 153, 168; coverage xvii, 44, 64; development 68; instruction 61, 64–65; interventions 44, 52–53, 58, 63; Islamic 54; journals 147; literature 39, 44; principle-based 123–125; research 35–36, 38, 40; subject matter 51, 55, 65–66; teaching of 45, 51, 53, 55–58, 67; training 54, 59–60, 62, 64–65; ethics *see also* accounting ethics; business ethics; ethics education; virtue ethics
ethics codes xvii; *see also* codes of conduct
ethics education xvi–xviii, xix, 44–47, 51–69, 120; business 90; importance of 58–60; *see also* accounting ethics education
ethics-unfriendly environments 100
eunomics 91–93; *see also* business eunomics
Europe 3–5, 8, 25, 53; medieval 3, 25
European Accounting Association (EAA) 109
experiential learning 57, 94, 96
external audit 36

Facebook 86
faithfulness 125, 129
financial planning 121
financial reports xvii, 26
fortitude (courage) 128; *see also* moral courage
Fourth Industrial Revolution (4IR) xvii, 83–87, 91, 93, 95–97, 95
France 5, 12

fraud xvi–xvii, 12, 18, 22, 26, 32, 34, 58–59, 61, 100, 147–148; tax 133n1
free will 41

games 56–57, 68
GenMe (Generation Me) 101–106, 113–115
Germany 12, 155, 162, 165, **166**
Ghana 54
globalization 60, 85
golden rule 130
Google 86; Doc 147; Scholar 46
governance 44, 84, 91–92, **95**, 97; agile 84, 87, **95**; *see also* corporate governance
guilds xvii, 12, 14, 25, 27n5

habits 15–16, 124, 127, 150, 153; bad 127; good 127
Halliburton 140
HealthSouth 58
higher education xix, 83, 91, 94, 96, 106
HIH Insurance 53
honesty xvii, 13, 18, 38, 62, 103, 125–126, 129, 146, 163
human-centered approach 84, 87, 89, 92, 94, 97
human flourishing 124, 126–127
human good 126–127, 131
human goods 120–121, 129–130, 132
human nature 125, 130, 132
human virtues 127–128, 131; *see also* virtues

impartiality 125
India xvi, 53–54, 60
Indonesia 54, 60
industriousness 125
Industry 4.0 83–97; impact on higher education 93–96; impact on society 84–87; and means-end relation 90–93; and technology and ethics 87–89; and value transformation 89–90, 93–96
Initial Professional Development (IPD) 108–109, 111
integrity xvii, 17, 23, 62, 64, 87, 102, 107, 111, 114, 122–123, 125, 127, 129, 149; *see also* integrity theory
integrity theory 97n7
International Accounting Education Standards Board (IAESB) 101, 107–109, 115, 116n3
International Code of Ethics for Professional Accountants 107, 114, 122
International Education Information Papers (IEIPs) 107
International Education Practice Statements (IEPs) 107
International Education Standards (IESs) 107, 109
International Ethics Standards Board of Accountants (IESBA) 107, 116n4, 122–123; International Code of Ethics for Professional Accountants 107, 114, 122–123
International Federation of Accountants (IFAC) 101–102, 107, 123
international money transfers 23
internet 86, 88, 90, 171n4
Internet of Things (IoT) 90, **95**
internship 94, 138, 143, 145–147, 150, 153
invulnerability 138, 148
Iran 54
IRS 141
Issues in Accounting Education 46, 48, 51
Italy xvi, 3–5, 12, 20, 25, 27n3, 102, 106; Florence 4–5, 7–8; Genoa 4; Lombardy 4; Naples 10, 13; Pisa 5, 7–8; Sicily 15; Tuscany 4; *see also* Venice

Japan 100
Journal of Accounting Education 46, 48, 51
Journal of Business Ethics 46, **48**, 51
justice 89, 125, 127–130, 144, 146, 148–149, 157
'just price' 11, 13, 27n7

Kantianism xviii, 123–124
Kantian theory 123–124
Kohlberg, Lawrence 52, 157, 161–164; theory of cognitive moral development 52, 63, 66, 159
Konstanz Method of Dilemma Discussion (KMDD) 168–170

Latin America 96, 100
lecture method 56–57, 109–110, 169
lifelong learning 93, 106
loyalty 60, 125, 129–130, 132, 140, 143–144, 152

Malaysia 53–54, 60
Manucci, Amatino 5
marketplace 36, 141–142, 144; cyber 89
means-end relation 90–93
Medici 8
Mediterranean trade 5
Menendez, Tony 140
merchant banking 11, 25
'Me Too' movement 137
Mexico 54, 165
Milgram, S. 163–164
MiniScribe 52
modernism 31, 34
modernity xvii, 31–33, 35–38, 40–41
modern moral philosophy 124
moral agency 145
moral behavior 123, 125, 128–129, 131–133, 137, 148–149, 157, 165
moral capability 56, 56, 63–64
moral character 120, 125, 127–128
moral competence 155–170; definition 157
Moral Competence Test (MCT) xviii, 158–163, 170n2; C-score xviii, 160–165, 171n3
moral courage xvi, xviii, 137–139, 153; accounting ethics course and 149–153; enablers of 140–143; inhibitors of 139–140; in public accounting firms 143–145; research about 145–146
moral cowardice 138, 149
moral decision-making 137, 147, 149, 153
moral decisions 149–150, 164
moral development 52, 54, 56, 63–64, 66, 68, 133, 147, 159, 163–164
moral duties xviii, 126, 146, 148
moral education 62, 125
moral exemplars 132, 143, 145
moral intention 137, 150
moral judgment 61, 122, 124–126, 128–130, 137–138, 143, 147, 149–150, 157, 161–162; *see also* Moral Judgment Test (MJT)
Moral Judgment Test (MJT) 170n2
moral motivation 125, 128–130, 132
moral principles xviii, 122, 124, 157–158
moral reasoning xviii, 54, 56, 56, 61, 63–64, 67, 123–124, 129–131, 137, 149; and cultural beliefs 100
moral rules 130, 133–134n3

moral segmentation 162
moral sensibility 125, 128–130
moral standards 59
moral values 14, 16, 19, 104, 125, 129–132
moral virtues 17, 129–130

Nassar, Larry 137, 142
natural law 133–134n3
Neo-Kantian theory 123
Netherlands, the 12
Nigeria 54
norms xvii, 12, 39, 120, 122, 124, 126; ethical xviii; group 150
novels 56, 68

objectivity 31, 107, 111, 122–123, 127, 129
omnipotence 138
omniscience 138
open-mindedness 125, 129
orders: illegal 163; immoral 163–164

Pacioli, Luca xvi, 10–11, 20–26, 27n8; *Summa Arithmetica* 10
Parmalat xvi, 53
pedagogical diversity 57
Pegolotti, Francesco Balducci 13, 27n6; *La pratica della mercatura* 13, 27n6
Philippines, the 54
phronesis 127, 139
Piaget 161
Plato 132, 139, 148, 156–157; threefold concept of wisdom 139
populism 87
Portugal 165
practical wisdom (prudence) xvii–xviii, 120–126, 126–129, 131, 139, 146, 148; *see also phronesis*
price fixing xvii, 12
principles xviii, 12, 44, 62, 89, 92–93, 116n3, 120–126, 129–131, 133, 138, 147, 152, 157; accounting 140; of agile governance 87; business 115; fundamental 107–108, 111; self-chosen 152; universal 124, 127, 129; *see also* ethical principles; moral principles
privacy 87, 89, **96**
private interest 36
proactive prosocial behaviors 37
professional competence 108, 111, 123, 127

professionalism 36–37, 44, 87
professional judgment xvii, 108–109
professional skepticism xvii, 101, 106, 109, 138, 141–142, 144
psychology 33, 41, 85, 101, 112, 160, 167, 167
public good 87, 122
public interest xvii–xviii, 31, 35–37, 44, 104, 106–109, 111, 114, 122, 132, 140–141, 146

rationalist theories 123–124
reliability 105, 125, 159–160
religion 12, 25, 31, 33, 35, 52–53, 162
research profiling 45–46
Rest, J. R. 125, 128, 147, 162; elements of ethical behavior 121; elements of good behavior 128–129; four-component model 61–63; Model of Moral Development xviii
right-answer syndrome 110
rights 23, 25, 35, 87–88, 130, 142, 147–148
role models 129, 132–133
role-plays 56–57, 68
Romania 54
rule of law 35
rules xvi, xviii, 20, 32, 37, 101, 105, 109–111, 115, 120–127, 129–133, 133–134n3, 146, 148, 150, 155–157, 168–169; see also ethical rules; moral rules; rule of law; standards

Sarbanes-Oxley Act 44
Satyam Computers xvi, 53
scandals 44, 52–54, 58, 68, 109, 114, 137, 142, 145, 155; see also names of scandals
Scheler, Max 157
Schwab, K. 83–87
scientific method 31, 33, 157
SEC 140–141
second-order desires 152
security 19, 84–89, 96; see also cyber security
self-interest xvii, 32–36, 38, 41, 61–62, 138, 146, 148, 150
self-regulation 36, 152
Seneca 18
sexual harassment 137, 143–144
Smith, Adam 36
social contract 35, 37
social identity 152

social responsibility 62, 66–67, 89, 93, 96, 121
social value 89, 93, 97, 100
Socrates 132, 157
South Africa 53–55
Spain 12, 60; Barcelona 5
Spotify 86
standards 26, 107, 126; accounting 115, 122; auditing 140; education 44, 107, 115; legal 121, 156; professional 104, 107–108; quality 85; technical xix, 101, 108; see also ethical standards; moral standards
surveillance 87–88, 94
sustainability 37–38, 66–67; environmental 96
Switzerland 165

technology 83–86, 90, 94, 123; -enhanced learning 57; and ethics 87–89, 96–97; learning technology platforms 68; nano- 90
temperance (moderation) 128
Ten Commandments 133–134n3
thinking, fallacies of 138, 146; see also egocentrism; invulnerability; omnipotence; omniscience; unrealistic optimism
transaction flows xvii, 87
trustworthiness xvii, 125, 129
truthfulness 125, 129–130, 132
Tunisia 54
Turkey 53–54; see also Constantinople

Uber Eats 86
United Kingdom (UK) 6, 52, 60, 110, 144, 166
United States (US) 44, 51–53, 60, 64, 100, 121, 137, 165
universal laws 41
unrealistic optimism 138
usury 12–13, 16, 18
Utilitarianism xviii, 123–124

Valley of Death 84, 90
values xvi–xviii, 31, 37, 60, 84, 87–89, 92–93, 95, 96–97, 96, 101–102, 107, 120, 123–126, 129–133, 139, 145, 148–149, 152, 155, 157; personal 44, 145, 152; professional 44, 108–109, 114, 116n3, 145; social 89; see also ethical values; moral values; value transformation

value transformation 87, 89, 93, 95–97
Venice 4–6, 9, 22; Venetian merchants xvi, 27n3
vices 17, 127–128
video presentations 68
virtue ethics 120, 125; theory 125
virtues xviii, 36, 120–121, 125–133, 152; agent-based 121; human 127–128, 131; person-rooted 121; self-mastering 128–129; transitive 128–129; unity of 128; *see also* cardinal virtues; ethical virtues; moral virtues; virtue ethics

whistleblowers 140–142, 144
whistleblowing 52–53, 61, 67, 140–141, 144
'white-hat' accountants 132
WorldCom xvi, 53, 58, 140, 142
World Economic Forum 83–84, 97n1
World Inequality Report 85

Zimbabwe 54–55